Slavery in the Twentieth Century

SLAVERY IN THE TWENTIETH CENTURY

Roger Sawyer

ROUTLEDGE & KEGAN PAUL
London and New York

First published in 1986
by Routledge & Kegan Paul plc

11 New Fetter Lane, London EC4P 4EE

Published in the USA by
Routledge & Kegan Paul Inc.
in association with Methuen Inc.
29 West 35th Street, New York, NY 10001

Set in Ehrhardt
by Input Typesetting Ltd, London
and printed in Great Britain
by Billing & Sons Ltd, Worcester

Library of Congress Cataloging in Publication Data

Sawyer, Roger, 1931–
Slavery in the twentieth century.

Bibliography: p.
Includes index.
1. Slavery——History——20th century. 2. Indentured servants——History——20th century. 3. Convict labor——History——20th century. I. Title.

HT867.S29   1986   306'.362   85–30037
British Library CIP data also available.
ISBN 0–7102–0475–2

CONTENTS

	Foreword by Lord Wilberforce	vii
	Acknowledgments	ix
1	Introduction: definitions and their origins	1
2	Chattel slavery	12
3	The slave as a disposable asset	32
4	Apartheid	53
5	Exploitation of children	77
6	Exploitation of women	100
7	Debt bondage and serfdom	122
8	Persecution of tribal minorities	144
9	Migrant workers and forced labour	168
10	Political/penal slavery	191
11	The role of the United Nations	217
	Notes and references	235
	Bibliography	253
	Index	262

FOREWORD

BY LORD WILBERFORCE

JOINT PRESIDENT OF THE ANTI-SLAVERY SOCIETY

We are living in a period of remembrance and celebration, of the abolition of slavery in the British Empire and of the emancipation of slaves 150 years ago. It is hard for us to appreciate that in spite of the great efforts made by the emancipators and their successors, in spite of the revolution in public opinion as regards all forms of slavery, in spite of the plethora of international agreements for the suppression of slavery (some 300 of them), this problem of slavery in the twentieth century is as great, indeed greater than it was in the 1830s. This is due to the increase in the world population, to the economic stresses resulting from that increase and to the recognition of conditions analogous to those of slavery proper which are just as cruelly violative of human rights.

So Dr Sawyer does well to give us, in this book, a wide-ranging and comprehensive overview, in eleven chapters, of all these conditions and practices which everyone devoted to the cause of human freedom should know about. At a moderate estimate the number of human beings living in slavery and analogous conditions is about 100 million.

The author tells us, too, of the individuals and institutions, governmental and non-governmental, who work so hard in the fight for freedom, encouraging and inspiring in many ways, and, with their share of success, discouraging in others in terms of slow progress, obstruction and ignorance.

I feel sure that this book will contribute to public awareness of facts which most people do not know, and, through greater awareness, to a strengthening of the humanitarian cause.

RICHARD WILBERFORCE

ACKNOWLEDGMENTS

The purpose of this book, which is more of a survey than a history, is to give some indication of the prevalence and diversity of slavery in the present century. It has within it the potential for many books, but it is hoped that a useful service will have been performed by bringing together consideration of the principal types of contemporary slavery between the covers of one volume. My own investigations, independent of written or published sources, were limited to making a fact-finding tour in southern Africa, conducting interviews and attending sessions of the United Nations Working Group on Slavery. For this reason I have many to thank, besides those who made first-hand contact possible and those whose names appear in the Notes and references and the Bibliography. While writing most chapters I was dependent on secondary sources, but it has been my good fortune to have been able to consult many of the authors concerned and to know from this experience, and the dove-tailing of their information, that their findings are reliable. Where relevant, the reports of investigators I do not know personally have been verified with the help of the Anti-Slavery Society.

My greatest debt is to this society, the world's oldest human rights organization, especially to Colonel Patrick Montgomery, its Secretary from 1963 to 1980. He read my typescript chapter by chapter as it was written, and was a constant source of enlightenment and encouragement. I thank him for his friendship and for giving me the benefit of the breadth and depth of a knowledge of slavery which must be unequalled. His mantle has fallen upon Peter Davies, the present Director (the title was changed as Third World leaders found 'Secretary' misleading), who, with his deputy, Maureen Alexander-Sinclair, has sustained me with a constant supply of reports, letters and other documents. Anyone who has watched Peter Davies exercising his skills at the United Nations, or observed Maureen Alexander-Sinclair keeping the wheels of the Society turning in London, will appreciate that William Wilberforce's successors are worthy of their heritage.

Members of other organizations have been generous and patient. The chairman of the United Nations Working Group on Slavery, Mr Justice Abu Sayeed Chowdhury, gave me the benefit of his advice, and at the International Labour Organization Klaus Samson produced a mass of useful information. He is not to be blamed for the kites which I have flown in the last chapter. For help with political/penal slavery I thank Dr Philip Walters of Keston College, Jack Lennard of the Wilberforce Council for Human Rights, Ursula Perry formerly of the International Society of Human Rights and Mandy Bath of Amnesty International. Malcolm Smart, also of Amnesty International, provided a number of documents which helped to widen my perception of the human rights position in southern Africa, and Stephen Corry, the Director of Survival International, gave me valuable information about missions to the Amerindian tribes. Because of 'political reasons to do with Khomeini and his regime' I can thank one of the founding members of the International Working Group on Women and the Family only if I use her pseudonym: R. Bahar. Leo Evans, Minister at the South African Embassy in London, was generous with time and literature. I only wish that I could have given his country a clean bill of health. What should be said, and understood more widely, is that men of his calibre have a conception of apartheid that has no connection whatsoever with the atrocities that are carried out in its name. To them it really is 'multinational development' for the benefit of all races. One lives in hope that their views will prevail, and reform will come peacefully from within.

Translators were needed from time to time and I express my appreciation for the assistance I received in this department from George Mansur, Elisa Marlowe-Dauncey and Peter and Sylvia Wilson. Others with specialist abilities which I exploited were Dr John Laffin, expert on Islam, and Dr Lilian Passmore Sanderson, expert on female genital excision and infibulation.

My investigations in southern Africa would not have been possible without the facilities provided by the government of Bophuthatswana. President Lucas Mangope, Paramount Chief of the Bahurutshe, extended the invitation, and T. M. Molatlhwa, his Minister of Foreign

Affairs, through E. J. Senne, Secretary for Foreign Affairs, saw that the arrangements were made and forgave me for playing havoc with my itinerary. In a continent that seems wedded to the principle of the one-party state it was refreshing to be able, despite difficulties of distance and terrain, to meet members of a vigorous opposition party, all of whom allowed their quarrel with the ruling party to be recorded on tape: Chief Toto (Leader), Paramount Chief Pilane (retired Leader), V. Sifora (Secretary General) and J. Seremane (Publicity). Sifora and Seremane had suffered terribly at the hands of the South African police. Ministers who gave recorded interviews were R. Cronje (Manpower), D. C. Mokale (Lands and Rural Development), Dr K. P. Mokhobo (Health and Social Welfare), K. C. A. V. Sehume (Posts and Telecommunications), L. G. Young (Finance) and the Minister of Foreign Affairs. I am especially grateful to President Mangope for allowing me to record his answers throughout a long interview. Others who provided invaluable information, nearly always on tape, were Brigadier C. S. S. Delport (Commissioner of Prisons), Mr Litheko, Secretary of the Baralong Tribal Authority, Christopher Milton (Ombudsman), L. S. Mogajane (Director of Information Service), Dawn Mokhobo (Agricor), Mr Molema (wise old man with royal connections), P. H. L. Moraka (Secretary for Education), L. Morolo (Bophuthatswana National Development Corporation), Audrey Renew (Curatrix of the Mafeking – or Mafikeng – Museum), Brigadier P. J. Seleke (Commissioner of Police), Theal Stewart (Chief Justice), S. I. Tire (Secretary for Internal Affairs) and H. Tlou (Secretary of the National Assembly). The finer points of apartheid law were expertly explained by the Dean of the University of Bophuthatswana and two of his specialist staff: Professor Carmen Nathan and Dr A. Naidu. Many others deserve thanks, in particular the Heads of three schools: Coloured, Multi-racial and White; and Ruth Rees, who made arrangements for me from England, L. L. M. Letlhaku who implemented them in Africa, and two of his staff who were my guides (and suffered some indignities on my behalf at the hands of South African police and security forces): A. Ditlhake and K. Sehularo.

Professor Mark Münzel, the authority on the Aché Indians of Paraguay, kindly wrote to bring me up to date with their condition. Ben Helfgott checked my chapter on slavery under National Socialism and spent most of a day recounting his experiences as one of Hitler's slaves. His recording, which is too harrowing for some to bear, is nevertheless worthy of publication in its own right. As well as my thanks, he deserves my apologies for making him live those experiences again.

There were others who helped in numerous ways which are difficult to classify. It is probably simplest to list their names in alphabetical order and state that their assistance is none the less appreciated: Swami Agnivesh, Dr Ruth Armitage, Bettina Bain-Watson, Kate Baker, Richard Chetwynd, Suzanne Cronjé, Michael Grylls, MP, Sally Grylls, John Martin, Marie Martin, Professor Sue Miers, Stanley Morris, Anne Negus, Ann Pilcher, Nicholas Thornton, Lieutenant Commander David Webb, Yvonne Willenberg and Stephen Winkworth.

Graham Heaney, of Southampton University Library, and John Westmacott, of the British Library, solved innumerable bibliographical problems for me. Librarians are the most reliable breed, and nowhere is that more easily proved than in the Bembridge branch of the Isle of Wight County Library. Mary Cullimore, Michael Cunliffe, Alan Philips and Adrian Wills are never defeated, however obscure the request.

Finally I am happy to record my thanks to Andrew Wheatcroft of Routledge & Kegan Paul for giving me so much encouragement and useful advice, to Jenny Penalva for producing the typescript on time, and to my sons, Charles and Rupert Sawyer, for checking the proofs.

Chapter 1

Introduction: Definitions and Their Origins

Slavery having predated and outlived so many civilizations, its apologists can almost be forgiven for believing it to be part of the natural order of things. Eve was told by God that Adam would 'rule over'[1] her and enslavement by a hypothetical First Man of a woman or enemy was seen by cultures older than Judaism as a necessary consequence of a law of nature. Ancient Egypt demonstrates an early tradition of slavery and modern Egypt has dramatic extant examples of what highly organized slavery can achieve; the pyramids which, to say the least, bear comparison with major structures of the industrial age, have also become the standard metaphor for a hierarchical society. Unfortunately hand in hand with the occasionally uncomfortable truth that some are born to lead, others to follow, goes Lord Acton's never comfortable saying about absolute power corrupting absolutely.

To see the institution not only in practice but also given serious consideration one must move from Egypt to Greece. Aristotle was a most persuasive believer in the idea that 'some are by nature free, so others are by nature slaves, and for these latter the condition of slavery is both beneficial and just'.[2] For many he proved to be the prime source of the intellectual respectability of chattel slavery, the complete ownership of one human being by another. By virtue of his broad and deep contribution to Western thought he has been treated with respect by serious and pragmatic students of theoretical and practical power. It is not fanciful to identify Aristotle as a fundamental, and powerfully reputable, source of inspiration for National Socialists or any other racist party, despite the fact that he believed that slaves should be treated kindly. He was, after all, a former pupil of Plato, who taught that no Greek should be a slave. Furthermore, by going on to say that although the slave was only a living tool there was a level at which it

was sometimes possible for a man and his slave to enjoy friendship, he inadvertently paved the way for recognition of different degrees of slavery.

Freedom of expression among the Greek elite, whose many freedoms were largely dependent on possession of numerous slaves, had allowed the beginnings of anti-slavery sentiment to develop before Aristotle's day. Unlike Plato, who took slavery for non-Greeks for granted, another student of Socrates, Antisthenes, inspired an anti-slavery tradition among his followers, one of whom was Diogenes, founder of the Cynics. A more remarkable Greek contribution to anti-slavery thought came from Epictetus, an ex-slave who became a leading Stoic and preached the brotherhood of man. He bridged the gap with Rome by forming an unlikely friendship with fellow Stoic Emperor Marcus Aurelius. Despite all the commendable libertarian ideas and ideals of well-placed intellectuals, slavery was not to disappear during the Age of the Antonines; for a while an imperial decree obliged gladiators to fight with blunt swords, but it was not very long before the customary cruelties returned to the arena in all their horror. However, the influence of Stoic principles should not be underestimated; in the short term it led to the passing of more humane Roman legislation, and in a later age Stoic beliefs in natural justice played their part in the development of democratic processes.

A separate, some[3] say less oppressive, form of slavery had been practised for many centuries under Mosaic Law. In Exodus it is plainly set out that a slave would only remain in bondage for six years, after which he might go free. But, 'If his master have given him a wife, and she have born him sons or daughters; the wife and her children shall be her master's, and he shall go out by himself.'[4] The possibilities conjured up by this stipulation are worthy of Harriet Beecher Stowe and detract considerably from the allegedly merciful attitude of Moses; nor is the situation greatly eased by the slave being allowed to say, 'I love my master, my wife, and my children; I will not go out free.' Then, as a special favour, he was allowed to have his ear (the symbol of obedience) nailed to the doorpost to signify perpetual attachment to his master's house. True, in Leviticus the master was advised, 'Thou shalt not rule over him with rigour',[5] but the stricture only applied to Israelite slaves; the enslavement of foreigners was an altogether different matter. Unlike Israelites, not only did they have a life sentence, but this passed from generation to generation. In theory Israelites could only be enslaved as a penalty for theft, though they could sell themselves or their children to alleviate debt or poverty, sell a daughter for marriage or be bought from a foreigner into whose servitude they had fallen. Foreign slaves were bought or captured at will.

Given though that the essential element of slavery, loss of freedom, was widespread, and frequently not limited to six years even for Israelites (as stated in Jeremiah[6]), one has to recognize that the Israelite system of slavery had some benevolent features. A principal right of a slave was that if he were seriously injured by his master he would gain his freedom, a privilege that could not be relied upon under any of the systems of slavery current today, unless the injury made the individual a wholly uneconomic proposition. Even then he might only gain the freedom to starve. Furthermore slaves had certain minimum religious, legal and even property rights, and, in their basic humanity were recognized as free men within the universal concept which under the Romans became known as *ius naturale.* This last may sound like an abstract privilege, more to do with Greek philosophizing than the real world, but it did mean that, unlike his modern chattel counterparts, the Israelite slave could not be equated with inanimate property, nor was he merely a beast of burden.

As was only to be expected, by the time the Roman Empire was at the height of its power slavery had become precisely embodied in Roman Law, that is the *ius gentium*, the embodiment of laws and usages found among, or imposed upon, the many peoples ruled by Rome. With the advent of the Stoics, *ius naturale*, the natural law of the universe, the source of perfect justice, worked, as best it could, through the practical limitations of the *ius gentium*. Under *ius naturale*, though it will have given him little comfort unless he was given much to contemplating the hereafter, the slave was as free as Caesar. In this world he was very much a chattel, the personal possession of his master for any of six reasons. He was most likely to be an object of title under Roman Law because he was born a slave; a child slave who was not born of a slave mother would have been either captured in war or voluntarily sold by impoverished parents. If the impoverishment of the parents was sufficiently degrading they may have made themselves objects of a fourth legal title by voluntarily selling themselves. The remaining titles were punishments for various crimes and for falling into debt.

Not greatly helped by the apparent difficulty of reconciling the two emphases of St Paul's teaching – 'there is neither bond nor free . . .

ye are all one in Christ Jesus'[7] and 'be subject to your masters with all fear'[8] – the Christian church followed Roman Law (with some voices crying in the wilderness) throughout the period of medieval serfdom and into the early seventeenth century, when an unsuccessful attempt was made to distinguish between chattel slavery, which was unjust, and ameliorated slavery which was morally legitimate. The basic tenet of ameliorated slavery was that you could buy and sell a man's work without appropriating his body, a cosy piece of rationalization which just did not square with the realities of life and simply contrived unsuccessfully to give a morally acceptable face to debt bondage and the other debt-based form of slavery, serfdom. But the church had not just been content to follow the imperial lead; it had postulated the 'just' war in order to vindicate the capturing of slaves and, in order to enforce clerical celibacy, it had added three more titles of slavery: the mistresses, children and wives of priests. The father of the Christian anti-slavery movement ought to have been St Gregory of Nyssa, who spoke out unequivocally against the system, and whose words fell on stony ground. He saw everything quite clearly and if Christendom had heeded him a large part of the world would have been spared sixteen or seventeen centuries of suffering.

The European colonial empires which came after imperial Rome's decline had, as part of their motivation, the wish to spread their religious commitments, which sadly lacked anti-slavery zeal, to the populations of the Americas, Africa, Asia and Australasia. Often they found, particularly in many parts of Africa, that slavery in one form or another was already firmly established and was very much to do with internal economics and social arrangements or inter-tribal warfare or trade. Whether or not the Europeans exported feudal serfdom is sometimes difficult to judge, and naturally there were many differences of imperial practice within each continent, especially where rival European nationalities were involved. The method, largely instinctive or accidental, of dealing with the North American Indian, for example, was to drive him out of the way to the west, kill the bison on which he depended and massacre whenever resistance was felt. Treaties were made and treaties were broken. Although all the cruelties of slavery were widespread, a coherent system was neither found nor introduced until the cotton plantations appeared in the south. In South America, however, the pattern was completely different; the Iberian invaders appropriated (as their descendants continue to appropriate) the agricultural land, and the Amerindian tribes either retreated into the forest or became serfs, tied by physical necessity and ultimately by the law to a particular plot. They did not own the land; in order to justify their own share of the crop they owed the landlord their labour.

Serfdom has evolved into many different types, partly because it has sometimes been combined with debt bondage. The fundamental difference between the two systems, however, lies in the peasant's relationship with the land. With serfdom he and his family are tied to it; in some cases one might say that he owes a hypothetical rent for it, but his situation is such that he is unlikely ever to be able to break free from his indebtedness, still less – short of radical land reforms, rigidly enforced – can he aspire to own the land. The system in which he is ensnared is today's counterpart of European medieval feudalism and, in South America at least, the landlords are normally of European descent. With debt bondage, although agricultural labouring is essentially bound up with the majority of cases, the key, though not the cause, is the moneylender. A classic example is the borrowing of money for a wedding: in order to conform with tradition the debtor may pledge to serve the moneylender night and day for five years. Written into the deed of service may be penalty clauses compelling the debtor eventually to repay the sum lent with interest, rate unspecified. Such deeds, even when pronounced illegal, have a traditional force that can bind whole families for succeeding generations.

Such are the semantics of slavery that the time is probably approaching when serfdom will be absorbed into the vocabulary of debt bondage; as it is, from time to time researchers find it necessary to use the term 'debt serf'. The system of peonage, formerly enshrined in the constitution of Peru, is still causing linguistic problems as some tenants of quite wealthy estates might technically be classified as 'peons', despite the insistence of dictionaries that peons are serfs. To eradicate this sort of confusion deliberate over-simplification may be justified; for the purposes of this stdy a serf is a prisoner of his landlord's land, a debt bondsman the prisoner of his moneylender.

Just as Latin American countries are identified as the territories in which serfdom survives, so is the Indian subcontinent regarded as the area of the globe with the greatest incidence of debt bondage. If the Iberian colonizers of Central and South America can be accused of bringing serfdom with them, can the British imperialists be held responsible for the present state of slavery within India? Indian government spokesmen repeatedly blame British rule for this addition to their problems. One may ask, though, as an International Labour Organization Observer asked the United Nations Working Group on Slavery in Geneva in 1984, whether, if British imperialism created the problem it is to be found in other countries which came under the imperial yoke. Although it is reasonable to suppose so, the evidence is not being produced. It is true also that ever since the phenomenon has been observed, creditor and debtor, unlike master and serf, have generally been of the same race, though not the same caste. The British fault does not lie in creating the system, which almost certainly predates British rule, but in allowing it to persist in accordance with the policy of indirect rule.

The Christian attitude to slavery in the various empires until the period of imperial decline was at best an influence for more merciful physical treatment, at worst outright support for the divine curse on the negro descendants of Ham. Independence, when it came to the former colonies, such as the United States of America, brought no benefits from church or state. Over 660,000 slaves are estimated to have been owned by American Protestant church members and ministers alone. And the Roman Catholic church was no better in its separate spheres of influence, that is until humanist pressures, which had begun to be exerted in the sixteenth century, largely in France, began to demand at least some form of intelligent reply. Jean Bodin led the way by attacking the church's support of the institution by refuting both the right to own slaves and the utility of doing so. But not until the eighteenth century, when another French philosopher, Montesquieu, developed the anti-slavery thesis, did Bodin find a worthy successor. Montesquieu even went so far as to deal specifically with Aristotle. Both men's works were banned by the church, as was the anti-slavery writing of the celebrated French contemporary of Montesquieu, Jean-Jacques Rousseau. Fortunately for the slaves the banning of the books did not prevent others from taking up the cause and repeating the arguments.

Concurrently with the literary efforts of the later French humanists there had developed a vital movement among Quakers, Methodists and like-minded Christian denominations, which steadily gathered momentum. Some preached and published, others, resident in the New World, were able to do something practical in the way of emancipating their own slaves and forbidding slave-owning by those of the same religious persuasion. Notable here were the North American Episcopal Methodists. The most impressive culmination of this type of Protestant activity came when William Wilberforce and his friends, collectively dubbed 'the Clapham Sect', sustained a long anti-slavery campaign, subject to many setbacks. This eventually brought about first the abolition of the slave trade and then the emancipation of the slaves throughout the British colonies in the Caribbean.

Until the Middle Ages the experience of Islam was similar in theory and practice to that of countries dominated by the Christian ethic. The Koran proclaimed the equality of man, but slaves were sub-human. Holy War captives were the only legitimate chattel slaves and they could gain freedom either by conversion to Islam or purchase. Official attitudes have undergone radical change during this century and found explicit expression at the Sixth Moslem World Conference held in 1964, when slavery of all types was condemned and support offered to all anti-slavery movements throughout the world. This was one year before the Roman Catholic church finally came out against slavery, after a delay of nearly 2,000 years. The Sixth Moslem World Conference and the Second Vatican Council removed the seal of religious approval from the institution throughout most of the world.

Having noted that serfdom remains endemic in many Christian countries and that Indian debt bondage is primarily a Hindu phenomenon (but not entirely; in Bihar, for example, 6 per cent of the masters are Moslem), it has to be remembered that although chattel slavery is now universally illegal its survival as a tacitly accepted part of traditional social and economic structures is now mainly limited to Islamic countries. And in this connection, as the use of children as property is a primary growth area of twentieth-century slavery, one must deplore the current use of child soldiers for clearing minefields in the Gulf War; the more so because, contrary to Islamic belief, this is done in the name of Islam.

Today the old traditional theory that slavery was good both for society and the individual slave has given way to an Orwellian double-think process: all states forbid it and many practise it. And those territories not influenced by Islam, Hinduism or Christianity are no better; one has only to look at the record of, say, China – of the mandarins or the People's Republic – to realize that the malaise is independent of religious or political creed. After the British Emancipation Act, which came into effect on 1 August 1834, the other  sovereign powers began to follow the British example as far as legislation was concerned, and there followed the period of the great illusion which persists to the present day. The mass of twentieth-century citizens in the developed world have long imagined that slavery went out with Wilberforce. When, in the reign of King Edward VII, Roger Casement exposed King Leopold II of the Belgians' slavery in the Congo basin, and the slavery of a British registered company in the Amazon basin, public opinion responded as though these were extraordinary anachronisms. The terrible truth is that the urge to enslave has been part of the dark side of human nature that dates from the beginning of history and, as far as one can tell, is common to all races and places. At times one feels that only an exorcist could remove the demon from the human spirit.

The 1930s and 1940s saw a resurgence of the lust for power that motivates the committed slaver. There was a fusion of former Roman and clerical ideas of title; the concepts of the chattel slave, penal slave and captive in a 'just' war coalesced into the concept of the slave as a disposable asset. Although the National Socialist period can be deemed to have been artificial and untypical, in so far as all its doctrine was concocted to serve political and national aims, and the whole episode was based on a calculated myth, it did demonstrate slavery pushed all the way to a ruthless logical conclusion. The lessons that can be learned are to do with constitutional machinery for the protection of minorities and democratic education for the enlightenment of majorities.

There are many organizations working in the field of human rights today, but only one is specifically concerned with slavery: the Anti-Slavery Society for the Protection of Human Rights, which traces its ancestry through the British and Foreign Anti-Slavery Society of Sir Thomas Fowell Buxton and others to the original society, which had leaders in common, but whose most famous leader was William Wilberforce. The types of slavery defined so far still demand much vigilance, but the society is often concerned with old forms of the institution in new disguises. Moreover during its long history it has gained sufficient experience to recognize that traditional slavery has its positive side. The benevolent slave-owner was always a special problem, but in Third World countries where the relationship between master and slave has come about by accident of birth in both cases and has led to an affectionate bond, like that between father and son, there will be mutual trust and dependence. In these cases compulsory emancipation could mean starvation and the disruption of a delicately balanced social system. This is not to say that such slavery is morally or even practically justified; the potential for abuse, particularly of women and children, remains, and inevitably power corrupts from time to time. But it does mean that the transition from slave to free man must be a slow and cautious process if the cure is not to be worse than the complaint.

As the senior non-governmental organization in consultative status at the United Nations, as far as this sphere of human rights is concerned, the Anti-Slavery Society naturally uses as its points of reference for its own definitions of slavery those laid down by the United Nations Supplementary Convention on the Abolition of Slavery, the Slave Trade and Institutions and Practices Similar to Slavery, 1956. The United Nations definitions are quoted below, at the head of the relevant chapters. The Convention defines a slave as someone 'over whom any or all of the powers attaching to the right of ownership are exercised', a definition which in the light of its experience the Society has tended to express more simply as 'one who is owned and thus has neither freedom nor rights' or 'one who, working for another, is not free to withhold his labour'.[9] The first of these is what is generally understood by the term 'chattel slavery'. In addition shortened versions of the four other principal types of slavery are preferred:[10]

> Debt Bondage is the state arising from a pledge by a debtor of his own personal services or of those of a person under his control as security for a debt, when the length and nature of the services is not defined nor does their value diminish the debt.
>
> Serfdom is the condition of a tenant who must live and labour on the land of another person, whether for reward or not, and who is not free to change his status.
>
> Exploitation of Children – any practice whereby a person under 18 years old is delivered by parent or guardian to another person, whether for reward or not, with a view to exploiting him or his labour.
>
> Servile Forms of Marriage – any institution whereby a woman, without the right to refuse, is promised or given in marriage on payment of a consideration in money or in kind, or may be transferred to another person or, on the death of her husband, may be inherited by another person.

The Society has had to widen its definitions of the exploitation of children and women in recent years in order that rapidly proliferating iniquities, sometimes as the product of urbanization, are not neglected. Whereas in the Society's older documents sham adoption, as practised in Syria, featured as a definition in its own right, now a form of words must be used to include buying and selling of children for use on farms or in factories or brothels. Vague expressions like 'Child Exploitation' have their shortcomings. They do, though, allow the disposable victims of child pornography to have a voice to demand their protection and denounce negligent or conniving governments. Similarly 'Servile Forms of Marriage' can be thought to be too obviously showing religious bias and it has given way for practical purposes to a wording more suited to dealing with a wide variety of violations of human rights (for example, Female Circumcision and Infibulation): 'certain types of abuse and exploitation of women'. Nevertheless the servile form of marriage remains a major problem.

For obvious reasons there is much overlap between the areas of responsibility shouldered by the Anti-Slavery Society. Forced labour, a human rights violation to which Communist governments are particularly prone, contravenes the 1957 Convention of the International Labour Organization, but it was already prohibited under the 1926 Slavery Convention. Also apartheid, variously described in United Nations papers as a 'crime' and a 'slavery-like practice', has attracted the attention of anti-slavery researchers working in the areas of child exploitation and forced labour, and there is another, stronger, reason for the Anti-Slavery Society to take an interest in the affairs of South Africa: the present Society was born of a merger which took place in 1909 between the British and Foreign Anti-Slavery Society and the Aborigines Protection Society. The protection of tribal peoples claiming or deserving human and civil rights is half its *raison d'être.*

The Anti-Slavery Society gathers information from all over the world (though little is forthcoming from the Communist bloc) in its attempt to eradicate chattel slavery, serfdom, debt bondage, exploitation of children, exploitation of women and the persecution of peoples whose basic territorial rights are threatened. The evidence is sifted and reports are written; these are then brought to the attention of the governments concerned. If the response is inadequate a decision is taken as to whether publicity or diplomacy will achieve the required result. In any event the matter is brought to the attention of the United Nations Working Group of Experts on Slavery, where like-minded non-governmental organizations from the United Kingdom, France and other states may well amplify the report with corroborative material. It then goes forward to the Sub-Commission on Prevention of Discrimination and Protection of Minorities with an appropriate recommendation. The valuable contribution of the other non-governmental organizations is not described here; their brief tends to be more specific, and their achievements deserve to be chronicled in their own right.

What follows is an account of slavery today, in accordance with the United Nations definitions and the Anti-Slavery Society's interpretation of them. Succeeding chapters deal with the different forms of slavery and at relevant stages some consideration is given to other twentieth-century manifestations of the institution. Slavery under National Socialism is described and the problem of apartheid, long the subject of much over-simplification, is reassessed in the light of recent developments. At the request of Communist delegates at the United Nations a specific chapter has not been allotted to Communist violations of human rights; instead they take their place under the appropriate definitions. If they predominate in chapter 10, it is only because the cap fits. Finally consideration is given to the role of the United Nations, its agencies and the non-governmental organizations, in the continuation of efforts to bring slavery to an end.

CHAPTER 2

CHATTEL SLAVERY

. . . the status or condition of a person over whom . . . the powers attaching to the right of ownership are exercised. . .

UNITED NATIONS SLAVERY CONVENTION

Although superficially the simplest form of slavery to define, chattel slavery evolved very differently in different parts of the world. Throughout the Islamic regions, where much survives today, the distinctions have been caused by discrepancies of national wealth, by the contrasts between nomadic and settled traditions, and by variations – sometimes opportunist – in interpretation of the Koran. Certain Arab countries bordering on the Gulf have sufficient recently acquired oil wealth to underwrite universal emancipation and rehabilitation. That liberation has not always taken place has been partly caused by an understandable wish not to disrupt a social pattern of great antiquity and complexity; freedom could bring chaos. It is also true, however, that oil wealth has stimulated the love of money that seems inevitably to be the root of much evil. Money brings power; power brings or renews a desire for status and there is no more effective status symbol than the possession of slaves. True, the condition of the slave can be improved until he is almost indistinguishable from a privileged servant, but if the basic democratic options of a free man are denied, perhaps by a purely economic sanction, the potential for unacceptable exploitation remains.

Even if cruelty never occurred, the conditioned subservience of individuals or groups from generation to generation, whilst picturesque, generally produces the mentality of a useful animal. Occasionally the animal is affectionate and loyal and these qualities are reciprocated by the master. This has been the inspiration of the romantic appraisal of the slave-master relationship. It is contended, however, that only if the formation of this exceptional bond is genuinely voluntary, and can be terminated by resignation at any time, is it worthy of sympathetic evaluation.

In the Gulf Great Britain has tended to interpret its protecting role comparatively strictly; hence the principles of indirect rule and co-operation with local custom were carefully observed. In the Foreign Office records for 1906, for instance, we find the following claim for expenses:[1]

> 'FEB 7. 1906 *MUSCUT [sic] DEC. QUARTER'S ACCOUNTS*
> CHARGE FOR SUBSISTENCE OF SLAVES
> Major Grey's No. 12 of Jany 5, 1906 Muskat [sic]
> £4:14:2'

The charge was sanctioned. And later, when this region was becoming one of the wealthiest parts of the Arab world, and of the world as a whole, and while Royal Naval ships continued during the 1960s to intercept slave-trading vessels plying between Africa and the Gulf states, it did not seem as though anything useful could be done by the protecting power about the ownership of people and their progeny on the land. Many male slaves had been castrated (blacks had had penis and testicles removed; the nineteenth-century influx of whites had been allowed to retain some penis) and a high proportion did not survive the operation, but, as one male could, if need be, fertilize many females, this feature of slavery did not greatly influence numbers. However, obstruction at sea proved effective and meant that slaves had to be transported by air.[2] Buraimi Oasis, a neutral zone jointly administered by Great Britain and Saudi Arabia, was a staging post manned by the Trucial Scouts, an Arab force with British officers. It was a British officer who informed the Anti-Slavery Society of his discovery that under cover of darkness up to 2,000 slaves per year were being imported to Saudia Arabia. Three aircraft per month supplying the Saudi contingent took on board lorry loads of negroes for the last stage of a journey from West Africa. Although the flights were meant to be strictly limited to military supplies and personnel, initial enquiries met with the excuse that the passengers were Buraimi residents visiting relations.

Prince Feisal stopped the Saudi air importations in 1962; in Muscat and Oman slavery officially ended in 1970. That slavery continues to exist in households within and without the Arabian peninsula is periodically observed by Western visitors and, more dramatically, is demonstrated by the evidence of slaves brought with diplomatic missions to London, Geneva and elsewhere. Occasionally it may even be found in England in non-diplomatic households which lack the protection of the Vienna Convention on Diplomatic Relations:[3]

> On 16 April 1984 in Marylebone Magistrates Court I heard the evidence for the prosecution in a case in which two Kuwaiti sheikhas were accused by their Indian and Sri Lankan servants of having taken their passports, forbidden them to leave the house, fed them irregularly and insufficiently, worked them very long hours, paid them nothing and beaten them both almost daily with a whip or with a length of electric flex.

Perhaps the most objectionable aspect of this abuse, apart from the fate of ex-slaves in general, is the vulnerability of women in slavery-orientated society and the plight of the most defenceless section of the community, the children of the slave class.

At the other end of the financial scale in the Arab area of dominance and far removed from the Gulf, although these priorities remain valid, the initial problem concerns the transition of the state as a whole from dependence on slavery to a social and political system in which voluntary co-operation (or non-co-operation) can replace the present fossilized structure of African feudalism. Although a lot is to do with changing a centuries-old outlook on life, in the case of both masters and slaves, the first stage in the process of emancipation should be economic – at a very down-to-earth level. The Gulf states have sufficient wealth to solve their own problems: they have only to adopt a more enlightened attitude to the Koran and change to a more equitable economic system. In short, all that is needed is the will to emancipate; oil has provided the means.

In and near the Sahel, according to an independent French witness[4] who addressed the Working Group of Experts on Slavery in Geneva in 1984, there are some 250,000 chattel slaves in the hands of nomadic tribes. He personally, having witnessed the sale of one of them, had managed to negotiate her freedom, a process which took seven years. Another Frenchman[5] was instrumental in recovering a girl who had been sold in Algeria by her father's owner to a Mauritanian. The girl was aged 7 at the time. Even with much influential backing (and, it must be admitted, much influential harassment) of the emancipator, the girl was 11 years old before she was returned to her parents. One cause of such delays can be best illustrated by the answers provided by Chad when, in 1964, a slavery questionnaire was sent to all member states of the United Nations on the initiative of the Economic and Social Council.[6] Asked, 'Does slavery . . . exist in the country?', Chad replied, 'Yes.' 'What are the causes or reasons for its existence?' 'Tradition.' 'What steps has your Government taken, or contemplated, for its elimination?' 'None.' Such honesty was, in a way, refreshing and is particularly so with hindsight as, since 1964, many of the states which self-righteously denied the existence of slavery within their borders have been caught *in flagrante delicto*.

The hypocrisy of states on this issue has been a recurrent theme throughout the ages and never more so than in the twentieth century. A notable exception is Mauritania, and its generally open response to investigations is one reason for its presentation here as principal example. Emerging from the colonial era Mauritania, the poorest and weakest state bordering the Sahara, was largely forgotten or ignored by the international community. For a short while, for a mixture of sometimes contradictory motives, it became involved in the struggle for the mineral resources of the newly independent neighbouring territory that had been Spanish Sahara. Extricated by the present rulers from this entanglement, it might have sunk back into the anonymity of other poor African states but for its adoption of the Shari'a, Islamic fundamental law. There then followed hand amputations, floggings and the sentencing of two men for murder. Photographs were taken and they attracted the attention of the foreign press and the usual temporary flurry of interest. On the surface there was nothing very remarkable about happenings of this nature which seemed typical of the resurgence of militant Islamic fundamentalism to be seen in a number of Arab countries. There was, though, one significant difference which influenced internal reaction: of the two men found guilty of murder, one was executed, one was not. The executed man was an ex-slave, the other a white Moor. Blatant use of a double standard reinforced the effect of the public sale of a young woman which occurred in February 1980.

Such events made a more permanent impression at the Anti-Slavery Society's office in London, whence came support for an investigation by John Mercer, author of two recent publications about conditions in adjacent territories[7] and a member of the Society. Mercer's findings were made public at the Society's annual general meeting in

December 1980, five months after Mauritania had, for the third time, abolished slavery. Mercer died shortly afterwards, but it was his findings that formed the basis for the action taken by the present Director of the Anti-Slavery Society, Peter Davies, by the United Nations team and by the Mauritanian government itself, which invited both the Society and the United Nations Organization to see for themselves the problems created by a long tradition of chattel slavery.

Mauritania, a country about twice the size of France with one and a half million inhabitants, occupies the largest portion of the western end of the Sahara, is mainly desert, and is bounded to north and east by desert countries. It has only one fertile area, the south-west region that lies in a right angle between the perpendicular of its coastline and the base line of the Senegal River. Along the coast, which extends northwards for some 750 miles, a disappointing yield comes from fishing; the rich waters of the Arguin Bank have been exploited over the years by Canary Islanders, Russians and Japanese. A similar story is to be told of the iron ore deposits at Zouerate in the northern desert. These are too far from the sea to be an attractive commercial proposition and the limited profits are siphoned off by an international company using the country's only railway line. The capital city, Nouakchott, was hastily created halfway along the coast just in time for independence; in addition to an essential desalination plant it has a few basic industries. At Nouadhibou in the extreme north there is fish processing and an oil refinery, but the oil is Algerian. Tourism awaits hotels and communications. Interested parties look forward to the sort of transformation which only occurs with a mineral miracle. Copper has been mined for twenty years but world prices have been disappointing. If phosphates or oil deposits were located Mauritania's feudal problems would soon be augmented by the very different ones brought by a too abrupt transition to a modern society. Would the example of the Gulf states be followed?

Agricultural products naturally fall into the two types representative of nomads and of oasis dwellers. With the camel as their beast of burden the nomadic tribes wander through the desert in search of pasture for cattle, sheep and goats; in the process they convey various goods or products from one oasis to another. The transhumance which governs their lives is no respecter of frontiers, which in any case are only lines drawn across a map. The settled peoples, who have long had a touchy relationship with the nomads, make use of them where possible; they grow dates and millet mainly for trading purposes. In the privileged area of the extreme south-west conditions will support several types of cereal crops, groundnuts and even water melons. Outside the few newly constructed coastal towns, although there is a decline in nomadism, life is apparently as it has always been, and there seems little reason for change. It is a traditional pastoral existence, deceptively attractive to the eyes of the hardier sort of European traveller with a romantic side to his nature.

The origins of the social structure around which this life revolves are ancient and yet one is reminded of them daily by the close correlation between skin colour and occupation. The Sarakolé, who now live in the valley of the Senegal River, are said to be the descendants of the original inhabitants, a claim which, as it refers to the period of myths and legends with which all histories begin, is not likely to be substantiated. Later the black inhabitants, known as Bafours, whether Sarakolé by blood or not, were conquered or driven south by light-skinned nomadic Berbers of the Islamic faith, and there followed a relentless extension of Berber dominance which eventually reached from Spain to Asante. The Berbers lost their supremacy after the twelfth century, forced to yield to an invading force which, being light-skinned and Islamic, must have seemed to the existing black slave population indistinguishable, save in numbers, from their former masters. In the long run that proved to be the case; by the end of the nineteenth century the Berbers had not only ceased to resist but had gone over to their Arab conquerors' ways in most of their culture and virtually all of their language. Of the four emirates which now make up the area known as the Islamic Republic of Mauritania only one, the Tagant, has not lost its Berber identity.

As with the rest of Africa, it was left to the Europeans to draw the national boundaries and at the beginning of the twentieth century France began a gradual occupation which was not completed until the northern territory was subdued in 1934. What the French found as their influence spread northwards from Senegal was a land in which a blend of Berber and Arab – Islamic, light-skinned and Arabic-speaking – known as Maures (Moors), ruled negro slaves. In the southern region there were black slave-owners as well, only too willing to collaborate with their Moorish counterparts in a closing of ranks designed to come to terms with French domination, particularly after France had gone through the motions of abolishing slavery in 1905.

The first President of independent Mauritania, Mokhtar Ould

Daddah, described his country as the hyphen of Africa, by which he meant that it formed some sort of link between Arab north and negro south. It was a wise saying, spoken with the tongue firmly in the cheek. His own slaves were kept behind the presidential palace and, as is well known, a large part of the history of Africa is about the capture by Arabs of black manpower either for local use or for export via markets as, for instance, in Zanzibar to the Persian Gulf or the Red Sea. The hyphen is a good metaphor for the pin in the shackle. By the time independence had come, although slavery was about to be nominally abolished for the second time, the minds of nearly all the people had been conditioned to accept slavery as part of the natural order of things. Shackles in the physical sense were no longer needed. The European wish to make the populations of colonies settle down to some work and keep out of mischief was best served by tacitly ignoring the status of the work force as dams were built and some new areas brought under cultivation. The wholly commendable French practice of freeing slaves who managed to embrace a flagstaff flying the tricolour, and then supplying them with plots of land and protecting them, was offset on the grand scale by granting deeds of land entitlement to slave-owners and subsidizing agricultural schemes carried out by slave labour. And those same titles inhibit emancipation today.

The hierarchy which evolved was to have several levels of servitude between the white Moors and the slaves, and much of the top level itself consists of descendants of warriors of Arab origin and holy men of Berber extraction. In the various periods of inter-tribal conflict before the feudal system became rigid the defeated tribes had to agree to regular payments of tribute to the victors. Again, although the French officially abolished this obligation, which was seen in terms of personal rights and duties, it went on throughout the colonial period and today some fishermen, for instance, still pay annual tribute to a visiting nomadic tribe. With the decrease in nomadism and the drift to the outskirts of the few towns, especially to the capital, the paying of tribute by settled debtors is a dying tradition; though it is unfortunately sometimes replaced by debt bondage, cruelly enforced. Below the tributaries but above the slaves are castes of formerly nomadic artisans, musicians and hunters discriminated against by Moors.

At the base of Mauritanian society are the slaves, part slaves, and former slaves. Today the supply of new slaves is almost entirely maintained by births to slave mothers. When sales occur there is an outcry among the ex-slaves (the *haratin*) and, since the notorious case of the sale of the young woman M'Barka mint Blail in 1980 and the international reaction which followed, probably the only ways in which the slave birth rate can be augmented are kidnappings or private purchase of children. The part slaves are the Mauritanian version of serfs, in so far as they are collectively tied to a settlement and must together raise the sum of money or proportion of harvest demanded. Elevation to part slave status may be granted by a benevolent master or acquired by means of payment made by a relative. To acquire complete freedom – that is to say such freedom as may be enjoyed by the *haratin* class – the price for the freedom of a woman of marriageable age may be as high as £2,000. Slaves have from time to time been sent abroad and have diligently, almost touchingly, sent remittances to their masters, some of whose standard of living may be inferior to their own. Among these there are some who eventually choose to escape; others, inhibited by the alleged opinion of Mohammad that only obedient slaves achieve paradise, will risk death rather than disobey. In the Mauritanian desert, where life begins and ends in a tent, and away from the influence of townspeople, one finds slavery in its traditional form, blindly accepted by master and slave alike.

The towns are not liberalizing influences as such; Western values – for good or ill – are not disseminated freely. The capital is, however, the usual haven for escaped slaves, some of whom banded together in 1974 to form an emancipation movement, El Hor, meaning 'Freedom'. Apart from the obvious reasons for its existence, El Hor may eventually find that it fulfils the nation's possible need for an effective opposition party. As the time of independence approached the French made sure that the Parti Populaire Mauritanien, with its pro-French leader, eclipsed the other parties. In short they set up what is commonly known as a neo-colonialist regime. As a result the method of changing government in Mauritania has had to be military *coup*. El Hor sees itself as a loyal national group, possibly as representing the most loyal section of the community. At the time of Spanish Saharan independence some Moors looked to Morocco for an extension of their Moorish power; some negroes feel affinities with Senegal. One day those who were weakest may inherit the earth. Officially El Hor does not aspire to anything more than genuine universal emancipation, and equality of all citizens in the eyes of the law, but it has links with the Union Démocratique Mauritanienne, an illegal black organization which operates from Senegal.

If feudalism perpetuates a balanced hierarchy with a docile base, one may ask what led to the birth of El Hor. The original impetus spread among the *haratin*, the ex-slaves, because their freedom lacked substance; in so many ways they were the 'untouchables' of Mauritanian society. In addition there were the memories and constant reminders of the circumstances of their own period of actual slavery. Slave life is not always easy to contemplate in the abstract; its physical realities can be distressing at close quarters. A slave mates with another slave under the direction of the master who will then own the children. A benevolent master will allow marriages and will not break up family groups; otherwise the offspring may be disposed of as the master wishes. A child may be given away, perhaps as a gratuity, or he or she may be exchanged; generally the transaction is a straight sale. Day-to-day life is not likely to vary much as a result of change of owner; the norm is unpaid labour from dawn until dusk with minimum clothing provided, and often discarded food for sustenance. There is no deviation from the repetitive regime other than is permitted or demanded by the master.

Punishment for disobedience can be harsh and is not governed by any systematic code. This is chattel slavery and a chattel is at the disposal of the whim of its owner; though arbitrariness may be tempered by fashion. There are reminders of the old penalties for witchcraft in England; an escaped slave[8] testifies that when sorcery is suspected a slave may be shot or otherwise executed. For less worrying offences he may find himself pegged out in the sun all day wishing he were dead, or savagely beaten with wet cord until the flesh begins to drop off him. Attempted escape has brought the worst punishments *pour encourager les autres*. One way of dealing with this offence against the institution is to stretch the offender over the back of a camel by cords which pass over the animal's stomach. The camel is then encouraged to drink until its stomach has swollen sufficiently to dislocate the slave's limbs. Alternatively the master's family may give him a collective beating or tie him up until he starves, perhaps to death. Sometimes castration or burning are used as punishments.

Specific examples of maltreatment[9] were collated by John Mercer not long before his death in July 1982. He named names and gave the addresses and dates which provide a valuable record for those upon whom his mantle has fallen. In one of his examples a slave woman ran off, refusing to go to the new master to whom she had been sold. The new master died and the old one therefore tried to get her back, using her two children and her mother as hostages; the mother was dragged about with a rope around her neck and one daughter was beaten about the face until she lost an eye. The escaped slave then tried to initiate legal proceedings and, as was only to be expected, achieved nothing. At this stage the former owner used, or rather misused, Islamic law, by declaring that the woman was his runaway wife. There was no disproving it and she simply fled to what might be termed the El Hor district of the capital, where she learned that her old mother had been thrown alive into a rubbish dump, where she was refused food and water, and eventually died. Another example is of a slave who had escaped and gone to the capital, where he was persuaded to enter into a debt bondage arrangement with his master, ostensibly in order that he might purchase his freedom. When, because of inflation, he fell behind with his payments, another slave lured him out of the town to a place where the master's family were able to kill him. Although the act was observed and reported to the police, there was neither trial nor punishment. The police interviewed the murderers, who admitted the killing, but a chattel proved to be no more than a chattel. From these and many other examples there emerges a constant theme of acceptance of the institution running right through police force, judiciary and society in general, notwithstanding recurrence of the atrocities inescapable from slavery.

Within Mauritania there are two sources of hope, which may ultimately help each other, provided that the *coup* which occurred on 12 December 1984 has not extinguished one of them. Among the ruling elite are some men committed to emancipation and it will be up to them to see that there is no turning back; they will have to win over colleagues and certain emirs. Dahane Ould Ahmed Mahmoud, an information minister of the government which proclaimed abolition, is on record as saying:[10]

> Slavery is the most primitive, hateful form of exploitation of man by man. We know it still exists in our country. The previous colonial and neo-colonial regimes tried to cover up the practice. It will take a long process before we are finally rid of it.

What is needed is the bridging of the wide gap between the

enlightened rulers and the other source of hope: the leadership of El Hor.

One of the founders of El Hor, Boubacar Messaoud, was originally the slave of a benevolent master who sent him to school. There he learned ideas in conflict with the accepted lore of tent and hut. Realization of the contrast between the possibilities of life in a free world and the almost superstitious acceptance of a servile role was a shock to him and to others fortunate enough to be exposed to education. A number decided to start a movement for emancipation and, as the word spread, a central committee was formed and representatives were found for the towns, the districts of Nouakchott and for sympathizers in Senegal. At first the movement gathered momentum only slowly, that is until a revolt took place in Choggar,[11] a settlement of part slaves in the Brakna emirate. The outcome of this confrontation was unsatisfactory when seen from either side of the feudal divide and the need for efficient spokesmen for the people who actually worked the land became more widely recognized.

A crisis had been created by the sudden imposition of heavy taxation to pay for the struggle for former Spanish Sahara. This was levied even on part slaves who decided that they could only survive by sending directly to the taxation authorities the proportion of the harvest that they normally paid to the masters. It was a direct challenge to slavery, or serfdom, and, after some rhetoric about cultivation rights, the masters reacted by destroying the irrigation dams, without which the part slaves were unable to cultivate. When the part slaves managed to gain concessions from central authority in the shape of certificates of cultivation rights, the local governor declared them invalid. Although he was dismissed his successor ruled that of the 200 part slave families in the settlement only seven men, from neighbouring Mali, were not slaves; these seven were expelled from the country, their families retained. Subsequently continued non-co-operation by the inhabitants of the settlement led to wholesale evictions from the village and imprisonment under military guard in a camp. Finally, after two children had died of starvation, some were allowed to go back to the land and resume their feudal existence.

After the Choggar revolt in 1977 it was a little easier for El Hor to convince Mauritania that there was a problem and its first task was to spread awareness. An early practical success, which added credibility to the young organization, was the freeing by means of a demonstration of two escaped slaves who had been taken into custody by the police. Then came the sale of the 15-year-old girl in Atar.[12] The demonstration of protest was on too large a scale for the authorities to pretend that it had not happened. Many *haratin* were arrested, charged with trespassing on the property of the slave's purchaser and imprisoned. Although some were soon released, others were to undergo a period of imprisonment with forced labour and a few, identified as ringleaders, were tortured. Harsh reaction to the Atar demonstration led El Hor to organize a series of protests all over the country which in their turn brought more arrests. By this time about 100 *haratin*, including Boubacar Messaoud, were awaiting trial and members of the government were considering a change of tactics.

The trial, when it took place in May 1980, succeeded in quelling much international disapproval. Suspended short sentences were awarded by a black judge. A few weeks later, for the third time in its history, Mauritania announced the abolition of slavery. World opinion was unaware of the continued imprisonment of the Atar protesters and the cruel conditions of the terms of imprisonment already served by those awaiting trial. If their testimony[13] is to be believed, and their injuries substantiate it, at least two were buried up to the neck at the tideline and beaten about the head until their hearing was permanently impaired. Some were forced to hold up heavy objects until they could do so no longer; there were beatings of the sort deemed suitable for disobedient slaves; one man, Ahmed Salem Ould Demba, went mad.

El Hor was not impressed by the abolition decree, nor by the terms of reference of the proposed commission to bring about emancipation and compensation. It wrote to Amnesty International who passed the letter on to the Anti-Slavery Society and, as has been seen, John Mercer decided to investigate. His findings, put before the United Nations Commission on Human Rights, had one immediately encouraging outcome: the official Observer for the Mauritanian government invited the Sub-Commission on Prevention of Discrimination and Protection of Minorities to send experts to verify the efforts the Mauritanian government was making with regard to slavery and the slave trade. That invitation was accepted and a delegation of two was appointed 'to visit Mauritania in order to study the situation and ascertain the country's needs'.[14] During the 1981 UN proceedings that country's representatives made many frank admissions and a few denials about the prevalence of slavery; from time to time one gains the impression that there is some division of opinion at the top level of government, and that, at least until the 1984 *coup*, the more liberal element has been in the ascendant. It is a new and long overdue departure for the United Nations to carry out field investigations into slavery at the instigation of a non-governmental organization. The expert chosen to set this important precedent was Marc Bossuyt from Belgium and the Mauritanian government asked that the Anti-Slavery Society be represented on the mission. UN protocol does not allow non-governmental organizations to perform in this way, but a means of avoiding the difficulty was found by arranging for the Society's Director to go as an observer specifically invited by the host government. Bureaucracy was thwarted.

El Hor has many specific aims, not all of which may turn out to be in the best interests of the *haratin*. Apart from the general obvious aim that slavery be brought to an end and that there be no discrimination against the ex-slaves, the leaders have expressed their belief in the need for recognition of the *haratin* as a distinct ethnic group, with its own culture. Against this it might be urged that integration with society, rather than retention of separate identity, might better serve the fundamental need to discard the unfortunate legacies of history. They are known to object to apartheid; they may regret going along with one of its tenets. Naturally they want an equitable share of the good land and they see this as just compensation for centuries of servitude. Less realistically they object to the idea of compensation for the masters. There is a moral argument against compensating a master for the loss of a slave; there are, however, sound historical precedents, especially within British experience, for hastening and guaranteeing emancipation by this means. And, though one can understand El Hor overlooking this aspect, some benevolent masters born into the institution barely at subsistence level do not deserve the starvation that emancipation without compensation might bring. Seemingly aware that its demand that financial compensation be paid to the *haratin*, the plaintiffs in the case, is over-optimistic, El Hor has expressed an alternative method of achieving roughly the same end: government grants for rural development and training, and also provision of schools, clinics and other amenities for the settlements (*edebaye*) occupied by newly liberated part slaves.

The great fear, stemming from the ineffectiveness of successive declarations of emancipation, is that yet again there will be a slipping back to feudalism. To prevent this El Hor wants a body of specific legislation designed to guarantee that in all ways former masters and slaves have equal rights; formerly, for instance, a marriage was only valid if the master had authorized it. One other demand is for the establishment of a centralized bureau to help freed slaves find alternative employment, should it not be possible or desirable for them to remain with their former masters as wage earners. Another important function of the bureau would be to promote labour-intensive government agricultural schemes.

The United Nations and the Anti-Slavery Society's Director were in Mauritania from 14 to 24 January 1984. One of the problems of such visits is the great danger that friendly relations with the ruling elite will lead to a report dispensing whitewash in all directions. However, a considerable advantage enjoyed by ex-colonial territories is the polite fiction that all can be blamed on the colonial power. That much having been assumed there is little point in hiding anything; quite the reverse, in fact. Whether or not such thoughts ever surfaced in the minds of interested parties, there is no reason to suppose that the official investigators were hoodwinked.

Mauritania has been considered in greater detail than other examples of chattel slavery because slavery has been, and still is, an integral element in the socio-economic fabric of the state and because evidence is readily available. There is now reason to believe that several other Sahelian states are similarly placed and the Anti-Slavery Society is pressing the United Nations to investigate the wider problem with a view to encouraging reforms in 'education, agriculture, animal husbandry and land distribution'.[15] But the way ahead is fraught with more difficulties than the general terms and cool language of official documents suggest. A healthy injection of emotion from the independent French witness addressed to the UN slavery experts sounded as though it was a reaction to a previous speaker's broadening of the definition of slavery to include standard advertising which featured attractive women. His comments did not refer to Mauritania but brought the Working Group's attention back to the basic issue of people who are property. To free them without compensation, education and land would be tantamount to a sentence of death. He went on to warn that, whatever the practical politics of compensating masters to sugar the emancipation pill, such compensation was hardly in line with Article 25 of Forced Labour Convention Number 29 (1930):[16]

> The illegal exaction of forced or compulsory labour shall be punishable as a penal offence, and it shall be an obligation on

> any Member ratifying this Convention to ensure that the penalties imposed by law are really adequate and are strictly enforced.

Sahelian states have ratified this Convention and the United Nations can hardly be seen to encourage the substitution of rewards for penalties. The ratifying of international Conventions may be an empty gesture on the part of some member states; nevertheless it involves a voluntary, if limited, renunciation of sovereignty.

In his report[17] Professor Bossuyt made fourteen recommendations to the Government of Mauritania. Firstly, having observed that since joining the United Nations Mauritania had not ratified all the international human rights instruments, he urged that this be done; on the face of it a mere formality, but it is difficult to encourage a state to toe the line if it has not explicitly yielded sovereignty on these issues. The next recommendation, if implemented, would cleverly defuse the compensation controversy without putting the United Nations in the position of having to go along with action contrary to the Forced Labour Convention: masters' compensation applications should not be accepted more than three years after the third abolition of slavery, or, to put it another way, the deadline should be 9 November 1984, only weeks after the publication of Bossuyt's report. El Hor would not have to suffer long before the door was closed for ever.

The third recommendation is for the establishment of an authority responsible for eradicating slavery on its own initiative and empowered to hear and act on complaints. As this is immediately followed in the report by firm advice that former slaves themselves should be involved in such activity, the point could be taken that El Hor and a government department should merge their interests. Next, radical modification is urged of the 'civil status legislation' being prepared so that the former slave is helped to realize that his status is completely transformed. At the same time it is important that the administration authorities be reminded by circular that slavery is illegal and that they must notify the judiciary of any irregularities.

To get across to everyone that the institution has really come to an end this time, Bossuyt recommends that measures be taken to spread awareness of all the necessary changes that this involves. Using every available means of communication the various implications of the abolition of slavery must be broadcast in all languages of the country, and religious leaders should be asked to explain to the faithful that these changes do not conflict with the *Shari'a*. An important part of the message is that any victimizer of his former slaves should know the criminal penalties (not specified in the report) that may befall him. Moreover increased vigilance must be exercised to see that where former slaves choose to stay on with their old masters as ordinary employees, there is no relapse or deterioration in the relationship. To this end careful inspection must be carried out. Much impetus towards change and new attitudes could come from the provision of new schools, especially in *haratin* areas.

There is a rather woolly recommendation that sociological research into Mauritanian society be developed and finally there are suggestions that handicraft enterprises be set up and that a system of loans on easy terms be made available to encourage former slaves to become livestock owners. But, knowing that his recommendations were being given to one of the poorest states in the world, Bossuyt then asked the Sub-Commission to draw the attention of UN member states and the relevant world organizations with funds for worthy causes to Mauritania's needs. How they will respond and whether money will underpin the country while it changes character and personality remains to be seen.

Africa and the Middle East are not the only areas of the world in which chattel slavery has persisted into the twentieth century. In 1977 Colonel Montgomery of the Anti-Slavery Society was asked by the Immigrants Advisory Service to interview a man who had arrived at Heathrow airport from Nicaragua and was asking for asylum on the grounds that he was an escaped slave:[18]

> When I asked what proof of this he could give he removed his shirt revealing a cruciform brand mark about two inches wide by three inches long at the top of each upper arm. He said that all of the forty slaves in the household of President Somoza were branded in this way and had their heads shaven to facilitate recognition in the event of escape. The penalty for attempted escape was death.

Somoza has since perished.

At much the same time in Altamura, southern Italy, a 14-year-old boy, sold for unpaid work as a shepherd, stole a shotgun and killed himself.[19] The ensuing publicity revealed that a slave market for shepherd boys had been held annually for centuries; the only concession to modern double standards had been a realization of the need for discretion, as far as the world outside this bleak corner of Italy was concerned. Even so the boys were examined physically, as though they were horses or negroes newly arrived in eighteenth-century New Orleans. The sales were recorded in writing and, when it came to a trial, all the old justifications of chattel slavery were resurrected. It was an ancient and good tradition upon which the locality depended. Spartan unpaid life in the hills is good for adolescents who are removed from the temptations of the modern world. The original sellers were the parents; after they had parted with their son he might be sold to a succession of owners at higher prices as he grew larger and stronger. It was frost bite and general debilitation which led to the suicide which brought the matter before the Italian court.

Such examples, as with much to do with slavery, could be dealt with under several headings. Italian shepherd boys might well have been considered under 'Exploitation of Children'. An alternative view, though, is that where sale of people occurs it is worth demonstrating that the common denominator is not necessarily one particular master race. All inhabited continents offend and while it is more effective to leave the buying and selling of the child prostitutes of, say, Asia to a later chapter, for the sake of impartiality it is desirable to quote from Europe an example of an ancient pastoral tradition using humans as property. Similarly the case of the Aché Indians, whilst relevant as an example of the persecution of tribal minorities, can also be used to show the existence of chattel slavery in a South American context.

While the *haratin*'s problems belong to the past and will give way to very different ones when emancipation is complete, the Aché (or Guayakí) Indians of Paraguay have much to fear from the present and little hope for the future. Forest Indians of central South America, their nomadic range is now limited to pockets of wilderness in the south-east corner of Paraguay near the frontiers of Brazil and Argentina. Although their history during and since the colonial period was of massacre followed by enslavement or retreat, it is the penetration of their traditional hunting grounds by roads and the destruction of their habitat by farmers and foresters which is accelerating their extinction. On the pioneer fringe a combination of commercial, military and missionary zeal has hastened the process of enslavement which, because of the nature of the tribe concerned, becomes part of the pattern of genocide.

The traditional response to the Indian presence by backwoodsmen was casual murder and the occasional manhunt, and the by-products of these activities in the early days were child slaves, sometimes an adult. The Aché defended themselves as efficiently as could be expected with bows and arrows; on rare occasions, when they interpreted encroachment as trespass, they helped themselves to the pioneer farmers' cattle. It was not long before a feature of the Aché tribe was identified and turned to the advantage of the advancing settlers: when free the Aché were strong fighters; when captured they became docile to the extent that they would co-operate in the hunting of their own tribe. Inefficient persecution went on until 1968, when the Native Affairs Department of the Paraguayan Ministry of Defence was founded and Indian affairs became part of the responsibility of the army. In 1974, when the United Nations had no machinery with which to attempt to implement the Convention on Slavery, the Commission on Human Rights was informed by the Anti-Slavery Society[20] that the Director of the Native Affairs Department, Colonel Infanzón, was trafficking in female slaves and that a Sergeant Pereira, accompanied by Aché slaves, was killing, torturing and enslaving more of that diminishing tribe. The information was attributed to Dr Mark Münzel, an anthropologist who had carried out an investigation in the Aché region, where what was euphemistically termed a 'reservation' had been founded.

The establishment of a reservation in which Aché could be confined has parallels with the setting up of extermination camps in Germany during the Nazi period. In each case the main purpose was to bring about the final solution of what was alleged to be a racial problem, and in each case sadistic human instincts came to the fore. Münzel[21] discovered that Jesus de Pereira had been placed in charge of the reservation because he was the principal slave-owner of the region and had put it about that the Indians had come to work on his farm to enjoy his protection. His position was naturally greatly enhanced by official recognition; for one thing he was able to draw food supplies from military sources, sell most of them for his own profit and keep the Indians not too far above starvation level. His own household resembled a brothel and, as camp commandant, he was able to murder and rape as the whim took him, which under the influence of alcohol it often did. His taste in girls included 10- and 11-year-olds and his taste in sadistic treatment, sometimes using a cage which prevented the prisoner from standing or sitting, at other times punching men in the genitals, was rationalized in his belief that breaking the spirit was necessary in order to civilize. All the cultural attributes of the Aché were seen as harmful to them: their lip ornaments, their music, even their language. If they were not sold or bartered there were only two options open to them: to become white men and catch or kill the wild Aché in the forest, or to sit down and die quietly.

As a result of Münzel's disclosures Jesus de Pereira was dismissed and imprisoned for a few days; he then resumed his activities in another part of the Aché region. His place was taken by Jack Stolz, of the North American New Tribes Mission, whose attitude to the Indians' culture is similar to his predecessor's. After his arrival, although there are no Aché within 100 miles of the reservation, uninvited investigators[22] took note of mysterious increases in the number of Indians in it. According to Stolz they just came in during the night; he implied that news of a congenial environment might have reached them. Physical conditions were appalling, at the outskirts of the reservation reminiscent of Belsen. The evidence of the photographs showed that witnesses had not exaggerated. In one of two huts said to be empty were found two dying women, abandoned in filthy squalor; in the other another woman lay dying with a hole in her leg. Stolz's son let slip that she had been shot while being brought into the reservation. The missionaries made no attempt to disguise their contempt for the Indians in their care. Stolz had no urge to learn their language, and hell fire surely awaited them if they did not learn his. The fate of the Indians was entrusted to a heartless Protestant mission in a largely indifferent Roman Catholic country, a situation which serves only to show that disregard for human rights is not peculiar to the adherents of any one faith.

Even if the pessimistic view is taken that the extermination of the Aché as an ethnic group is inevitable despite the protests of almost all relevant human rights groups and many individuals, including church leaders, there are other Indian tribes under threat. And, furthermore, there is the problem of the *criados*, children orphaned by the murder or enslavement of their parents. Many remain concealed as chattels with Paraguayan families. As for the surviving 'tamed' adults, living outside the reservations, Münzel estimates that in 1985 between 100 and 150 'are in bad situations of some kind of bondage'.[23] The position is complicated as each Aché labourer needs to be investigated separately to find out whether or not he is working of his own free will, and 'the Paraguayan authorities do not seem to be very interested in finding out'.

What lessons may be learned from these examples of chattel slavery? As the story is still unfolding, early conclusions must be tentative. Where atrocities occur the roots are much the same: greed and weakness – especially the weakness induced by poverty – are juxtaposed; eventually the phenomenon of slavery brings out the worst in all men, regardless of cultural or religious heritage. Where it is truly an institution, as in Mauritania, it perpetuates itself until outside influences enable change to begin. Elsewhere the potential for cruel enslavement seems to lie within the kernel of original sin until opportunity causes it to germinate. Love of money may be the root of much of the evil, but money itself, in terms of international aid, properly dispensed, is a large part of the cure of traditional organized slavery today. The United Nations, said to be a club of governments rather than peoples, once given access to the people, has machinery which could help. Under the pressure and guidance of non-governmental organizations, whose function is often to try to protect citizens from governments, it would be possible to alleviate poverty and curb greed. For this to be a fact of life instead of a dream, a mechanism has to be devised to enable United Nations officials to gain admission to a country if there is reason to believe that a Convention is being ignored by a government which has ratified it. As things stand, obligatory inspections are out of the question: national sovereignty is paramount and the United Nations has neither the wish nor the power to interfere without an invitation. If access on demand was built into the wording of Conventions, would they be ratified?

CHAPTER 3

THE SLAVE AS A DISPOSABLE ASSET

Work brings freedom (Arbeit macht frei)

INSCRIPTION OVER THE GATES OF AUSCHWITZ

The twentieth century has seen the rise and fall at the very heart of civilization of slavery at its worst; the phenomenon was carried to the uttermost limit. Under the Third Reich the chattel slave was the property of the state, its agencies or its industrial concerns, and, according to official policy as expounded by Hitler and practised by the *Schutzstaffel*, as far as the Jewish slave was concerned, his destination was the gas chamber as soon as possible; another, less powerful, school of thought urged the necessity of his contributing to the war economy first. It was, however, not as simple as that. Memories tend to be short and it needs to be emphasized that National Socialist use of slave labour was not born of expediency. From time to time it yielded to short-sighted aims assumed to be expedient, but there remained an apparent contradiction between the wish to exterminate and the wish to exploit; and this can only be understood by taking into account racial policy as originally proclaimed in *Mein Kampf*.

Very much the product of an anti-semitic culture and thoroughly disillusioned by his own early failures and the contemporary failures of his country, Hitler devised a crude interpretation of Darwinism in which the Jews were the principal race unfit to survive an inevitable historical process. As his argument was developed one can see that, if the premises were translated so as to apply to other societies, any race could emerge as dominant or doomed, without the validity of the argument being threatened. Like more respectable thinkers before him, Hitler simply postulated what he wanted to prove. The first wholly fictitious premise was that there exists an Aryan master race, possessing a monopoly of virtue and a white skin. The alleged scientific basis of supremacy was the Aryan's recognition of the natural law that races only mate with their own kind. Miscegenation is evil: mating across the racial barrier 'is a sin against the will of the Eternal Creator. And as a sin this act will be avenged.'[1]

Given an enlightened interpretation, Aristotle's precept that some were born to rule, some to obey, can be seen to be true and probably harmless. One of the dangerous elements of Greek belief and practice, the conviction that we rule, foreigners serve, was translated by Hitler into a biological or anthropological imperative without any attempt even to manipulate laboratory evidence. In Volume 1 of *Mein Kampf* the author expresses the truth as though it had been revealed to him from on high; in Volume 2 it is reinforced by an illogical jump from biological necessity to geographical necessity. Not all foreign races are grossly inferior to the pure-bred Germanic Aryan, but by a coincidence of biology and geography those living in territories adjacent to the German frontiers of 1918 are dependent, impure non-Aryans ripe for subjugation: to the west is France, undergoing 'the progressive disappearance of the best elements of the race',[2] to the east is Russia, contaminated by the ideas of the Jew, Marx; since the French are bent on self-destruction, Germany's positive urge for expansion must be directed to the east. Volume 1 contains the most coherent exposition of the development of the master race. Social progress, within races and between races, depends upon the survival of the fittest, that is to say those with pure blood; conversely, hybridization leads to decay. The historical process leads to a three-fold stratification: 'founders of culture, bearers of culture and destroyers of culture'[3] or Germans, dependent races and Jews. Although Hitler strongly denied that man could control nature,[4] for a short period of history he found it easier to initiate violent action than did the Marxist with his belief in an inevitable outcome. His policy could be construed as co-operating positively with the laws of eugenics as he saw them. If his followers were not vigilant the Aryan race would be contaminated by miscegenation and cease to have the potential for world leadership. He gave a paradoxical warning about the culture destroyers,[5]

> the Jewish people preserve the purity of their blood better than any other nation on earth. Therefore the Jew follows his destined road until he is opposed by a force superior to him. And then a desperate struggle takes place to send back to Lucifer him who would assault the heavens.

Although *Mein Kampf* had no scientific evidence to support its claims, Hitler's timing was such that his exhortations for pride in being German and identification of a scapegoat for Germany's ills ensured much popularity for his ideas, if not for the book itself. The linking of racial superiority with the need for territorial expansion gave his supporters ambitions as they looked out at the world. Equally what applied between states applied between groups within the state: the man to whom the truth had been revealed must lead, helped by an elite of loyal disciples; the purified race would follow. The all important priority was the purification of that race and, once in power, National Socialists made sure that legislation aimed at eliminating undesirable elements began. In 1933, as had been specifically urged in *Mein Kampf*,[6] much sterilization followed the passing of the eugenic laws. Two years later the anti-Jewish legislation began to take its effect; if a German had one or more Jewish grandparents he was not fit to marry a German; Jewish property was confiscated; Jews lost their citizenship; and so on until the concentration camps gave way to the extermination camps.

At first the idea of actual physical elimination was not fully grasped even by those within the elite. Many deportations occurred and Jews were useful as slave labour; only later, as the Third Reich extended its boundaries and the middle layer of Hitler's hierarchy began to form an essential part of the war machine, did the racial plan run into difficulties. Certain key passages in *Mein Kampf* provide the best indication of the part which slavery would play in the future:[7]

> Had it not been possible for them to employ members of the inferior race which they conquered, the Aryans would never have been in a position to take the first steps on the road which led them to a later type of culture.

That road, which within twenty years was in places literally constructed from the bones of subjugated races, and built by others destined for the crematoria, was to lead with the help of slavery to the imperialist victory of the racially pure: 'Only after subjugated races were employed as slaves was a similar fate allotted to animals.'[8] Hitler was at pains to trace a continuing historical process and in his switches from past to present and thence to future he is rather more clever than when attempting reasoned argument:[9]

> It was not by mere chance that the first forms of civilization arose where the Aryan came in contact with inferior races, subjugated them and forced them to obey his command. The members of the inferior race became the first mechanical tools in the service of a growing civilization.
>
> Thereby the way was clearly indicated which the Aryan had to follow. As a conqueror, he subjugated inferior races and turned their physical powers into organized channels under his own leadership. . . . While he ruthlessly maintained his position as their master, he not only remained master but also maintained and advanced civilization. For this depended exclusively on his inborn abilities and, therefore, on the preservation of the Aryan race as such. . . .
>
> In this world everything that is not of sound racial stock is like chaff.

It is the method of the orator; analysis of the past slips easily into urgent demands for changes in the present national arrangements to ensure that Germany fulfils its natural destiny, as summed up in the Epilogue: 'A State which, in an epoch of racial adulteration, devotes itself to the duty of preserving the best elements of its racial stock must one day become ruler of the earth.'[10] Even in the mid-1920s, when these words were first drafted, it was clear that the Jew was not to be equated with the slave. When the orator's aims were being fulfilled with astonishing rapidity, the Jew's only temporary salvation was to prove himself worthy of slavery; and even as a slave he worked for the success in war of his own executioner. Hitler's supporters in his anti-semitic campaign, Alfred Rosenberg, Julius Streicher and Joseph Goebbels being among the keenest, had early success in identifying the Jews as a sort of racial poison, and persecution did not wait upon international disturbances; it was first priority and only in Germany's darkest hour would a small proportion of skilled Jews be able to look upon slavery as providing a frail possibility of survival. Their only hope, it appeared, lay in a sudden German collapse before the SS had time to carry out Hitler's order that there should be a last-minute comprehensive massacre. One Jewish estimate[11] is that some 200,000 Jews, having worked as slaves and thus avoided the gas chambers, survived the war; and they survived despite a modification of the SS position which allowed work itself to be the means of extermination.

Such were the cruel standards of the Third Reich that, until defeat was in sight, slavery could be regarded as the merciful alternative to suffering the conditions of the extermination camps. There, apart from relentless progression towards the crematoria, there was arbitrary torture and sometimes laboratory experiments of satanic imagination. And within this world Lucifer's work was aided by the advanced technology of the German firms as they competed for the crematoria contracts, and by a physical lust for cruelty thought quite unbelievable until the revelations of the Nuremberg Trials. National Socialism required the dependent conquered races to labour for Germany during and after the war. Poles, Slavs and Russians bore the brunt of forced labour and Belgians, Dutch and French played their part, though the terms agreed at the capitulation of France created a fudged contractual relationship which made Frenchmen nominally volunteers. The contribution which Jews might be allowed to make to the German war effort was a controversial matter even within the ranks of the SS; policy varied with the degree of success or failure experienced in the conflict and sometimes with the personal motives of those with vested interests in an unpaid labour force. To the purist, though, a Jew was always destined for the gas chamber without delay.

To many of those who survived, the merciful alternative proved to be a living hell. Some were given heavy, meaningless tasks, like carrying rocks back and forth for no other purpose than to occupy them and satisfy the sadistic cravings of the guards.[12] Most worked in the armaments industries and were either in privately owned factories or rival concerns set up at the concentration camps. Heinrich Himmler, enthusiastic about the idea of an SS industrial empire, autonomous within the state, planned to employ 25,000 prisoners from a number of camps including Auschwitz and Buchenwald. It was a project which, although only partly realized, greatly worried Albert Speer, Minister for Armaments and War Production. Speer, who was still struggling with his deceased rivals as late as 1981, the year of his own death, pronounced Himmler's enterprise a failure because it was 'too brutal' and 'too amateurish'[13]. Although hardly a reliable witness, Speer eventually arrived at the correct conclusion that brutality had been counter-productive; and yet, despite daily demonstrations of the inability of maltreated slaves to equal production rates of free workers, the radical change of policy needed to stave off defeat was never seriously entertained. Those employers who did improve conditions did so on their own initiative. Himmler was distinctly irritated by the general assumption that slaves only yielded half the production of free workers: 'It is not clear why the imprisoned skilled worker cannot achieve the same performance as the skilled worker who lives in freedom.'[14] He had only to look at the mortality rate to find one answer.

To see chattel slavery as it has survived until today, one has only to look at the small traditional society of Mauritania. To understand the National Socialist concept of the slave as a disposable chattel, one needs a smaller example than is provided by the Third Reich as a whole, with its endless proliferation of cruelties. Many German firms made use of slave labour; to some it was a golden opportunity for profit and they may even have had sufficient self-interest to feed their workers adequately. But one firm had had a special relationship with the fatherland going back several centuries and it lay at the centre of Germany's industrial heartland; without it Hitler could hardly have contemplated war in the modern manner. About the same number of slaves passed through the hands of Krupp as are to be found in Mauritania today; general suffering was, however, much greater and can be regarded as typical of practices inflicted on the forced workers throughout the armaments industries of the racist totalitarian regime. Poverty and greed are prominent features even of this artificially created and transient manifestation of slavery. The influence of poverty was unusually diversified; firstly, much bitterness had been generated by the post-Armistice shortages felt keenly by the German ex-soldiers and other unemployed, whose plight it was felt needed to be avenged. Then there was the deliberate reduction to poverty of the Jews and the inevitable impoverishment of the conquered peoples. Greed is less easy to discern. Himmler's wish to construct an SS industrial empire was to do with establishing an independent power base, but is not the difference between love of money and love of power largely a question of degree rather than of kind? Himmler scored both ways: during 1943 the firm of Krupp was paying the SS three or four marks per worker per day.[15] Some slaves went to ancillary industries. There greed took its toll; not every entrepreneur who headed for the rich pickings of the Generalgouvernement (the Polish territory under German rule) was an Oskar Schindler, busily diverting men and women from their part in the Final Solution.

Ideally there should have been no conflict of interest within the slave market; foreign workers were for the factories, Jews for the extermination camps. But a dilemma was created by the high sickness and mortality rates among slaves generally and by civilian manpower shortages caused indirectly by losses at the front and directly by allied bombing. At first official policy was to replace Jewish workers by foreign workers, and this became easier as the boundaries of the Third Reich widened; but Jewish brains and efficiency were valuable in their own right and a policy of replacement meant that weeks or months of output were lost while the new work force was trained. If suffered generally across the armaments field, such delays could alter the outcome of the war. It was Alfried Krupp, leader of the famous dynasty during the crucial war years, who made the professional recommendation that a policy of annihilation through work should be adopted. As he saw it, to work a Jew to death in a few months reconciled the twin goals of racial purification and economic efficiency. Given an endless flow of replacements, disposable slaves could, in theory, have won the war for Germany. One reason that they did not was the inhuman treatment which they received.

Throughout the period of racial persecutions, as though with an eye on the day of reckoning, a vocabulary of euphemisms for what was actually happening to Jews and other doomed categories became current among Nazi officials. 'Evacuation' was one evasion, 'Final Solution' another. The Krupp family's firm, with confidence accumulated over more than 300 years, had no such qualms. After an interval, when early arrivals were treated almost paternalistically because their status was not appreciated, Krupp officials went to the logical extreme and took the newcomers for what they were, slaves, and labelled and organized them accordingly. As they emerged from the trains at Essen in the Ruhr, much the worse for wear after a long journey in goods vans from the east, a plentiful supply of slaves began to be subjected to the Krupp version of a dehumanization process similar in fundamental respects to what was practised in many places throughout occupied Europe; it ran counter to traditional Krupp practice, but the new proprieter was a loyal Nazi.

Arbitrary rough handling began immediately, regardless of physical condition. There were four main classes of prisoner: Jews, Poles, Russians and other eastern races. As the lowest form of life, the Jews bore a different form of label, a yellow tag; the others were distinguished by large initial letters on the prison uniforms which all wore. Those who fell outside the principal racial classifications were differentiated by arm bands of various colours. Names were now things of the past; numbers, which in many cases had already been tattooed on the arms, were now stitched on to uniforms. All were provided with clogs and blankets. After the twilight period came fists and boots; as the war economy warmed up these soon gave way to truncheons and steel whips, and neither uniforms nor shoes of any sort were provided for eastern workers. Unfortunately for the supposedly volunteer workers, or *Freiwillige*, from the western European countries, France, Belgium and Holland, the careful categorization of prisoners defeated its own object; the diversification was too great and guards tended to make one distinction only: between Germans and others. Later, when *Freiwillige* had served their full term and attempted to leave, they found that their contracts had been compulsorily extended and their lot was soon little better than that of the despised eastern races.

Likewise accommodation steadily deteriorated. Russian tribal peoples, drawn into a war about which they knew nothing, died from a number of causes, including bad sanitary arrangements. Their quarters were saturated in excrement, a state of affairs which encouraged the diseases which, in their exhausted condition, they were unable to survive. Some 600 Jewish women from Ravensbrück were kept in a work camp which allied bombing had damaged to the extent that Italian prisoners of war could no longer be held there. They were visited by Krupp's senior medical officer, Dr Wilhelm Jaeger, who at Nuremberg described what he had found.[16] In his affidavit he said that the women had no shoes and wore only sacks with holes for head and arms. Their heads had been shaved and they had untreated open septic wounds. Restrained by barbed wire and SS guards they had little food and no medication; they were diseased and infested with fleas.

Another Krupp work camp was in Noggerratstrasse at Essen. There French prisoners of war fared little better than the Ravensbrück Jewesses. Many of them lived for about five months in dog kennels three feet high, six feet wide and nine feet long; there were five men to a kennel. Others had to live in urinals. Jaeger gave testimony about eight camps for Russian and Polish slaves. The conditions were such that they made a mockery of the perverse policy of annihiliation through work; the workers who might have saved the Reich by their labours were dying instead from diseases caused by overcrowding, a starvation diet, lack of water, general filth and, in winter, absence of heating. Other causes of their deaths were brutality on the part of their masters; gratuitous beatings by Krupp foremen or SS guards contributed to physical and emotional decline. And one did not have to be an experienced industrialist to see that output fell far short of its potential under such a regime; terror never yielded the expected profits in the realm of skilled labour. Unskilled workers employed in fields and forests could be driven hard by it; and yet the only area in which slave labour may have been of general and consistent value to the ruling power was agriculture where, because of the unavoidably open character of much forced labouring on farms, conditions were on the whole far less severe. This is not to imply that the ordinary citizens of Essen were unaware of what was going on. They knew only too well. In the Ruhr, however, they had become prime RAF targets, and whatever sensitivities had survived the propaganda machine were soon numbed.

When British bombing began in earnest at the beginning of 1943, instead of protecting the work force out of self-interest, Krupp staff simply worried about the effect on the local populace, should slaves escape during the raid. Initially the absence of shelters did provoke unrest among the slaves during the actual bombardment. It was not very long, though, before lack of protection was accepted as just another facet of the New Order. The slaves accepted that burial of the dead and reconstruction of the damaged plant were now part of their day-to-day existence. Slit trenches, which could save many lives, were allowed, but the opportunity to dig did not always precede the onset of the raid. In 1944, Krupp lost some 600 Russians because there was no form of refuge in their camp. Slaves soon learned to scoop holes in the ground with their hands. Other camp inmates were lucky enough to live within reasonable distance of railway tunnels. Capacity was limited, which meant that, true to National Socialist principles, as raid followed raid, only the fittest arrived in time to be sure of survival.

Although national responsibility for mobilization of slave labour was vested in Fritz Sauckel, and carried out by fanatical underlings, the Krupp firm identified itself so strongly with this aspect of national life that it entered into the field in its own right. Not content to confine itself merely to production in the Ruhr and leave the task of providing forced labour to others, it went directly to the camps, both for labour acquisition and to minimize communications problems by bringing the factory to the labour source. The Krupp directors decided that Auschwitz would best satisfy their needs. The original plan was to make fuses, but so vast and varied was the available labour pool that the scope of the factory was extended to include the parts of automatic weapons. By choosing Auschwitz they had inadvertently ventured into an area of industrial expansion which Himmler had coveted to further his own SS industrial ambitions. There were some unnecessary delays, for Auschwitz held enough talent for all; the only real problem was to divert it from the gas chamber to the factory floor.

During April and May 1943, the firm of Krupp was allowed to take possession of a sizeable portion of the most comprehensive extermination camp. Within it the firm built its own railhead, manufacturing sheds and sanitary block. Barracks were hired, as were the prisoners, from the SS. The terms of the arrangement allowed for the rejection of Jews whose physical condition fell short of minimum Krupp standards, a wise precaution. Selection, formerly an SS prerogative, was not only shared with Krupp, but Krupp had the last word. Twenty-five Krupp officials were alloted[1] to the Auschwitz branch of the Krupp empire, charged with organizing and training the 500 Berlin Jews whose life expectation had been increased by a few months. Krupp and the Auschwitz commandment, Franz Hoss, were at one about the temporary nature of the stay of execution. Before the war ended, experience here had paved the way for many similar enterprises, in other parts of the extended Reich, combining Krupp and SS expertise: an unholy alliance of work and death.

Despite Alfried Krupp's precaution that enabled him to reject slaves who were beyond repair, he never fully realized that working to death was inefficient if the worker was perpetually unfit. At Auschwitz the prisoners were nightly in the care of the SS, who delivered them at dawn and remained on guard throughout the day; lack of food, and inadequacies of clothing and shelter sapped strength and the smell of burning flesh from the crematoria demoralized everyone. Although the industrial empire had the common feature of degradation, as Germany's difficulties increased there was less and less uniformity from camp to camp, contrary to the nation's reputation for obsessive regimentation. The Auschwitz factory was not in action for long before the Russian advance forced evacuation in the conventional sense of the term; and that and other westward migrations brought the lowest levels of life to the Ruhr where the accommodation problem was acute: some prisoners slept in the open air; luckier ones might have a bombed out house, a shed or a tent, in which they would huddle together for warmth. In Essen, as elsewhere, the quality of the slave, on and after arrival, declined. As the last stages of the war approached desperate attempts to maintain production meant that the very young were exploited. In 1943 12-year-olds were employed, in 1944 the youngest slaves were aged 6.[17]

Although the Nuremberg judges have had to live with the uncomfortable fact that the victors were trying the vanquished, the wealth of written, oral and filmed evidence was so great that serious endeavours could be made to explore the genesis and expansion of the National Socialist system of slavery; the trials had a value over and above the need for justice to be done. The verdicts and sentences can usefully be put out of one's mind when considering the crimes against humanity, though the characters of leading participants should not be ignored, nor allowed to divert the student of the phenomenon from the thought that the guilty may have been numbered in millions. The guilt of the industrial proprietors who practised slavery is not in doubt; those industrialists who preferred free labour to slave were never penalized, however inconvenient their preference may have been. Their position is comparable to that of those members of the SS who could not stomach shooting Jewish children; they were not shot themselves, they were transferred to other duties.

Mention of the iniquities of Krupp was made at the Nuremberg Trials, but Alfried was not obliged to appear with the surviving leaders of his country because his senile father, Gustav, was erroneously held responsible. Gustav was not fit to plead and Alfried was not properly charged. However, it was not long before Alfried was summoned before an American military tribunal and charged with war crimes, including crimes against humanity. Soon the extent of Krupp slave trading and treatment was revealed, partly from his own files, despite efforts to destroy the most incriminating records; precise details remained of transportation of Jews from concentration camps to factories, and often the factories were simply fenced off areas of the camps. The three American judges heard how, when the end of the war was in sight, the accused had thought it proper that 520 Jewish girls, some aged 14, should work in cruel conditions in Essen. Krupp had never been ignorant of the atrocities carried out in his name; medical officers, including the family physician,[18] had reported on the reasons for the deaths of slaves. Starvation was one cause; a post-mortem might reveal complete absence of fatty tissue and no evidence of disease. But usually disease played a prominent role. One routine report analysed the causes of death of fifty-four eastern workers:

thirty-eight died of tuberculosis, two of malnutrition, one of haemorrhage of the stomach, two of intestinal diseases, one of typhus, three of pneumonia, one of appendicitis, one of liver disease, one of an abscess.[19]

Armed with good legal advice and sympathetic witnesses, it might have been possible to attribute a proportion of the starvation, disease and damaged accommodation, perhaps even lack of clothing, to the misfortunes of war. It would not be so easy to explain away spontaneous or calculated sadism. Special premises were reserved for the physical torture of those who were no longer able to co-operate adequately. Remarkably, or so it seems, these were in the cellar of the Krupp administration building in Essen, not, as one might have expected, in the anonymity of a distant suburb. There a metal box, known as the Cage, had been purpose-built. It contained two miniature cells, each five feet high and twenty-two inches square. Slaves would be confined there for hours or days, unable to stand or sit, with one hole in the lid through which to breathe. The crueller type of guard was known to pour water through the ventilation hole, or confine more than one prisoner in a cell. In one case it was used as punishment for a woman who was seven months pregnant: conceiving for a second time was her crime. Beatings also took place in this cellar and the cries of the victims were heard by staff working in Krupp's offices overhead.

Other evidence at Krupp's trial referred to the hosing of Ukrainian women with ice-cold water to waken them long before dawn; cold water was a popular means of winter punishment which could kill. By the last days of the war the hoses were used as whips for beating the breasts of women and the genitals of men. In the workshops wooden truncheons were used and impossible physical tasks were given to the weakest workers, for no other reason than to satisfy lust for cruelty and to avenge the imminent defeat of the Aryan race. Savagery accelerated as the end approached.

Individual examples of cruelty may be grasped, if not forgiven, but the statistics, though they can be discussed dispassionately as statistics, representing as they do a vast accumulation of personal tragedies, baffle comprehension and leave the imagination numb. Hitler's special regard for the Krupp family meant that these horrifying excesses continued even if there were opposition from rival interests within the state, as when obstacles temporarily delayed a plan for Jews to build the Krupp howitzer plant in Silesia. Construction of the Berthawerk, named after Alfried Krupp's mother, went forward because it had Hitler's personal blessing. And again, Krupp took advantage of his privileged position in the state when it came to labour supplies at many other camps, including Ravensbrück, where Jewesses were traded by the hundred. To take delivery of, say, 700 women at a time needed guards with special skills and Krupp female staff were therefore despatched to Ravensbrück for SS training. It is doubtful if training of any kind was given to the staff whose function it was to care for the children of Krupp slaves at Buschmannshof. Seventy-four per cent of the initial admission died.

Having refused to take the stand, Alfried Krupp was found guilty as far as the slave labour part of his indictment was concerned, and this included 'exploitation and maltreatment of large masses of forced foreign labour'. He was sentenced to have his property confiscated and to go to prison for twelve years. The statistics of slave labour employed by Krupp were as follows: 4,978 from the concentration and extermination camps, 23,076 prisoners of war and 69,898 foreign civilians. They constituted a fraction, but a meaningful one, of the figures for Germany as a whole: 4,795,000 foreign workers. To this figure may be added the 6 million Jews who were put to death. Krupp emerged from Landsberg Fortress after serving less than six years in the comfortable environment in which his lifelong hero had dictated the draft of *Mein Kampf*. He came out unrepentant and very soon his property was returned to him.

Who was responsible for the European resurgence of slavery? The catalogue of misery is pointless unless it gives some indication of the way similar systems might arise. Since all power was theoretically vested in the Führer, it seemed simplest at first to pass the blame up to him, particularly as he was dead. Anyone who could write, in 1926, 'if twelve or fifteen thousand of these Jews who were corrupting the nation had been forced to submit to poison-gas . . . the millions of sacrifices made at the front would not have been in vain'[20] could not have claimed after the extermination camps that he was carried along by mysterious forces of history. His commitment was total, in practice as well as in theory, and that is where he differed from philosophers like Schopenhauer, whom he used to give his thesis the mark of respectability. But for one man to hypnotize a nation the necessary precondition, as he knew well, was a responsive populace; although he set out using illegal means, he finally achieved power by popular acclaim, having made no secret of the sinister elements of his master plan.

Below the dictator were many individuals to whom responsibility for justifying and co-ordinating the New Order was delegated. An obvious candidate for blame was the chief of the SS, Heinrich Himmler, whose attitude to slavery was indicated in a 1942 directive: laziness 'should be penalized by special treatment. . . . Special treatment is hanging . . . a certain number should attend the special treatment.'[21] And although he gave frequent and fervent exhortations in favour of stepping up the extermination programme, he often of his own volition diverted tens of thousands of Jews to slave labour factories. He proved to be a rival in this respect to Albert Speer, to whom slaves, despite his first-hand contact with them, remained no more than essential parts of the assembly line; their human attributes were best put firmly out of mind. To Bormann, Goering, Goebbels, and others of the upper hierarchy, Jews were marked for death, conquered peoples for enslavement, true to the tenets of *Mein Kampf*. And Goebbels made sure that ordinary people, and some extraordinary people, knew what had to be done. As one moves from the tip of the pyramid to its base complicity does not lessen. Sauckel's gathering of the slaves demanded active physical co-operation from men and women of all walks of life, down to the workers of Essen, and beyond them to the criminal elements of society ripe for the messier tasks of the regime. Here the cruelties of those unaccustomed to power came to the fore. Although each guilty act was an individual matter attributable to personal wickedness or frailty, one has to turn in the end to the social creature to see how it was that the peculiar nature of the state contributed to the degradation of citizens on such a scale.

Hitler did not invent the totalitarian state; he did, however, shed much light on how one can be created in a very short time. His ideas and actions, once the inspiration of millions, now have value only as warnings. Translators of *Mein Kampf* have always hesitated when confronted by certain of the author's terms, and often they have simply allowed the German word to stand. *Volk* is one of these words; it means a lot more than 'people' and has within it the idea of the fundamental essence of a national breed. Another word much used by Hitler is *Weltanschauung*, literally 'outlook on the world'. As used in the National Socialist period it conveyed a wealth of meaning; it blended spiritual, cultural, political and economic ideas into a mystical entity that was ideal material for use by a good orator. Shorn of its romantic trappings it represented a totalitarian philosophy of life.

Today 'totalitarian' is a term of abuse, bandied about indiscriminately at the United Nations. In the 1920s and early 1930s, however, widespread disillusionment with general disorganization and poverty made the idea of a tightly organized society, in which government would direct the activities and policies of individuals and groups for the purposes of national aggrandizement, deceptively attractive to many. Mussolini, 'the great man beyond the Alps', seemed to have paved the way in practical terms:[22]

> We fascists have had the courage to discard all traditional political theories, and we are aristocrats and democrats, revolutionaries and reactionaries, proletarians and anti-proletarians, pacifists and anti-pacifists. It is sufficient to have a single fixed point: the nation. The rest is obvious.

The Italian leader was no theorist; he put the concentration of power first and only secondly tried to find intellectual support for his actions. Hitler tried hard to create or locate natural justifications for the totalitarian view of life and, for a brief period, he succeeded. The extent of state control is sometimes forgotten; nothing lay outside the state's authority. To be one of the *Volk* was to have all aspects of personality embraced by the state apparatus. And all associations, educational, political, commercial, fulfilled the wishes of the supreme authority. Leisure pursuits were directed towards state goals. Trades unions effectively ceased to exist. Censorship was all-embracing; nothing could be said or printed, no meeting could be held, without state approval. This meant, of course, that there could be no independent judiciary to which, say, an escaped slave could appeal, no parliament in which the conditions of slaves could be debated, and certainly no form of opposition of any sort. In the end, whilst some slaves were more comfortable than others, all became slaves to the system, which from time to time claimed its victims from the upper echelons of society. The rule of law gave way to interpreting the will of the state and conforming to it. By way of reaction to this, those seen to be slaves were pushed to the extremities of suffering. It was within this scheme of things that Krupp functioned.

Was Hitler's Germany an isolated aberration? European Common

Market psychological and economic pressures might lead many to believe that this is so, but all the evidence is to the contrary. 'The slave state', as Speer later called it, had essential characteristics which were not unique, as can be appreciated by looking at the example of its principal opponent. The alleged opposition between the doctrines of National Socialism and Bolshevism, although from an early date fervently believed in by the faithful, merely provided an excuse for territorial expansion. In reality the two ideologies, despite subsequent 'right' and 'left' labelling, were similar not only in superficial respects; the analogy of the circle, though hackneyed, remains apt: whether you went round to right or left you arrived at the same place – the totalitarian society.

The evolution of the Third Reich and the Russia of Stalin had many parallels, although Bolshevism was imposed on a peasant society and National Socialism drew its main force from an urban environment. Each made full use of writings which acquired the status of Holy Writ. The dialectic of the Marxist, which to put it at its simplest had substituted a class struggle for the struggle between nations, was nevertheless transformed easily into a form of imperialism justified by the need to stimulate the class conflict on an international basis. In practical terms the territorial expansion of Communism, strictly speaking a unification of a class on a nation-to-nation basis, differed little from the racial domination of Hitler's New Order. And within the nations there was little to choose between the systems when it came to the survival, and dominance, of those fit to rule: the party elite.

The concentration of power in the hands of the leader and ambitious party members, whether they were ruthless racial purists or the intellectual agitators of the working class, differed mainly in the way it was represented to the people. While dictatorial power resided in the hands of Stalin, much was made of the dictatorship of the proletariat; by way of complete contrast in Germany the nature and person of the Führer were proudly proclaimed; the difference was one of semantics. In order that power should not be diluted at the top, each elite found it necessary to develop an extensive system of secret police and the lower levels of society were held firmly in place, often deceived about national and foreign events. Propaganda naturally played a large part in diverting the proletariat from awareness of the degree to which their freedoms had been eroded. Both nations exterminated dissenters, both eliminated the basic human rights of their own citizens, both created within their region of control a network of camps in which countless slaves laboured in appalling conditions. As the declared political philosophies of the two governments were opposite and the methods and achievements were so similar, one is inclined to take the view that the evils observed are inseparable from the totalitarian structure itself. The machinery of the state, devoid of democratic safeguards, gives power to the ruthless and drains freedoms from the majority; and experience has shown that corruption can permeate to all levels, until the morality of the supposed victors of the class war is sapped away too.

The increase in totalitarian regimes, one of the dominant themes of the mid-twentieth century, did not produce, as might have been expected in uniformly rigid societies, closely similar systems of slavery. And this was not only because the German experience was confused with genocide, the crime that is frequently the partner of slavery and which took precedence in the Third Reich. Prophetic novelists had correctly foreseen and warned against the advent of the huge and impersonal apparatus of state, within which oppressed classes of workers and undesirables laboured for some hypothetical and long-forgotten common good. When it arrived the framework of the state was much as forecast, but the ingredients varied. While under the vague laws of Hitler's Germany the slave made armaments or released others to make them, the occasion never occurred when he helped to build the new world after a National Socialist victory. Elsewhere, under Stalin's very different laws, the slave was punished or kept out of circulation for speaking out of turn, despite the freedoms guaranteed to him under the constitution. His energies, when peace came, were mainly devoted to forestry or industry, but his profitability was not be realized until after Stalin's death, and then only in certain isolated pockets of the economy.

Although National Socialist slavery was wholly dismantled by force in 1945, slavery as a constituent of totalitarian systems gained a new lease of life during the post-war era. While fugitives from justice at Nuremberg made their way via the Vatican escape route to congenial employment under South American dictators, developments within Stalinist Russia were much more ominous. In both continents the dictatorships made use of slavery in its most crude form, but Stalin developed it with imperial vision, modifying and extending its scope to meet imagined needs. Racial persecution had no place in the theory behind the Soviet collection of camps, the Gulag Archipelago, but that did not stop the system from absorbing members of Russian national minorities, like the Crimean Tartars. The Soviet authorities took great pains to prevent the international community from learning of the existence of the Gulag. When the information did leak out, the obvious tangible slavery of the camps, with all their inefficient squalor, caused widespread alarm and concern. Connections were made between the employment of slave labour and a totalitarian political system, but it is doubtful whether the revelations served to draw attention to the lack of fundamental human rights enjoyed by ordinary Soviet citizens at that time. Fortunately today that state sometimes feels the need to take world opinion into consideration, though one has to be wary of its motives. During Stalin's reign it seemed that a self-perpetuating system of vicious balances and checks had halted political evolution. Once the totalitarian edifice has been constructed, easing of restrictions on individual liberty can seldom be achieved except by a brave speech from a Khrushchev at the top or slow and even more courageous pressures exerted from below by those who have retained independence of mind and spirit.

The Latin American dictatorships are not totalitarian in the full sense of the term, but in so far as they practise authoritarian rule, usually by one man or a military junta, and permit no effective opposition, a cynic might say that they aspire to membership of this group; their extensive denial of personal liberty is limited only by inefficiency and frequent *coups d'état.* In Bolivia and Paraguay, for instance, slavery has been either an instrument of terror or used against the Amerindians for short-term profits. And it was in these countries that former SS officers knew that they would find a welcome and opportunities to relive old memories. Traditional slavery is not likely to last very much longer because destruction of habitat is completing the work begun by those who used to capture or kill the Indian. Again, though, the nature of society is such that the mixed breeds that form its broad base are likely to be kept firmly at a level bordering on slavery for some time to come. They are the urban social equivalent of the serf, and economic slavery, capitalism's and automation's contribution to the institution, restricts many of them to a rubbish dump existence on the outskirts of the towns. International aid never seems to filter down to them and the system and technological progress deny them the means to change the status quo.

It is the rigidity of totalitarian societies which makes the process of democratization within them so tortuous. History gives no encouragement in this field: ancient Egypt became almost fossilized for centuries, and the balance of fear within the Third Reich meant that notwithstanding the efforts of Count Klaus von Stauffenberg and his group the state could only be destroyed from outside, and that destruction could only occur because it had overreached itself territorially. Moreover, to take heart from the thought that physical expansion inevitably brings fragmentation and the possibility of freedom for some is to indulge in a false sense of optimism. It cannot be assumed that technology will never develop sufficiently to extend control of the proletariat to the sort of boundaries dreamed of by Hitler.

Technology applied to the field of communications is a two-edged sword. It gives greater power to the controlling authority, but it also helps with the dissemination, between and within states, of information about the true state of affairs. Dr Goebbels did not have television in his arsenal. He would have welcomed it, though the corporate environment of the cinema served his purposes better. It is difficult to imagine this medium helping to democratize an authoritarian society from within, but it is only too easy to see how, transmitted across national frontiers, it can be used to remove some of the illusions of peoples about the actions of their governments. When Bophuthatswana television beams uncomfortable BBC news items to South Africa the mobile nature of the populace makes jamming a futile exercise.

Democratization of existing totalitarian regimes to the extent that slave labour camps can be abolished is unlikely to occur until ratification of international Conventions involves giving guarantees of access to United Nations officials for purposes of inspection – currently a remote possibility. How else can the Marxist's belief in the distortion of truth as a means to achieve ideological ends be overcome? Until the day of objective truth dawns, action is limited to subtle underground pressure and the brave gestures of dissidents. One lives in hopes of liberation from within; external pressures, apart from those which give valid verbal support to human rights issues or are purely economic, tend to be counter-productive, and are potentially cataclysmic.

Prevention of the spread of totalitarianism, with its consequent enslavement of classes and ethnic groups, is a less dangerous undertaking, in so far as world war is not a likely outcome. Here the role of the Christian church, which still has deep roots in many Third World countries, particularly in Africa, is no longer ambiguous. The Reverend John Maxwell, a Catholic priest and member of the Anti-Slavery Society, has pointed out[23] that if Hitler had asked the Vatican authorities whether use of slave labour camps for condemned criminals, and use of enslaved non-Christian foreign prisoners – captured in a 'just' war – was morally justified, he would almost certainly have received a 'probable opinion' in the affirmative. All that changed in 1965 when the Second Vatican Council corrected the teaching of many centuries. At last there was no hedging:[24]

> Whatever violates the integrity of the human person, such as mutilation, torture inflicted on body or mind, attempts to coerce the will itself; whatever insults human dignity, such as subhuman living conditions, arbitrary imprisonment, deportation, slavery, prostitution, the selling of women and children . . . all these things and others like them are infamous.

But in former colonial regions the church is now often rejected, along with the imperial power with which it was associated, and its warnings may well go unheeded. Its interference with traditional beliefs often alienated it from peoples for whom the tribe has affinities with a political party. After independence loyalty to the tribe, given instinctively, as well as by rational commitment, caused a tendency towards the one-party system of government. This may be natural for Africa; it still gives cause for concern.

In order to be legitimate, ways of countering from without the growth of a form of society which enslaves its citizens have to respect the autonomy of the state in question. Again, international Conventions have a part to play and membership of international organizations with powers to fund development can help obliquely to deter short-sighted curtailment of human rights. Hitler needed poverty, resentment and chaos to get his movement going. Poverty can be eradicated by external means, given the goodwill of government and people, and its disappearance can avert opportunist seizure of power. However, creeping totalitarianism, which threatens all forms of society as the administration of citizens becomes increasingly complicated and bureaucratic, can only be averted by the vigilance which comes from a democratically educated electorate blessed with constitutional safeguards.

Of all the forms of slavery which await abolition, that which is part and parcel of the political philosophy on which the state is founded is the most dehumanizing and is the hardest to eradicate. Fortunately Hitler's slavery policies proved to be self-defeating. He cleverly exploited racial prejudice and the sadistic element of human nature, but he failed to learn from his narrowly selective study of history that slave states have had a vested interest in keeping their slaves alive and reasonably healthy. His dependent races died unnecessarily by the thousand, and the temporary reprieve reluctantly granted to the despised Jewish remnant failed to achieve its purpose; because the asset was disposable the National Socialist war machine was deprived of much needed brawn. Even those with brains capable of inventing an atomic bomb were sacrificed on the altar of ideology. The cruelties inseparable from the institution had helped to bring about the destruction of the society itself.

CHAPTER 4

APARTHEID

... apartheid is a crime against humanity ... inhuman acts resulting from the policies and practices of apartheid and similar policies and practices of racial segregation and discrimination ... are crimes violating the principles of international law, in particular the purposes and principles of the Charter of the United Nations...

INTERNATIONAL CONVENTION ON THE SUPPRESSION AND PUNISHMENT OF THE CRIME OF APARTHEID

The gulf which exists between South Africa and most member states of the United Nations has been caused by, and has contributed to, the growth of two main interpretations of the concept of apartheid, or separate development, to give it its simplest English rendering. Vociferous opponents of the present South African regime see it as the most systematic denial of human rights in the modern world and United Nations debates and publications repeatedly drive home the message: 'South Africa is the only country in the world that proclaims the inequality of its citizens in its laws';[1] it is 'in the opinion of many people the most oppressive manifestation of slavery that exists in the world today';[2] and the 1984 report of the United Nations Working Group on Slavery was only using the generally accepted terminology when it described apartheid as 'a collective slavery-like practice':[3] any argument about the use of '-like' would not be on aesthetic grounds.

Although the current official South African yearbook candidly states that 'multinational development of the population groups ... was considered to be the only means by which the continued existence of the White South African nation could be safeguarded...',[4] its frankness uncharacteristically underestimates the case for apartheid. Dr D. F. Malan, the prime minister whose government created the legislative framework which gave precise form to apartheid, left it to his Minister of Native Affairs, Dr H. F. Verwoerd, to add flesh to the skeleton;

and this he did with a conviction that got through to the lexicographer: while Oxford kept carefully to the bare bones of 'racial segregation', others spoke of 'a political, economic, cultural, spiritual and racial separateness, as apart from mere physical (or geographical) separateness'.[5] Cynical Afrikaners of humble origins might hint that any system that kept the kaffir in his place was worthwhile, but, to the thinking man, apartheid was not merely a device for maintaining white supremacy. The races, it was hoped, could be separated to the advantage of all. The more respectable United Kingdom newspapers were selected to carry a series of advertisements which put forward the rationale (or rationalization as critics might claim) of separate development. A question and answer format presented powerful arguments barely distinguishable from Anti-Slavery Society recommendations for protecting threatened primitive peoples from exploitation. While reading them one felt that ancient cultures were in danger of being swamped by harmful twentieth-century interests and that barricades should be erected to prevent cultural genocide. 'Separate but equal' was the essence of the doctrine and the creation of autonomous bantustans seemed the ideal solution. A problem of race was being translated into a problem of sovereignty.

As with most issues which generate heat for a long time, received opinion on each side eventually crystallizes into over-simplification. Most people who casually dismiss apartheid as evil mean either that cruelty to racial groups is bad, or that universal suffrage regardless of boundaries is the only possible democratic solution to a political problem. While readily agreeing that racial persecution is not to be condoned, informed apartheid supporters might reasonably attempt to justify their cause by pointing to the artificiality of many of the world's frontiers. Given, say, ten main tribal groups, all of which wandered into the same large area over the course of many centuries, why should the twentieth century be the time when the European imperial line which surrounds them all is fossilized? Would not ten enclosed spaces (one white) allow the preservation of traditions and the development of maximum individuality and freedom? As is invariably the case, the truth is somewhere between these notional extremes and attention to the evolution of the practice and dogma of separate development can help to clarify matters.

On the basis of that often meaningless term 'indigenous', South Africa, or at least the Cape region of it, would have to go to the Bushmen, as their rivals for the title deeds, the Hottentots

(Khoikhoin), subsequently retreated into Namibia. However, although the chronological criterion is loudly urged in other parts of the world, there is no clamour on behalf of the Bushmen; their numbers have diminished to a minute statistic and common sense has been allowed to prevail as far as their entitlement is concerned. The third immigrant group, the Europeans, make much of their early arrival, and the fact that they did not wander off again, but run into difficulty when defining the extremities of the territory which they have peopled. The trouble is that these races were all, to some extent, migrant or nomadic; while whites of several nationalities moved northward, blacks of even more varied ethnic origins were moving southward. There were many inter-racial clashes and where these were between black and white the superior technology of the whites usually prevailed over the iron-age artefacts which faced them. It is not popular to say so, but much of the land over which these people fought was *terra nullius*, empty land, which had either had no previous settled or nomadic claimant or had been abandoned for centuries. Archaeological investigation does reveal evidence of ancient use in certain places, but only exceptionally can it be attributed with precision to today's inhabitants.[6]

The seeds of apartheid were sown very early. A principal occupational difference between black and white was immediately apparent; to the white observer the blacks' agricultural method was a loose pastoralism, mainly nomadic; on their side the blacks were at once upset by the whites' habit of enclosing land. When the people of European origin migrated, their purpose was always to put some sort of fence around new territory – and even more disconcerting, the fences around the old territories remained. The blacks streamed southwards, leaving the north; the whites expanded northwards, retaining the south. Penetration and enclosure by whites can be traced with the aid of a wealth of documentation, and the historian can isolate and date fairly accurately the arrival of Dutch, German and French groups and individuals. Unfortunately the same cannot be said for the black peoples; bold southward pointing arrows emerging from some vague central African source or sources have been painted across maps to indicate the movements of some eight ethnic groups – North Nguni, South Nguni, Transvaal Ndebele, North Sotho, South Sotho, Tswana, Venda Lemba and Shangana-Tsonga – but the best that can be said for these lines of migration is that they represent probable migratory trends over long periods of time. Moreover, the chronology is disputed; order of arrival in what is now South Africa has not been established with any degree of confidence.

The tribes were often at war with one another and, in the absence of written records, accounts of detours, delays and conflicts are little more than folklore. It is therefore something of a relief to be able to give a definite date to the drawing of a boundary line between two contenders for territory. Collision between Xhosa-speaking blacks from the north and whites moving inland led to a proclamation in 1778 that the Fish River should separate black from white. To Europeans this was only normal and just; to the blacks it was alien and well-nigh incomprehensible. An African version of the Hundred Years War was to take place before boundary lines were to achieve anything approaching general acceptance.

From the early days of Dutch settlement, black slaves had been imported to the Cape and this process continued until 1807. The institution then continued in its legal form until the British abolished it in 1834, some twenty years after they had taken over the Colony. Although there was never any need for slaves to become a crucial element in the agriculture of a temperate region, their sudden emancipation by a government alien to the white majority ruined many colonists, and contributed to a widening of the rift between British and Afrikaner. The following year the Trichardt Trek began, and 1836 was the year of the Great Trek. White tribal migrations now led to bloodshed between blacks and whites and eventual establishment of the Boer Republics. These, in turn, generated white inter-tribal disputes which eventually caused the South African War and its magnanimous sequel, the establishment of the Union of South Africa in 1910. There were, however, some forebodings about the selective nature of the magnanimity which brought the new dominion into existence. In London the Anti-Slavery Society, anxious about safeguards for the black peoples, withheld its blessing. The Crown gained its imperial diamond, but the Society sustained a heavy blow, the loss of its royal patronage.

Before the founding of the dominion relations between blacks and whites had been instinctive or pragmatic, distorted by the paternalistic aftermath of slavery and by physical confrontation. Pragmatism of a ruthless sort was common to both white traditions: the Matabele stood in the way of the Voortrekkers, the Zulus in the way of British interests; the Matabele were soon in Rhodesia, the Zulus suffered the same fate as they had inflicted on innumerable black tribes. But the

Afrikaner, who had been in Africa longer than other whites, had identified more closely with the continent and his views were eventually to predominate as the haphazard rivalries of the past gave way to a more systematic approach to the future (especially after the Second World War had caused the deaths of so many British South Africans). The new state, although shorn of the High Commission territories, Bechuanaland, Basutoland, Swaziland and Rhodesia, had enviable assets and was soon to expand its frontiers still further, to include the substantial colony known as German South West Africa.

The modern legislative foundation of apartheid was the Native Land Act of 1913, which specifically reserved certain areas for black ownership. Lines were drawn around pockets seen to be *de facto* enclaves of particular tribes or groups. The law simply made official some physical separation; it did not provide for black political development. However, in 1936, the Development Trust and Land Act set aside sufficient additional land for later legislators to use the zones as a basis for evolution towards black autonomy. With the 1936 additions about a seventh of the land went to peoples who, collectively, outnumbered the whites by three or four to one. It has been said that the allocation amounted to a quarter of the non-desert land, but this is misleading as increasing exploitation of mineral resources has meant that desert is not to be excluded from any calculations. Territorial division was in the same year reinforced by a far-reaching measure of political separation. The Representation of Blacks Act demonstrated that Anti-Slavery Society fears about inadequate constitutional safeguards had been justified. Although it had been laid down that the non-white franchise in Cape Province and Natal could only be abolished if there were a two-thirds majority in the Senate and House of Assembly sitting together, the necessary arrangements were made and the Act was passed. The blacks of Cape Province came off the roll and new black registrations were prohibited in Natal. Black participation in government was limited to the establishment of a Native Representative Council, and to the right to elect three white representatives to the House of Assembly, and four to the Senate.

These developments engendered discontent among the politically aware, but it was left to a great external upheaval to bring matters to a head. The Second World War had a major impact on the theory and practice of race relations within South Africa. Freeing Europe from a racist totalitarian regime gave great impetus to those who sought independence for imperial possessions in Africa and elsewhere.

The Empire had played a vital role in the defeat of National Socialism and citizens were not slow to translate principles of emancipation to their own country. Almost inevitably with the cessation of hostilities in Europe came clamour for imperial withdrawal, and generally the criterion for liberation urged upon European rulers was majority decision by current inhabitants. One after another the colonies of Africa were liberated, with varying degrees of goodwill or hostility. Many had no sooner achieved freedom than they reverted to barbaric internecine squabbles or their new rulers submitted whole tribes to cruelties that echoed the excesses of the recent German occupation of Europe. South African leaders watched the outcome of majority rule with some foreboding.

A more fundamental effect of the Second World War arose from the divided loyalties of the white population. Although the three races most affected – Afrikaner, German and English – had originally arrived with distinct European cultural traditions, naturally these had been modified during their time in Africa and the balance between them had altered. It was not simply the South African War which had distanced English from Afrikaner; imperial trappings of dominion status did not help, nor did the language barrier. Furthermore another important cause of division had been the acquisition during the First World War of German South West Africa. British insistence that this be done had led to South Africa's own Curragh Mutiny, but the long-term effect of annexation had been a merger of some German and Afrikaner aims and methods. There was already a common philosophy expressed in both languages by the same word, *Volk*. Not surprisingly, while the forces of the British Commonwealth Dominion played a brave role defeating Hitler's *Volk*, there were many in South Africa whose sympathies were firmly with the Axis powers. A hard core of Afrikaner opinion had always hoped to sever links with the British Crown, and Great Britain's European wars gave additional stimulus to separatist ideas. Such sentiments now gained enthusiastic support from German settlers, about to be doubly defeated, as it were. Neither Afrikaner nor German inclined towards power sharing with blacks; while Dutch slave ownership had evolved into rigid Afrikaner paternalism, the German record in South West Africa had been far more repressive. A policy of genocide had used as one of its aids what were officially described in the early 1900s as concentration camps.

As South Africa was not anyone's colony, and the Afrikaner had no means of retreat, should he ever think in those terms, the immediate post-war period was a time of entrenchment. White survival was uppermost in white minds, but it was closely linked with the quest for a political arrangement which would give all ethnic groups the autonomy to which they aspired. Almost by definition, separation had to precede development and the renewed process did not start well: the Native Areas Act, 1945, which restricted black admission to towns and obliged city blacks to live in special locations under the control of white superintendents, took a one-sided view of the colour divide. Three years later Dr Malan's party came to power and apartheid was soon a precise doctrine that was spawning a proliferation of major laws and minor regulations. Almost all the innovations, including the recent Native Areas Act of the previous administration, were based on earlier legislation. It was, however, disturbing to note that among the first fruits of the new government were racial purity laws reminiscent of a perverse system that had only just been dismantled in Europe. The Immorality Act, 1950 had its useful clauses, but its purpose, and the purpose of the Prohibition of Mixed Marriages Act, 1949, was to prevent sexual intercourse and marriage between whites and non-whites. There was already a large Coloured (mixed race) population, but to the purist separate development means what it says. Accordingly, 1950 also saw the passing of the Population Registration Act, which obliged all South Africans to be racially classified and created special courts for the investigation of borderline cases. This Act has widespread relevance to apartheid, but its use in assessing the acceptability of marriage partners or other domestic relationships has generated more resentment than any other aspect of its implementation. Although apartheid has many enemies, apart from the atrocities of interrogators and evictions there is probably no facet of the system that has alienated public opinion more than legislative intrusions into personal and private habits. Even those who jib at miscegenation on traditional aesthetic grounds draw the line at governments prying into the bedtime behaviour of their citizens. The absurdities of the Act have at last been appreciated by the South African government, and a decision has been taken to repeal it.

Had the purists had their way, virtually all contact between white and non-white would have ceased during the 1950s and, in a sense, the problems would have evaporated. Multinational development would have occurred, the homelands would now be established members of the United Nations and all would be separate and equal. That was all part of the theory. What in fact happened, apart from the growth and activities of various black opposition groups, was the commonsense realization by white business men, industrialists and farmers that black labour was indispensable (in the pre-automation period) to a degree that in its own right resisted the tenets of apartheid. It was the tug-of-war between separation and interdependence that made apartheid legislation so complicated. Ubiquitous overlap meant an increase in separate amenities, which necessitated yet another Act of Parliament. The whole process now accelerated and diversified as one measure created an artificial need for another. The Native Abolition of Passes Act, 1956 (which achieved exactly the opposite of what its title suggests) was partly the consequence of the Native Areas Act, 1945; together they begat the Group Areas Act, 1956, which empowered the government to establish ghettos in which people of mixed descent might live and own property. And so it went on; but through it all ran a consistent policy believed to be unavoidably inequitable in the short term, wholly desirable and democratic in its final outcome. First the vestiges of black representation had to be removed from the old apparatus of state; then black nations should be re-established and encouraged to evolve to full independence. The Bantu Authorities Act, 1951 abolished the Native Representative Council and in its place set up tribal, community and regional authorities in the specified areas of the Native Land Act. The culmination of basic apartheid legislation was the Promotion of Black Self-Government Act, 1959. This ended black representation in the Senate and House of Assembly and transferred responsibility for internal legislation to the homelands. Henceforward these territories were to develop to full independent nationhood.

Few would claim that the process so far described was a democratic one, but to what extent can the South African authorities be accused of practising slavery? The ultimate aim is certainly compatible with democratic principles. If devolution goes according to plan until it reaches the stage when homelands are as independent as, say, Lesotho and Swaziland – and Bophuthatswana is already more independent than these UN members – the charge of slavery will not be applicable to the dismantled system. Land consolidation and referenda will have occurred, frontiers will have been redrawn and somewhere in the south of what may be a loose-knit federation will be one African state with a white majority. The trouble is that, having embarked on a policy of separation which was intended to lead to this over-simplified yet widely misunderstood goal, it was necessary to separate the peoples in all aspects of life. Integration anywhere would hinder or reverse the process.

The iniquities of apartheid, which have rightly enraged human rights organizations the world over, have arisen from the practical problems of the intermediate stage, a circumstance which in no way mitigates their evil. Paradoxically where slavery has occurred it has done so in defiance of apartheid principles and has been perpetrated by ignorant sections of the community, initially motivated by prejudice. Discrimination, not slavery, has been the general rule, but its extent has been alarming. If separation were to be based on cultural differences, it was believed that the ethnic groups would have to have different systems of education. However, instead of being distributed among ten or so systems of education, the bulk of the populace were subject to 'Bantu' education, generally regarded as different in quality rather than in ethnic suitability; *per capita* expenditure on white education was far higher (over five times as much); and Coloureds and Indians were the only differentiated groups. Putting the pupils in different buildings was consistent with the dominant creed, and the same can be said for racial segregation in lavatories, bus services, railway facilities and the like.

In many ways these developments were no more than institutionalization of behaviour patterns which already existed. One tends to associate with like-minded individuals and it is highly probable that these will be members of one's own race. The physical process might have continued peacefully for an indefinite period, but for the most disruptive separation of all, that of residence. Large numbers of blacks had accumulated on the outskirts of rich cities like Johannesburg, where they were needed in the mines and elsewhere. Natural apartheid had occurred, as it does everywhere; but then came meticulously enforced localization, as ordained by the pass laws, and soon, as the policy moved into its next stage, compulsory migration became a factor in the lives of both urban and rural blacks. This, in turn, led to further complications. With the development of the homelands, some were compulsorily shifted before the land on which they were obliged to settle was handed over to the new rulers; others went voluntarily; later, when the world refused to recognize those homelands which had achieved independence and scant foreign investment was attracted, some breadwinners had little option but to migrate again to the old townships. When the family was split, inevitably those who suffered most were the old, the women and the children. Many of the children were virtually abandoned and became increasingly vulnerable to those in search of cheap or free labour.

Apart from child exploitation, which should be adequately prevented by existing South African laws, these features do not amount to slavery as the term has been defined. As has been indicated, they are part of a highly organized scheme of discrimination, said or thought to be justified because it is temporary and its eventual result will be independent sovereign states. It is because of widespread belief that a black caste has been doomed permanently to subsist at the bottom of its pyramid that South Africa stands accused at the United Nations of embodying an unusual form of slavery in its constitution. Putting to one side the acceptability or otherwise of transforming 'a crime against humanity' into Multinational Development, it is penal slavery which gives the greatest cause for concern. And here, although criminals and political prisoners have frequently been intermingled, it is necessary to make a distinction between the methods used when dealing with the two types of detainee. The South African prison service has long been accused of abusing or insufficiently protecting many who have been placed in its care, and as far as the criminal, non-political cases have been concerned, it has been the lease or parole system which has attracted the most condemnation. The practice is based on the perfectly sound belief that it is better to have prisoners on farms than in cells, but as the parole system uses private farms it is contrary to the International Forced Labour Convention, 1930 (no. 29). This exempts from its provisions:[7]

> any work or service exacted from any person as a consequence of a conviction in a court of law, provided that the said work or service is carried out under the supervision and control of a public authority and that the said person is not hired to or placed at the disposal of private individuals, companies or associations.

The Committee of Experts on the Application of Conventions and Recommendations of the International Labour Organization subsequently modified this prohibition[8] to allow voluntary agreement to undertake private employment, subject to stringent safeguards, but during its period of membership of the ILO from 1919 until 1966 South Africa did not see fit to ratify the Convention.

A prisoner in the hands of a brutal employer is a chattel slave, and there is reliable evidence of the cruelties which can occur when power is concentrated in this way:[9]

> 'I lost my Reference Book. . . . I placed my thumb on a piece of paper when it was placed before me. We were told by the official that we were to work on the farm . . . for six months . . . we were allowed to drink water from a certain big oil drum which was outside the prison. . . . The premises were filthy and infested with vermin . . . two drums . . . were placed within the prison to be used as lavatories . . . our bedding consisted of dirty sacks and dilapidated blankets. . . . I was given a sack with armholes to wear . . . assaults were committed on me or one of the other workers regularly and daily. . . . When the workers used to faint X [one of the 'boss boys'] would urinate into their mouths to revive them . . . the boss boys would use their sticks to beat the workers to make them work faster. This was done in [the white boss's] presence. . . . I was called with the other workers to where one, John, was lying. . . . I gathered from the talk that he was dead.'

This abbreviated extract from an affidavit used in connection with a habeas corpus case reflects the horrifying side of the lease system; with other similar testimony it helped to initiate reforms.

Private sector actrocities have come to light much more easily, and therefore more frequently, than those in the public sector. Within prison walls it is much easier to hush things up. A factor contributing to the abuse of the lease system has been inadequate punishment awarded to those found guilty of cruelly treating farm labourers generally. And although brave journalism helped to ameliorate matters, the parole system as it now functions still attracts much adverse criticism. However, there have been improvements and these are not always acknowledged by the lunatic fringe of the anti-apartheid lobby; complaints levelled against current procedure are sometimes based on assumptions which are dubious. As the law stands at present a prisoner who opts to work on a farm has the right to change his mind and return to the prison. Farms are subject to inspection and, should a prisoner lodge an official complaint against his employer, the prison authorities are obliged to investigate. To this extent the prisoner is technically better protected than the free labourer. Moreover, the record of state prisons the world over being what it is, there is no reason to suppose that private supervision of prisoners will be more harsh. Opponents of the South African constitution are sometimes so anxious to discredit the regime that they forget that the persons whose welfare is under discussion are convicted criminals. Admittedly it has often been the case that the laws transgressed would not exist in any other society and would never warrant prison sentences. That is another matter altogether.

Assuming that actions universally accepted to be crimes have been committed, a hard day's work on a farm is a healthy way to achieve redemption. The system can be humanely administered. Regular inspection of farms, with opportunities for prisoners to make confidential complaints, is a way of ensuring that conditions are acceptable and that the profit motive does not lead to exploitation. It remains true, however, that the crimes committed by many prisoners are on a par with United Kingdom parking offences, and the imposition of prison sentences by whites on blacks for trivial transgressions of pass laws has created a class of, albeit transient, penal slaves. Conditions may have improved appreciably, so that the circumstances are those of benevolent slavery, but the punishment is out of all proportion to the petty bureaucratic disdemeanour and is reserved exclusively for non-whites.

One unfortunate consequence of giving work to prisoners is its effect on the employment prospects of law-abiding citizens, and this applies equally to prison farms, as opposed to private farms which employ prisoners, and to the various types of contract work done within prison compounds. Payment and provision of food, clothing and accommodation are ways in which the private employer eases the burden which the prison community places on society in general; the prisoners' practical achievements make matters worse for the unemployed in particular. It is argued in the homelands that a poor farmer could only afford to employ prisoners; if they were not available the work would simply not be done. The flaw in the argument is that it will be a long time before social security is introduced that will enable the jobless to be discriminating about poorly paid opportunities. If the prisoners are doing the jobs, the unemployed must suffer and/or migrate. And if prisoners are doing the jobs, cheaply, what is the effect on wage levels generally? On the face of it this problem only affects the homelands; it is claimed by the South African Prison Department that parolees are now paid the normal local rate for the job. Lack of remuneration was one of the essential features of penal slavery.

The Prison Act, 1959 helps to conceal the links between those parts of a service which are enlightened and have their share of enlightened personnel, and other parts in which staff members have indulged in cruelties on their own initiative and have collaborated with South Africa's gestapo. Instead of realizing that more than any other place a prison must be subject to scrutiny, by genuinely independent bodies, the legislators placed a high premium on secrecy. Part of the impetus to impose censorship came from revelations of conditions in what are known as farm jails, built by farmers with a vested interest in acquiring labour in large numbers to meet special demands. In one case[10] conditions were such that forty-five prisoners were reported to have severed their own Achilles tendons to escape the rigours of their employment. The Act made it an offence even to photograph a prison and, by a 1965 amendment, its clauses were made applicable to aid centres, establishments which specialized in directing pass law offenders to employment in rural areas. The Act is not, of course, binding on the independent black states; some have introduced similar legislation, but one can wander at will and photograph what one likes in, say, Rooigrond Prison, Bophuthatswana.

Farm jail scandals revealed the existence of an unholy alliance between a public service and private enterprise; even worse, in standards of inhumanity, has been a liaison between two public services. The prison department has the onerous responsibility of playing host to the torturers of the South African security police, but for whose actions it is conceivable that the world might eventually have come to terms with Multinational Development. To a significant degree the security police have done for South Africa what the Provisional IRA have done for political harmony in Ireland. Like the Provisionals these policemen are destroying the cause which they serve. And like Marxist and Fascist interrogators the world over they have become obsessed by the extraction of confessions, the purpose of which has long since been forgotten. However embarrassing it is to those who are doing excellent work in those prisons to which overseas visitors are taken, the prison service must take its share of culpability for the forced interrogations. It is no excuse that interrogation goes on in separate sections of the prisons or in security police buildings; at some point in the process normal prison staff become accessories to torture.

Although comparisons with aspects of National Socialism or

Stalinism seem exaggerated, they are apt in so far as departments of state have acquired sufficient autonomy to enable them to break the law usually with impunity. However, when the excesses of the torturers come to light, the upper echelons of the white South African legitimate power structure seem as horrified as anyone else; so horrified, in fact, that the immediate response is defensive disbelief. However, observers will be inclined towards scepticism unless dismissals of high-ranking officers and resignations of ministers follow judicial pronouncements to the effect that atrocities have occurred. Naturally all interrogation excesses are prohibited by law, but a network of legislation has provided limitless opportunity and erected a screen behind which abuses occur. The following is from a tape recorded interview with the author:[11]

> 'I was blindfolded and gagged, and then they applied electric current. . . . One of them . . . was beating me solely for the reason that I was talking English. . . . He was Afrikaans-speaking. . . . I have been attacked by township thugs, but I say I have never been assaulted that way. [The electric current] was applied somewhere above my ears, here. All that I could hear was the sound and that shock, you know. And that left my whole head, including the neck, just moving on its own accord and I feared that I was going to snap my spinal cord.
>
> 'And the torture – some of the things it's very difficult for me to say – for instance, I found myself, when they unfolded me . . . just wetting myself and I hardly felt it. I could only see it on the floor, as it was just flowing on the floor, because they had started with me at something like eight o'clock in the morning and at about four-thirty it was still going on. . . . I'd gone through all sorts of forms of punishment. They had forced me. . . . I had put on all my clothes. "Put on all your clothes; you are going home." Then they took me from the cell and I dressed up with my coat, my jerseys (because prison cells are very cold and it was during winter time). So I put on all my clothing, even an overcoat. When I got there I was told, "No, no, no; you get on with the exercises." I did floor tips; I did all sorts of exercises and they left me completely soaked wet . . . and from there they started assaulting me. And then they handcuffed me. I had to squat and my hands were handcuffed in front of my legs and they passed through some sort of broomstick between them and I was suspended in

> mid-air: what they call the "helicopter treatment" – that's what they were saying – and as they were kicking me I was suspended. That stick was the fulcrum and I was just swinging this way and that way, being kicked all the time. And they also tried to force in water through my nostrils . . . so I must choke.
>
> 'Some of them are . . . real sadists; you can see it in their faces. They get satisfaction. . . . Very few get touched when they have overdone it . . . one or two in my whole experience of prison life. . . . They look very sad and they tone down. And, for instance, in my case one just never wanted to do it any longer. . . . It was . . . in Pietermaritzburg. . . . They made it quite a point that they don't use their names in the presence of detainees or when they do that to you. But I pointed it out, you know, to one of them. . . . "This is a whole set-up. You are very careful, you white interrogators, very careful not to call each other by your names, but when you come to your black counterparts you just call them any. . . . I know quite a number of them because you mention their names". . . . I spotted once when one black guy mentioned one of his white colleagues' names. He got so annoyed with him . . . meaning they are trying to keep their identity secret.'

The laws which most protected and encouraged the torturers began to appear after the banning of the African National Congress and the Pan-Africanist Congress led these two organizations to adopt violent methods. The General Law Amendment Act, 1963 permitted arrest without warrant and incommunicado detention without trial for successive ninety-day periods. The most sinister feature, as it turned out, was the 'incommunicado' element. In 1965 matters worsened dramatically with the Criminal Procedure Amendment Act. This doubled the period of detention, and witnesses proved to be fair game, whether or not suspected of complicity in the alleged offence, which might be political or criminal. Again the detainee was held incommunicado and, as if the interrogator was not already sufficiently shielded from justice, the hitherto independent judiciary was barred from pronouncing on the legality or otherwise of such detentions. Two years later the torturer's charter was greatly strengthened by the Terrorism Act (retroactive to 1962). This was an entirely logical development: anyone could be detained incommunicado without charge indefinitely. Terrorism was broadly defined and included actions which may prove to be an 'embarrassment' to 'the administration of the affairs of state'.[12] The burden of proof is placed upon the detainee, who would be held, perhaps in solitary confinement, until he had replied 'satisfactorily' to the questions of the interrogators.

As the definition of terrorism gave almost unlimited scope to the security police to arrest on impulse or intuition, the preventive detention clauses of the Internal Security Act, 1976 were really superfluous. The main purpose of the Act was to make more widely applicable the machinery whereby people or organizations could be banned, and it was intended to replace the Suppression of Communism Act, 1950. Nevertheless, detention incommunicado and without trial for renewable periods of twelve months was added to the statute book; the interrogator's shield was reinforced in law. Communist activity had been defined very widely under the 1950 Act and included omissions or threats which might bring about social or economic change; the new Act authorized preventive detention of anyone regarded as a threat to security or the maintenance of public order. There remained the problem of acknowledgment that the prisoner was under interrogation; the interrogator could still be inconvenienced when his victim's identity became known to organizations which might agitate, perhaps internationally, for information about physical welfare. Such inconvenience was not suffered by, for instance, the torturers of Argentina, and the deficiency was remedied by the Second Police Amendment Act, 1980, which prohibits unauthorized publication of detainees' names. Security legislation has since been consolidated in the Internal Security Act, 1982, which provides for the protection of detainees, but retains the objectionable features listed above.

The South African government is not insensitive to the allegations frequently made about security police atrocities. Minister of Law and Order Louis Le Grange was sufficiently worried in 1982 to issue a directive to all police officers about those held under Section 29 of the Internal Security Act. This drew attention to provisions for access by detainees to a review board and medical facilities, and access by various officials to detainees. It then went on to lay down regulations about standards of care. However, apart from a blanket prohibition of torture, the wording of practically every regulation contained an escape clause or was in some way naive. There is little point in saying that the prisoner must have sufficient sleep unless he can be given a cell in which the temperature permits it and be guaranteed a minimum number of hours – improvements which are unlikely unless members of the legitimate prison service have the final say. Similarly although notification of the nearest relative is authorized, it need not occur if it is believed that it may hamper police enquiries. And it is no consolation at all that a second interrogator should always be present; many of the traditional sadistic contortions require two pairs of hands. Somewhere between apparent ministerial intention and its translation into reality the regulations have been emasculated; in any case they lack the strength of law, and the laws themselves, when it comes to the protection of prisoners, are riddled with loopholes. The situation has reached the stage when only limitless powers of access, granted to bodies like the International Red Cross or Amnesty International, could prove that the government's wish for reform is genuine. Internal efforts are too easily frustrated by hardliners convinced that if there is any relaxation in the apparatus of terror they will be swept away by a black tidal wave.

As detention without trial is used in the great majority of cases against the black population, it runs counter to the apartheid principle. Moreover, in theory there should be black jails administered by blacks and white jails administered by whites. It is believed that this will happen when Multinational Development has been achieved, but during the present transitional stage, this cannot be. Although the ideology continues to be expressed in terms of vertical strata, in its practical expression the system is a horizontal one. Even in the everyday details of prison life this is the case; as a general rule, for instance, whites have beds and mattresses, blacks have mats and blankets. It is argued that cultural differences make this distinction desirable.

Since the reforms the case against the practice of apartheid may have been over-stated as far as penal slavery for the common criminal is concerned, but only in so far as by internationally accepted standards of natural justice he was a criminal. Failure to carry a pass hardly places him in that category. Political slavery, where a man or woman becomes the chattel of a regime, liable to be physically violated at the whim of the state's agents, is a charge against which the state can offer no defence. But what of the black citizen who picks his way carefully through the minefield and makes quite sure that he does not fall foul of the authorities? How is he to achieve genuine freedom? Among his many grounds for complaint are lack of proper wage negotiating machinery, inferior educational opportunities and liability to compulsory migration. His wife is even worse off; black and white traditions have something in common when it comes to women's rights and she is discriminated against as a woman and as a black. There is no doubt that apartheid at this stage in its evolution has too many unacceptable features for it to be borne much longer. International disapproval has only served to make the Afrikaner more determined. What, then, short of a bloody revolution which could usher in another Idi Amin, is to be done?

A look at three of the four independent homelands gives little support for the solution foreseen by apartheid devotees. No state which is the child of devolution starts from a *tabula rasa*. Inevitably much is inherited from the parent state in the social and political domain; in particular, a range of legislation on matters great and small is likely to remain intact on independence day. Ciskei, granted independence on 4 December 1981, had among its security measures Proclamation R.252 of 1977, granting the Minister of Justice powers to authorize incommunicado detention without charge or trial for renewable periods of ninety days. Access to lawyers was denied, and there was no independent court of appeal. Within a year laws of this nature had been repealed, but the legislation replacing them, the National Security Act, 1982, had provisions that gave the security police even greater scope for torture and murder.

Detentions under the new Act, which was closely modelled on the South African Internal Security Act, 1982, were authorized by Life-President Lennox Sebe's brother Charles, head of the Ciskei Central Intelligence Service, until he was himself detained under suspicion of planning a *coup*. The Act has also been used against trade union officials, many of whom were involved in a boycott of bus services. Torture has been widely used and there has been a degree of co-operation with the South African security police which casts doubt on the genuineness of Ciskei's independence. In keeping with the customs of twentieth-century torture, detainees have been made to strip before being subjected to physical cruelties including strangulation, electric shock, sleep deprivation and suspension from handcuffs. Detention without trial has also been used extensively in Transkei and Venda. In Venda interrogators have their own refinements with regard to water and electricity, and, in common with most torturers they have found that sadistic satisfaction can be derived from directing attention to the genitals. They have not, however, proved sufficiently skilled to prevent all their victims from dying prematurely.

The trouble with discovering that life in the independent black states has many of the worst features of life in South Africa is that, while it discredits apartheid, it can also be taken as a prediction of what the whole of South Africa might be like after the advent of simple majority rule: a pessimistic view made credible by the deterioration of so many African states. Grounds for optimism, on the other hand, may be found by looking at the one former homeland which has not only refrained from violating human rights Conventions, but has managed to achieve economic viability despite nearly four years of drought: Bophuthatswana.

Seen from the air or on the map, Bophuthatswana seems an unlikely candidate for viable nationhood. Like Kwazulu, which has not taken its independence, it is in seven pieces, though at least two of these will soon be linked. A large amount of land has been withheld by the white government and, during the period of internal self-government, the people and the chiefs were divided on the issue of which should come first: consolidation of the national territory or independence. Those who wanted immediate sovereign rights won the day, but only the South African government recognizes the new young state although, apart from its fragmented condition, it satisfies every social, political and economic criterion that the United Nations could devise. The world shuns it because of the manner of its birth. The other independent black states had the same parent; what has made Bophuthatswana different? The answer lies in the genuineness of its tribal integrity and its historical right to its land.

The dominant tribes of Bophuthatswana are the Batswana ('the scattered ones'), known to their Victorian British rulers as the Bechuana of Bechuanaland. Many of them lived in the south, in what became British Bechuanaland; others lived in the Bechuanaland Protectorate, now Botswana ('the place of the scattered ones'). When it became known that the British government was planning to hand over British Bechuanaland to Cape Colony, the people's wishes and fears were summed up by Chief Montsioa:[13]

> 'I thank and praise the Great Queen of England, and I rely upon her. I now ask her with great earnestness not to give us over to the Government of the Cape, for if the Queen does that she throws us away. If we remain under the Government of England, we live, I and my people. We shall not be divided into small locations'.

And his words were echoed by many others, including Moyhkoane Mokgoetse of Mafeking (strictly 'Mafikeng'): 'I love the British Government . . . because it treats both black and white alike.'[14] Nevertheless in 1895 the nation was given to Cape Colony, the people were divided into small locations and blacks and whites were not treated alike.

The Batswana have as great a historical claim as any other African nation to the land which was theirs when the present sacrosanct imperial boundaries were drawn. In fact their century-old agitation for a Bophuthatswana (a 'gathering together of the scattered ones') is the stronger for being based on a judgment of Governor Keate who, after a legal dispute in 1871, gave the most generous definition of their land entitlement. The first real opportunity of regaining jurisdiction over their territory came with the passing of the Promotion of Black Self-Government Act in 1959. South Africa's alleged motives were of no concern to them. Their entitlement seemed to parallel that of Botswana and their economic viability proved to be superior to that of the Batswana's other land.

The international community believes that Bophuthatswana is artificially supported by a South African subsidy, that its President is a puppet of Pretoria, and that it amounts to no more than a cheap labour pool. It is true that a subsidy did help to get the economy going; it is also true that this has dwindled to less than 3 per cent of annual income/expenditure, and that Bophuthatswana regards this as a small but useful contribution towards payment of ground rent which is long overdue. Although the Minister of Finance will hang on to it as long as he can, it is not crucial to the state's survival. The nation's wealth derives from four other sources: a remarkable investment in tourism centred on the Sun City complex; rich deposits of platinum, gold, silver, diamonds and other minerals; rapidly growing industrial complexes funded by the Bophuthatswana National Development Corporation; and community agricultural schemes organized by Agricor, whose technology is still defeating the drought.

Having seized an opportunity which history was not likely to offer them again, those Batswana who live in Bophuthatswana have been determined to make the state work; consequently they have brought in much expertise from overseas. Agriculture provided the greatest initial challenge and Taiwanese help was sought so that wetland rice could be grown in the desert. Israeli guidance has enabled community projects for mixed vegetable production to be introduced, using computerized drip feed irrigation of the type developed in Middle Eastern war zones. Despite lack of official recognition, investment has been attracted to extensive labour-intensive industrial concerns, especially in Babelegi and Selosesha. Put together these schemes have made Bophuthatswana far more independent than many internationally recognized states.

Important as the physical quality of life is to the citizen of Bophuthatswana, more fundamental is the fact that he is free: no longer a slave in any sense of the term. No time was lost in repealing all apartheid legislation and in addition to the new democratic constitution a Bill of Rights has provided much needed reassurance. The judiciary is independent and an ombudsman took office in 1981 as a further safeguard of individual rights. Where these have been threatened, and there have been a few cases, so far the Bill of Rights has prevailed. Penal slavery being one of the major sins of the parent state, the prison service is where one looks immediately for signs of inherited wickedness. The parole system is used, but no abuses have been detected. Parents of children at state schools, where prisoners create gardens, have complained not that their children are in danger of criminal assault but that the wages of sin are altogether too attractive. On the prison farms prisoners produce much of the food needed for their own consumption, and plants are cultivated for the decoration of public buildings, not for private sale. Within the prison compound much is made of the self-help principle, as a means of reducing the cost of the service while teaching skills which help towards rehabilitation.

Bantu education has been replaced by multi-racial schooling with high aspirations (though the late transfer of Mafeking to Bophuthatswana brought with it two apartheid schools which have not yet been relinquished by South Africa), and the only state-enforced migration is the deportation of illegal immigrants. There is, however, much economically motivated migration, mainly to Soweto, because the state needs much more investment from overseas. This causes some child neglect as many migrants leave their children behind, rather than expose them to apartheid. Another disadvantage, the supreme disadvantage, is the existence of the South African corridors between the segments of Bophuthatswana. Free citizens lose their freedom while travelling from one part of their sovereign state to another, and harassment does occur.

Internal faults of this former homeland are potential, rather than actual. Lack of opposition representation in the parliament is one possible source of trouble. The ambiguous manifesto of the opposition National Seoposengwe Party led to the defeat of all its candidates at the last election. As far as can be judged, this was caused by fears that the state might be handed back to South Africa; in fact most opposition spokesmen say that the only South African link that they wish to retain is something akin to EEC citizenship. More serious is the passing of the Internal Security Amendment Act, 1984 which could lead to severe limitations of Freedom of Assembly. As if it was feared that this might have been the first move on a slippery slope, enlightened amendments to the Amendment are already in train.

It is difficult to know which should come first: consolidation or international recognition. Both are essential, but one would presumably lead to the other. International recognition would certainly give the state added muscle in her negotiations with South Africa about land transfers. At some stage a UN supervised referendum would legitimize the whole process and Bophuthatswana would have pointed the way to a solution of the present South African deadlock. In its unrecognized fragmented condition it is exceedingly vulnerable. If any neighbour were to march in to capture the mineral wealth, not one official voice could be raised in protest, for officially Bophuthatswana does not exist. And yet here is a state with no pass laws, no compulsory migration, no political prisoners, no interferences with marital arrangements, no detention without trial, no torture by security forces, no slavery. The police are generally polite and all citizens are equal before the law, regardless of pigmentation. Even those Batswana in Soweto who disagree with independence now comment that 'the cattle get fatter every year'.

Simply because it was their misfortune to end up with the wrong colonial master, between 2 and 3 million Batswana are collectively rejected by other free nations. Because of their human rights record Ciskei, Transkei and Venda are partly to blame for this; they have misled foreign observers. Having lumped all the independent homelands together, few are willing to admit that in one case they may have been wrong. If they were to do so, the bestowing of official recognition would help in the restoration of Botswana's smaller, though richer, sister. Once recognized and consolidated Bophuthatswana could be a model for the transformation of the other homelands into what South Africa professed that they would be. Nudged by the world into practising what it had preached, South Africa would have to make substantial realistic land transfers, without resorting to compulsory migration. As soon as viable economic units had been constructed or reconstructed, in accordance with tribal wishes and historical claims, the time for meaningful referenda would have arrived and the people would have the opportunity to opt for complete independence or some form of federal link. The magnitude of the task is to be compared to that of the partition of India. Remembering the bloodshed that that entailed, South Africa is right not to be rushed. At the same time, if the tribes are to be patient, current inhumanities must cease; the state must repeal totalitarian legislation and make its security police subject to careful control.

Apartheid has not been kept within the confines of the Republic of South Africa; it was, and is (in a modified form) practised in Namibia, the former German South West African colony ruled illegally by South Africa since 1966. Here what has been said about Multinational Development is unlikely to have any relevance whatsoever, unless after independence the new state opts for economic links with the hypothetical federation. Although in theory South Africa could walk away from the problem and leave it to the United Nations to sort out, in practice the position is no less complex than the Republic's internal affairs; furthermore it is made more difficult by the existence of a state of war in the north of the country, by rebel camps in Angola, and by the absence of an alternative to South Africa's Administrator General. Contenders for power are either too weak or have strengths uncomfortably similar to those of the worst elements of the regime they wish to oust. All the concomitants of apartheid are to be found within Namibia, even miniature homelands, though compulsory migrations of Bushmen and other ethnic groups have been fewer in recent years. The features of the system that reduces people to the level of chattel slaves are there: incommunicado detention without trial and torture when under interrogation. 'Disappearances' occur and the creation of a now notorious counter-insurgency unit *Koevoet* (Crowbar) has done nothing to improve the situation. When security torturers and murderers have come before the courts, their crimes have only cost them fines. The United Nations needs to involve itself much more intimately with its foster child, so that the Cuban-Angolan and the South African forces can disengage. Unfortunately the UN will only recognize the South West African People's Organization (SWAPO) as representative of the Namibian will.

Namibia will go its own way in the end, and the Republic will then be in a stronger position to put its own house in order. The plural nature of its society is such that it is not so much a country as a continent of many countries and in future dialogues this should be taken into account; moreover, fears of domination by a warlike tribe mean that relationships between black and black are as much to be considered as those between black and white. Day-to-day practices of apartheid[15] are evil, but there is nothing evil about nations developing separately, and related tribes refer to themselves collectively as 'nations'. Instead of imposing sanctions which inevitably damage the economies of those who have succeeded in breaking free, the world would be better employed ensuring that slavery cannot return.

Chapter 5

Exploitation of Children

Prohibition under Section 1, Article 1, (d) of *Any institution or practice whereby a child or young person under the age of 18 years is delivered by either or both of his natural parents or by his guardian to another person, whether for reward or not, with a view to exploitation of the child or young person or of his labour.*

UNITED NATIONS SUPPLEMENTARY CONVENTION ON THE ABOLITION OF SLAVERY, THE SLAVE TRADE, AND INSTITUTIONS AND PRACTICES SIMILAR TO SLAVERY

At a recent Anti-Slavery Society AGM, when Lord Wilberforce was in the chair, a member stood up, announced herself to be a 'true Wilberforce', gave her married name and complained that it was high time someone spoke in favour of child labour. It was, she believed, a thoroughly good thing. After an initial hush, she gained support, even from the platform, and, in the context of what was discussed, she was right. In both advanced and Third World countries it is often good for children to make a constructive contribution to family and, indirectly, national welfare; a main proviso, of course, is that it must not deprive the child of other essential ingredients of education. To deny that there is such a thing as legitimate child labour is to undermine the efforts of those who seek to remove some of the most inhumane forms of modern slavery. Perhaps, as will be seen later with female circumcision (one of the worst misnomers with which anti-slavers have to cope), child labour, as an important human rights issue, needs a more accurate title.

Use of children for adult labour and for labour which is too tedious or otherwise unsuitable for adults is the major part of human rights activity in the field of what may be termed child exploitation; though in his report to the International Labour Conference in 1983, the Director-General of the ILO said that 'Exploitation is an over-used term; its existence and its extent in any given situation can always be points of contention.'[1] He did, however, go on to say that he would not quibble about the use of the term with regard to work which endangered physical or mental health, unpaid or poorly paid labour, and the exclusion by work of normal childhood opportunities, especially education. Supporters of the anti-slavery cause naturally concentrate their efforts on situations where there is a consistent pattern of inexcusable exploitation. While this is their first criterion, they also seek to show that few if any cultures are blameless, that what is inexcusable in a developed country may be acceptable in a poor one and that there is a wide range of occupations which offer scope for exploitation. The Director-General listed examples including cases of young girls losing their eyesight in industrial work requiring the handling of fine wires, of children working down mine shafts, of bonded children, of children working in fields heavily contaminated with insecticides or in sweat shops, and of subcontracted shepherd boys working a fifteen-hour day. 'That is child labour. Not teenagers working for a few hours to earn additional pocket money; not children helping on family farms; not youngsters doing household chores.'[2] The true Wilberforces would agree with the point he is making, would say that exploitation is the name of the crime, and would add some alarming examples, particularly in connection with forced labour in pornographic film making and in brothels. The Slavery Convention quoted at the head of this chapter encompasses too limited a field of exploitation to suffice for those actually engaged in combating modern manifestations of the institution. One of the ways in which it is deficient is in the use of the word 'delivered'. Although many children enter slavery by straight sale or lease, many others are stolen, abandoned or orphaned by famine. Those inherited are generally the traditional chattel slaves (chapter 2).

What is a child? The slavery convention is right to direct attention to all those who are under 18, especially as in some ways adolescents are even more vulnerable than young children; but the International Labour Organization has had to be realistic in defining the minimum age, particularly with regard to Third World countries. A principal aim of the Minimum Age Convention, 1973 (no. 138) is to close the gap between schooling and employment at a reasonable level: 'The minimum age . . . shall not be less than the age of completion of compulsory schooling and, in any case, shall not be less than 15 years.'[3] But this is modified in the next paragraph for the benefit of those countries 'whose economy and educational facilities are insufficiently developed'[4] and, although hedged about with recommendations about 'light work', the net result is a substitution of 12 years as the effective minimum age for much of the world. Absence of reliable methods of birth registration and commonsense elimination from the scope of the convention of 'employment in family undertakings'[5] has further blurred the distinction between what is, and what is not, acceptable. Even so, by 1985 only twenty-nine states had felt able to ratify the Minimum Age Convention.

The wish to draw a specific age line is derived from the negative aspect of child exploitation. A child who is working before reaching the age of 15 or 12 may well be physically or mentally stunted or educationally deprived as a result; a common abuse is sleep deprivation. Alternatively the child may benefit from vocational experience that is in itself educational. In what follows, however, emphasis is on the positive abuse of the child. Enslavement of adults is a crime; enslavement of children is worse to the extent that because of their helplessness they can more easily fall into the category of disposable assets. A man enslaved late in life, possibly for political reasons, may have a future if he is eventually released; but if, for example, a 5-year-old prostitute survives physically, he or she has nevertheless been psychologically injured or destroyed.

Whereas with other forms of slavery it is sometimes possible to select one country as a principal example, with child exploitation the practice is so widespread and diverse that it is better to take the opposite approach. In order to give some attention to a wide range of abuses, examples are taken, continent by continent, mainly from Africa, South America, Asia and Europe. Although mention is made of North America, in most cases its sins are best recorded as offences against migrant children from outside the continent and children of tribal minorities; and much the same can be said of Australasia. The only part of the world allegedly free from child exploitation is the Soviet bloc. A stream of information reaches the United Nations Working Group on Slavery from almost all countries in the world about non-political human rights violations, but not a word from the Warsaw Pact nations. All, except Czechoslovakia, have ratified Convention 138 and all are apparently without sin. When challenged privately as to why this large segment of the world was silent on these matters, a communist delegate replied, 'We run a well-disciplined society.' A colleague added, less discreetly, 'If you want to know the true position, you must ask about "minority groups", not "slavery".' Children do not constitute a minority group; hence the silence, perhaps. The only clear evidence of their human rights being violated comes when they are related to dissidents or are part of a religious or racial minority out of favour with the regime.

As mentioned in chapter 4, one consequence of apartheid which comes within the narrower definition of slavery can occur when migration splits families. Despite protective legislation, the exceptional vulnerability of children of South African migrant labourers has reduced them to slavery on certain farms; and in a society where dates of birth are often unrecorded it is difficult to see how the loopholes in the laws can be sealed. The Black Labour Act, 1964, attempts to curb contractual employment of blacks 'apparently under eighteen years'[6] and, in keeping with the spirit of ILO recommendations, a lowering of the limit to 16 for agricultural work is subject to the issue of special permits 'to recruit Bantu youths of the apparent age of 16 years and under 18 years'.[7] The words 'apparently' and 'apparent' in the Act and the permit can be compared in their effectiveness to United Kingdom regulations about sale of cigarettes and alcohol to minors; they render statutory minimum ages ineffective in the absence of goodwill. Another cause of present irregularities is unwillingness to break free from an old established land tenancy system, officially abolished at the end of 1968. A common arrangement was for black families to pay for the right to live on the land by giving six months' labour to a white farmer; for the rest of the year they either subsisted as best they could or depended on remittances from a migrant bread-winner. The residual system limits the white farmer to five resident families, regardless of the acreage of his farm, and they must work for him full-time; the others are supposed to be resettled, though in fact many remain.

Without an effective age restriction, law enforcement starts from a grave disadvantage. One way of tackling the problem once compulsory education is universal would be the appointment of schools attendance officers with wide powers of inspection. Provided that the curriculum fulfilled the needs of the children, such an inspectorate could perform a dual service for children of farm labourers, and its brief could be extended to include children engaged in factory work, trade and domestic services, where good laws[8] are not always enforced. However, removal of child earners could impoverish a black family unless legislation were introduced guaranteeing realistic minimum wages for the parents. Given that there are acceptable forms of child labour, a more sensible initial approach would be to make sure that conditions, hours and wages of child workers down to age 12 were satisfactory, and that work done by those younger than 12 was strictly 'within the family circle' and of benefit to the child.

Anti-Slavery Society investigators visiting the Msinga district of central Natal, half of which lies in Kwazulu homeland, were told by a local researcher of some 8,000 local labour tenants. With the advent of the five families limitation and compulsory settlement of the remainder in Kwazulu, many blacks have had to adapt rapidly in order to survive, and child exploitation, sometimes approximating to slavery, has been one of the results. The Anti-Slavery Society report[9] shows that the children tend to fall into three categories; some are taken by truck daily across the Kwazulu-South African border for a dawn-to-dusk day, excluding time spent travelling; others become boarders in compounds on the farms for weekly or six-monthly periods; others are exported to other parts of the country, again by truck. In terms of recompense the first group usually fared worst; their pay was generally in kind, tomatoes or potatoes. But children are liable to receive nothing at all in their own right. In one case, rather than agree to resettlement, which would have put elderly relatives at risk, a labourer negotiated for permission to stay outside the homeland. It was agreed that he could move on to a white farm with the condition that he supplied the farmer with two children for six months' labour. As his own children were too young, he paid two of his neighbours R90 (£50) each and acquired substitutes who were in his opinion old enough. They worked unpaid for the agreed term, after which they were summarily dismissed and the labourer, who had worked elsewhere in the meantime, was told that he must leave the farm as well.[10]

Transportation of the children in open trucks may take little account of their physical welfare and lead to accidents. In 1979[11] two boys were frozen to death while being driven 400 miles after helping with the harvest, and there have been other tragedies with vehicles caused by insufficient care and supervision. To the boarders, though, travel is usually the least of their worries. Inadequate food and poor accommodation can be continual sources of unhappiness. In many areas porridge, potatoes and thin soup constitute the daily diet, with protein rarely added; and sleeping conditions on an eastern Transvaal farm have been described as 'atrocious. . . . It was just a hole; boys and girls chucked together in an uncemented place. . . .'[12] A schoolmistress commented, 'It's camouflaged slave labour. It is taken that the child has volunteered, but he has not.' In fact often, elsewhere, he has volunteered, but only because he has jumped to the wrong conclusion, or been misled, about pay. And when he decides that he has made a serious mistake, he may find that his homeland passport has been confiscated.

Here, as with everything else to do with apartheid, there is a broad range of interpretation of what is conceived to be the proper way to deal with blacks. As the *Cape Times* commented on this topic,[13] 'Their wages and working conditions differ widely, from near slave labour to the most favourable treatment that unskilled workers could hope to receive. The point is, however, that payment . . . and . . . conditions rest almost entirely at the discretion of employers.' Some employers clearly retain Dr Verwoerd's belief that 'There is no place for the native in the European community above the level of certain forms of labour',[14] and will not worry about treating black children as inferior to cattle. This end of the spectrum was illustrated (literally) in 1983[15] when an Afrikaner farming in Namibia put his legally employed 18-year-old farm hand in chains and cut off pieces of his ear to make him say he was a SWAPO sympathiser. Later he gave a drinks party at which he posed for a photograph while aiming a gun at his victim. He then shot and killed him and was subsequently sentenced to six years' imprisonment (less remission). Others will go to the opposite extreme and create employment where none exists, sometimes turning a blind eye to the age of a child for morally commendable reasons. It is this type of farmer who will provide a reasonably well-built farm school, which will be run by the Education Department according to its lights. Taken as a whole the situation is mixed, but indefensible. Failure of the state to enforce existing legislation which could cleanse the whole farming system and extinguish the objectionable element makes it guilty on this count of practising slavery.

At the other end of the continent, in Morocco, the environment of child exploitation is more obviously industrial than agricultural. Commentators with Marxist inclinations have always been quick to point out why a large proportion of capitalist big business spokesmen has long called for the abolition of child labour: forced by trades unions to pay improved minimum wages to adults, manufacturers were liable to be seriously undercut by competitors with a negligible wage bill. However, with the arrival on the scene of multinational corporations, whose far-flung organizations could profit directly from the sweat of an anonymous unseen child labour force, capitalism may be tempted to return, more discreetly one assumes, to the position of the West Indian parliamentary factor in Wilberforce's day. This cynical interpretation of capitalist motives is a gross over-simplification; nevertheless unacceptable capitalism is to be seen writ large in Third World countries where vulnerable tribal peoples occupy resource-rich territories, and in transitional economies such as Morocco, where a traditional domestic craft has penetrated a lucrative world market.

In Morocco emergent industrial capitalism can be observed in terms of one key industry, carpet making. What was, in feudal times, a family-centred occupation has been moving into the twentieth century, carrying some of its medieval features with it. Before the development of the factory system there was a stage when children would go, perhaps as boarders, to the house of a skilled weaver, known as a *maalema*, or *maîtresse*, to be taught the skills of the trade until they were able to practise it in their own right. Like black children on white South African farms today, some were slaves and some were privileged, with many grades between, but generally it was in the *maalema*'s interest to care for a productive workforce of unpaid apprentices. Unfortunately the benevolent element was partly withdrawn with the invention of modern looms and the move from house to factory. The system evolved in such a way that the factory owner operated through the *maalema*, who recruited and organized the labour supply. He paid the *maalema* for the number of square metres produced and was in every way cut off from the children.

Like the biblical tax gatherer, the *maalema* has every incentive to extort as much as she can from the children in her power. And her employer, whether he be private entrepreneur or public official (for some factories are state-run), can take as much or as little interest in the weavers as he likes. As with similar middleman arrangements, from Irish tenant farming to Peruvian rubber gathering, the system is fraught with potential for exploitation and some state-run concerns have abandoned it, risking the probable decline in profits. Whether this contributed to a recent decline in numbers has not yet been discovered. With or without the middlewoman, the industry as it stands is dependent on cheap labour to keep the product competitive in the European market and two laws[16] are working against each other to prevent reforms. The first of these is simply a dead letter, ignored in state and private enterprises alike; it states unequivocally that children under the age of 12 may not be employed as paid workers or as apprentices. The other sets the minimum wage for adults and decrees that children from 12 to 15 years receive half pay. Ideal recruits for the unscrupulous are well-built under-12s who will work hard unpaid in the hope of eventually graduating to the pay roll.

Anti-Slavery Society teams visited Morocco twice[17] and compiled detailed reports which, after considerable delay in the hope that the country would respond in a positive way, appeared in print in 1978.[18] Seventy-nine factories were visited, including many back street workshops which worked for large companies. The practices of the less respectable multinationals were reflected in a crude microcosm. The teams had found that, partly because of the absence of compulsory education, the industry was employing children aged 7 and upwards (on their first visit they had seen some looms attended by 5-year-olds) and sometimes the children, exclusively girls, were made to work a seventy-two hour week. If they were on the pay roll their pay was equivalent to the price of a loaf of bread; but most were illegal apprentices who received nothing for their labour. The Society observed that matters were getting worse and made two principal recommendations: that the *maalema* system be abolished, and that the existing labour inspectorate be given real powers to improve conditions and see that laws are enforced. It appears, however, that the inspectorate itself is ill-staffed and in need of reform; it is alleged that inspectors rarely visit factories, and when they do they expect to receive bribes for turning a blind eye to irregularities. Widespread exploitation is likely to remain, at least until the country has found the means to provide many more schools.

Conditions described in some Anti-Slavery Society reports indicate the degree to which the children's health is threatened:[19]

> The looms, numbering about one hundred and seventy, are placed in rows close together. . . . The noise and dust created by these machines contribute strongly to the unpleasant and unhealthy working conditions. Festoons of wool dust, created by the spinning machinery, hang from the rafters of the forty foot high roof. The clothes and hair of the children are soon covered with this dust. The building, at the time of investigation in March was intolerably cold and the noise of the machines almost prevented the possibility of conversation.
>
> The children, three, four or sometimes five to a loom, worked

> fast and without stopping under the watchful eyes of their supervisors. More than half of the children were between the ages of five and ten.
>
> When the children emerged from the factory at the end of the day it could be seen that their health was affected by the conditions in which they had been working. Many of them had colds and sores on their faces, their complexions were pallid and their eyes bleary. They breathe in the dust from carding and spinning machines for six days a week. Although the machines stop in the afternoon, the air is never free from this all-pervading dust.

Other factories had healthy facilities, but several nervously refused access to the team.

As one moves from Africa to Europe one enters a completely different pattern of child abuse. In the Mediterranean lands the situation is complex and often subtly concealed and in parts of the continent children may be exploited, often indirectly, as dependants of migrant workers. Common to both continents is callous undermining of children's health, though the short step across the straits of Gibraltar is sufficient for an investigator to discover that this is achieved in different ways. While the main Moroccan method of exploitation is the use of unpaid apprentices, and is therefore within a narrow definition of slavery, Spanish practice in the unpaid sphere is to work children hard within the family setting and thus relieve the farm or shop from having to take on paid labour. The Spanish Basic Education Law, 1970, which makes school attendance obligatory from 6 to 14, is resented by some parents, particularly in rural areas, and has not always been strictly enforced.

It is not, however, within the family that the child's health is most likely to be at risk. The trouble arises when dissatisfaction with a dreary and apparently unprofitable life leads to a break with the family. Many children are then attracted into back street industries, some of which require the workers to handle toxic materials during the manufacturing process; an example of this is the glueing of soles and heels to cheap shoes. Eventually disillusionment can lead to a second break; the comparatively lucky ones may find employment in the hotel industry, where under-aged labour will be welcomed, or they may find opportunities in domestic service. Those not so fortunate go into the self-employed category as shoe-shine boys, scavengers or beggars.

Once completely on their own, some drift into prostitution. In many states such a situation would call for legislation. Some may well be needed, but when Susan Searight investigated Spanish child labour for the Anti-Slavery Society nearly all her recommendations[20] simply emphasized the need for existing laws to be enforced.

Italy is another European country which has been investigated by the Anti-Slavery Society. The suicide of a chattel slave shepherd boy (see chapter 2), had made the world aware, for a time, of rural exploitation of child labour in this state, though it is doubtful whether the extent of the practice outside a medieval enclave in the south was fully appreciated; there was a strong local tradition in the Bari region around Altamura, but 9-year-old boys were working sixteen-hour days unpaid in the north as well. Dramatic disclosures were not only short-lived in their effect on public opinion, they also diverted attention from the main environment of child exploitation. Marina Valcarenghi, who carried out the investigations for the Anti-Slavery Society, found that a minority of Italy's estimated one and a half million child labourers work in farming. Far greater numbers are working in commerce, handicrafts and industry. At the time of the Anti-Slavery Society's investigations, the results of which were published in 1981,[21] there was no official statistic for Italian child labourers under age 14. They were everywhere, but in theory they did not exist. However, partly with the help of three other sets of statistics – school absenteeism, industrial accidents and illnesses caused by work – it was possible to arrive at a more realistic estimate than the 100,000 that had previously been postulated.

Although poverty plays its usual role in stimulating exploitation, greed enters the labour market from above and below in a peculiar way. At the base of society lies the belief, common in poor regions or countries, that children are property. Many peasants, or people of recent peasant origin, feel that education – certainly the sort that has been on offer in Italian state schools in recent years – is diverting the child from his true function as a contributor to family welfare. At the other end of the economic scale, a ruthless industrial corporation can reap vast profits from the use of child labour provided that it decentralizes, that is to say keeps the children off the main industrial sites, working in a small empire of clandestine workshops. Moreover, although it sounds melodramatic to say so, the top and bottom of this unregistered and officially non-existent edifice are held together by the Mafia's concept of *omerta*: the strict code which demands a total commitment to confidentiality. Children sense that it is more than their life is worth to divulge the name of the firm for which they work.

The financial advantages to big business of decentralization of production extend far beyond the employment of cheap labour, though children are the most essential ingredient of the arrangement. As Marina Valcarenghi's report stresses, the illegal aspects of such enterprises increase profits in a variety of ways: there need be no premises to maintain, no taxes, no national insurance contributions, no liability for employees' health or accident risks, no contractual obligations and no overheads of any sort. Furthermore the nature of the bond between the outlying workshops and the central organization is such that hours remain flexible and nothing resembling trade unionism is ever likely to develop. The imagined advantages to the child are less obvious; in a sense, as he is not eligible for paid employment, all remuneration is perceived as a bonus. His parents would say that he was better off out of school, off the streets and (they hope) learning a trade. He would share their enthusiasm about missing school and doubtless derive some pride from having been accepted into what is technically an adult environment.

Investigations have revealed the degree to which one of the major advantages (in a Machiavellian sense) of decentralization is removal from the firm receiving the manufactured goods or parts of any legal responsibility for the workers' health. A principal industry exploiting child labour is shoe manufacturing and, as in Spain, toxic glues are used by the children. The industry is extensively developed in Italy and there have been many cases of glue polyneuritis. Marina Valcarenghi cited several of them, including that of Letizia,[22] who started working a ten-hour day at the glueing bench at the age of 13, when her father was unemployed. Before long she had skin problems with her hands, eye trouble and stomach pains. After three months she was constantly debilitated, suffering from nausea and irritation in her arms and legs. Then her legs became paralysed and she collapsed. She also suffered from paralysis of her arms, to the extent that she could not feed herself. After five months' treatment in hospital she was able to walk with a support and could just manage to take food unaided. Ten years later, when the Anti-Slavery Society report appeared, she was still a semi-invalid.

Similar experiences of two girls at another workshop have been recorded. Maria, aged 12, suffered the same nausea and paralysis of her arms and legs, and her condition was eventually diagnosed as glue polyneuritis. A critical stage was reached when she stopped breathing and had to spend two days in a resuscitation unit. Since then her condition has fluctuated between respites and relapses. She has never recovered. At much the same time, Francesca, a 14-year-old who had been doing the same work in a different section since she was 12, was unaware of the risks she was taking. The weather became cold and the only window was closed, preventing the escape of the poisonous fumes; and it was not long before the child was feeling sick and experiencing tingling sensations in her arm and leg joints. As with Letizia, it was about three months before she lost the use of her legs.

Just as the child labourers have no legal employer to whom to turn for industrial injuries compensation, so there is also no one officially obliged to see that the conditions in which they work reach minimum standards. The Anti-Slavery Society report says that every workshop visited was 'bad in the extreme' and singled out the old centre of Naples as one of the worst areas. Frequently workshops are not only back street, but below ground, located in badly ventilated basements, usually with no more than a window through which noxious fumes may be released. Letizia's workshop was thirty metres square and had twenty-two people working in it; Maria applied her poisonous substances (three brand names are mentioned in the report) in a room of forty square metres, shared with nineteen others; Francesca was working with twenty-four operatives in a ten-metre square section. The premises in which Maria and Francesca worked were subsequently inspected by a commission including two doctors from the hospital to which Francesca had originally been admitted. The commission's verdict was that the place was a health hazard; it was inadequately ventilated, too cramped and unhygienic.

At this particular workshop the children were working from 8.00 a.m. until 6.00 p.m., with half an hour off for lunch, sticking shoes or bags together as rapidly as possible. In the leather industry the emphasis on speed has two tragic consequences: it is the toxic glues which stick quickest, and the pace of production encourages the children to use their hands instead of the brushes which are provided. As well as having to breathe in the fumes all day, they leave work in the evening with hands and clothes contaminated. But although it is by far the greatest source of danger to them, glue is not the only threat to their health. Because they are so often below street level, workshops are frequently damp, and some are verminous; spiders, cockroaches and rats share the environment. Rooms tend to be excessively hot in summer and cold in winter, while lighting may be poor all the year round. All the workshops have machines and little effort is made to shield the work force from noise which achieves an injurious pitch; moreover, the dust problem is as acute here as in the Moroccan carpet factories. Scientific development, so often confused with progress, has made matters worse; increased use of synthetic materials in place of leather has meant that glue, though still the main enemy, is now one of several with which the workers come into contact. The children are exposed to poisons which may enter their bodies via nose and mouth or pass through the pores of the skin.

Objections to Italian child labour practices are supported by a remarkable statistic: despite the illegality of the relationship between the worker and his firm, and the clandestine scenario of Italy's open secret, compensation for permanent disablement was granted to more than 6,000 children over a fifteen-year period. About 3,500 disablements were the result of industrial accidents, while 2,500 were agricultural. As the traditional way of dealing with accidents in the illegal sector is a private settlement, one can only begin to imagine the true number of accidents which have occurred. The leather industry is the best researched, but the same statistical source has revealed that child labour is widely exploited in heavy industry and in methods of production which involve advanced technology – and both these areas are fully unionized. Many cases show that electrocution is a special hazard for the under-aged worker.

Italy has the highest rate of child labour in the EEC and although its legislation, like that of Spain, is pointing in the right direction, the physical and psychological consequences of its ineffectiveness are alarming. Law 977 of 1967 and Decree 36 of 1971 define the light work that children may do, provided that health and schooling do not suffer, on the premises of wholesalers, retailers, chemists, travel agents and hoteliers (provided that the hotel does not have a billiard room). '*Commercio in commissione*'[23] is also permitted, and errand boys and shop assistants are named as performing specifically approved tasks, subject to the various restrictions which limit hours and eliminate the harsher physical burdens. That legislation has been largely ineffective is reflected in the medical condition of the many children who have suffered accidents at work, as discovered by doctors employed by schools and insurance companies. This ranges from extensive damage to heart, lungs and spine to a wide variety of occupational diseases arising from contacts with toxic materials which frequently affect brain and eyes.

Filling gaps in the law will not in itself bring about reform. However, the granting of additional powers and finance to the existing labour inspectorate could help to give life to a dead letter, always supposing that the inspectors themselves would be inspected from time to time; and the inspector's task would be made much easier if the gap between the school-leaving age and age of eligibility for employment were closed. For this to mean anything there would have to be something of a revolution in the nature of what is taught in the schools. An essential prerequisite of reform is that parents and pupils shall come to see school attendance as a desirable and profitable route to life in the real world.

Turning one's attention to the other side of the Atlantic gives no more grounds for optimism than were perceived on crossing the Mediterranean. In the Americas several slavery traditions have interacted and created a tangible pattern of exploitation which pervades both continents. While in parts of North America old habits of enslavement have generally survived in the areas of pornographic film making, forced prostitution and preying on migrants, South American practice is much more complex. Serfdom deserves its own treatment (chapter 7), although it is the children who suffer most under its several regimes; as far as the other current forms of slavery are concerned the continent seems to have shown a predisposition to exploit the child. The preferred ways in which these helpless members of the community are most often exploited are easily observed among both Spanish- and Portuguese-speaking peoples.

When the Anti-Slavery Society reported to the United Nations Working Group of Experts on Slavery in the International Year of the Child (1979),[24] the estimated number of child labourers in Colombia was 3 million. Despite the theoretical protection of laws prohibiting employment which could damage the health of those under 18, some three-quarters of the children under 10 had no days off and a quarter of the child work force worked a thirteen-hour day. Somewhere between a third and a half worked a nine-hour day and, although it was expressly forbidden, the same proportion was solely committed to working at night. Figures for Bogotá showed that a third of the children never attended school, and this reflected the proportion of urban child workers for the nation as a whole, though it did not include the number of children involved in casual labour. In the countryside half the children were working.

Colombian statistics in this field give some indication of national economic dependence on child labour. What is more remarkable, though, is the nature of the work the children are obliged to undertake. Some details, supported by photographic evidence, recall Lord Shaftesbury's complaints about the sufferings of English children during the nineteenth century. It was revealed that child coal miners were working deep underground in tunnels without the most basic safety precautions. Roofs and walls were unsupported by props, light came from candles in open tin cans balanced on ledges in the walls and there was no provision for ventilation. For eight hours a day the children hacked away at the coal surface with hand tools, filling sacks at the rate of about thirty a day and then dragging them to the top of the shaft. While they worked in the lower regions, often mothers and sisters were working at higher levels, operating hand pumps which drained the tunnels. With their feet perpetually in cold water, they too worked an eight-hour day protecting those who worked beneath them. As is so often the case, the ultimate slave-driver was economic necessity; frequently the children come from one-parent families and their physical survival depends entirely upon ability to fill enough sacks at the given piecework rate for the job. In 1979 seven pesos was paid for a sack which fetched 180 pesos when received by the synthetic fibre factory which was a major customer. The question of school attendance did not arise. Once a miner, one was likely to be a miner for life. Education could only deprive a child of the means of survival.

Although whole families may be employed, the mines naturally make greatest use of the boys. The fate of girls is precarious in a culture which has not yet developed a concerned respect for the weak; and girls can suffer because they are young, because they are mere females and sometimes because they are servants. Domestic service sounds a much softer life than coal mining; it can be equally soul-destroying, as witness the testimony of an unpaid 7-year-old:[25]

> 'They leave me alone, locked up all day long. I have to get up at about four in the morning, to make coffee and breakfast for the boss. Afterwards I do it for his wife and the child. They all leave very early. Afterwards I wash dishes, I make the beds, and when I have finished I look out of the window. Afterwards I make dinner

and I go to bed at around eight o'clock in the evening. They pay me nothing because the boss is a friend of my mother.'

Although technically the children may be paid, the actual passing of money is more likely to be from new owner to parent, sometimes a lump sum for outright purchase, sometimes a regular fee for services rendered. As the child involved may be bought or hired from the age of 3, he, or more usually she, can soon be conditioned to accept the new status without question. If the owner has a conscience, it can be salved by the knowledge that payment has been, or is being, made; the fact that the money bypasses the child altogether can be forgotten. This is sham adoption, the form of slavery defined in the Supplementary Convention quoted at the head of this chapter.

Because the life of the rural poor is harsh in South America, particularly on the plantations, an illusion of comparative ease has drawn many to urban environments, where large numbers of children seek employment on almost any terms. At the less dramatic end of the child exploitation scale is the example of Armando, who has worked in a brickworks since he was 6. At first he carried water and prepared the ash; as he grew older he graduated to moulding and cutting, after which, when he had grown strong enough, he moved on to loading the lorries. During the International Year of the Child he was getting between twenty and twenty-five pesos for putting 2,000 bricks on to each lorry. As he had to start his day at the factory at 4.00 a.m. he had no alternative but to pay his employer thirty-five pesos for meals provided on site. Even when the legal age for working has been reached, his right to a minimum wage is thwarted by inability to raise the 100 pesos necessary to satisfy the essential precondition: possession of an identity card. Unless he can work harder and stop eating, he is unlikely to be able to break out of the vicious circle.

Scavenging and begging are the seemingly inevitable occupations of those who are outside the organized conventional child labour market, and even here predatory adults have sought to exploit. Police investigations in Bogotá in 1974 brought to light two houses using over fifty children as professional beggars. From this life it is a short step to prostitution which, with the almost inevitable presence of the procurer, soon moves from a degraded type of economic enslavement to the more precisely defined form of slavery known as forced prostitution; there is no glamour, there is only short-lived profit, and there is disease, mutilation and death. Jean Fernand-Laurent, in his 1983 report to the United Nations, gave some explanation of the existence of a special market for children:[26]

> There has always been a demand for children for sexual purposes because of their freshness and simplicity. Our age, which is 'permissive' and at the same time surfeited and sexually vulgarized in the extreme, seeks all kinds of erotic refinements. There is a great demand among our contemporaries for the sexuality of the child, through which they seek to renew their thoroughly jaded sensuality. Hence the universal flourishing of child prostitution. . . . The prostitutes most in demand in Latin America are between the ages of ten and fourteen.

Setting aside the mining industry, Brazil, as might be expected, tends to be Colombia writ large, and the larger scale has meant that each form of exploitation has been pushed further towards an extreme. As in other continents, plantation agriculture has retained many of the worst features from which it gained its notoriety in earlier centuries. Isolated from the rest of the country, plantation communities have developed like independent islands; their old established ways have led to acceptance of values derived from looking inward at their archaic world, and they have become cut off, physically and psychologically, from the world at large. The internal economy of the plantation requires either that a family send its children to work simply in order to ensure survival, or that employers establish a contractual link with the family as a whole; the difference is between being pulled and being pushed. The result, as far as the sugar-cane plantations of Pernambuco State are concerned, is that children from 7 years of age form a sixth of the work force. They work from dawn until dusk during the season and tend to be inadequately fed, receiving a third of the calories necessary for normal physical and mental development. According to the latest information,[27] the heavy work commitment prevents children from attending the generally substandard schools provided by the plantation management; the presence of a school building does, however, serve to disarm critics of the system.

Unpaid child domestic servants are common and give prestige to Brazilian families with social pretensions. The middle ranks of Brazilian society, anxious to widen the gulf between themselves and their often humble origins, may well acquire their human possessions as infants. A mythical link is commonly established between a wealthy urban family and a poor rural one; some form of godparent relationship may be mooted, or there may even be a genuine, though tenuous, distant blood connection; the rural family gains some money and has one less mouth to feed, the urban family gains a slave and social enhancement, the child loses what protection it had and is now entirely at the mercy of the new owner. Unfortunately, it is those who are unaccustomed to such power who are most likely to abuse it.

Brazilian children from poor backgrounds also run the risk of being drawn into prostitution. Unlike the other forms of slavery, prostitution, in its initial stage, brings money to the child, but in eight or nine cases out of ten the intervention of a procurer transforms a free agent, whose earnings are potentially considerable, into a helpless victim. Some children, in the Colombian pattern, gravitate from scavenging to prostitution, but others are procured from the beginning. Sometimes the method parallels the domestic servant arrangement and payment may be made to the parents, who may be unaware of the nature of the services they have sold. When it comes to outright possession, it is the Amerindian children who are most liable to be victimized. For most of recorded history they and their parents, especially in the north-western corner of South America, have been outside the law, regarded, as Roger Casement discovered during his Putumayo investigations,[28] as animals. The traditional attitude has survived and its victims are known euphemistically as *criadas* or maidservants. The *criadas*, captured, bought or received as gifts, start life as domestic servants in the guise of adopted children. As they grow older they can be used by the sons of the house and, as they are not allowed to marry, any children they bear ensure the perpetuation of the system. Those who escape are well prepared for a life of prostitution.

The two Asian countries which provide the most thorough assessments of the prevalence of child exploitation are India and Thailand, both of which were investigated for the Anti-Slavery Society by Sumanta Banerjee.[29] Though the two states could hardly be more different, and the independent research carried out was not part of a comparative study, there are similarities in the way in which present problems have developed. The first of these is the part played by strong religious traditions, having little in common but their strength. In India two case studies were made, one of a mainly Hindu industry, the manufacture of bricks, another of the *zari* embroidery industry, dominated by Moslems. The former has a known history of 3,000 to

4,000 years and division of labour in the manufacturing process reflects the hierarchical nature of Hinduism. Scheduled caste families have been conditioned by history to perform the humblest task, the shaping of the bricks from the fresh clay; a slightly higher caste transports them to the kiln, where one or two more categories of worker see to the firing and dispersal of the finished products. As with plantation workers elsewhere, the employer's contract is with the family unit; the children themselves, who carry the wet clay, are not paid, neither do they attend school. The wealthier *zari* embroidery industry, which uses gold and silver thread, also has a long history subject more to Moslem traditions about the role of the female than the place of the child. The very young children employed in it are more fortunate when it comes to earnings (Rs3 (15p) for a nine-hour day in 1979), and they at least are learning a useful craft. But here too education has been sacrificed, and both occupations have their health hazards. At the brick kiln these are silicosis, tuberculosis and general accident; at the hand loom spondylitis, eye complaints and lead poisoning are risked.

Buddhism has had an unforeseen effect on child exploitation in Thailand. The idea of giving away or even selling a child, repugnant to most religions and races, has been a respectable Thai tradition for many centuries. Presenting a boy to a monk was seen to be a worthy gesture; in times of famine it seemed only sensible to part with more children to those more able to care for them. No stigma attached to such an act and it was accepted as natural for a fee to be paid. The modern extension of this activity is evil. It has been partly caused by the almost total separation of the worlds in which urban and rural Thais live. Most poverty-stricken peasants in the north-east, when they have sold or leased their children through an employment agency, have had no idea of the true nature of the likely destination. They were brutally informed during 1984, when the destruction by fire of a brothel in which the children had been chained to the beds led to the death of five young prostitutes and some publicity. As well as demonstrating the hazards of a life which has been falsely glamorized for centuries, the tragedy gave an insight into the economics of child prostitution. One of the five girls had been handed over by her parents for an advance equivalent to about £20, conditional on her performing unspecified tasks. She happened to be literate and soon wrote to her mother describing what was required of her and saying that she had been beaten to make her comply. She pleaded for the money to be returned so that she might be bought out of slavery. Unfortunately the money had already been spent and the fire intervened before the matter could be resolved. Some of the girls were merely injured and their survival enabled sympathetic organizations to learn about the conditions of slaves required to service five to ten customers each twelve-hour session.

The problem of rural and urban poverty is shared by India and Thailand, but whereas the scale of Thai difficulties indicates that solutions can be imagined, the vastness of India means that nothing short of a revolution in principles of distribution of world resources can make it possible to lift the burdens off an estimated sixteen and a half million children. It should not be beyond the bounds of possibility for Thailand, having been able to dominate the world's rice market until the late 1960s, and being economically less dependent than India on its three and a half million child labourers, to provide its own solutions, if the will were there: but it is not. As a minister and chairman of the National Youth Council of Thailand put it, 'we cannot be too rigorous in opposing the use of child labour because it would reduce productivity and harm many businesses.'[30] On the subject of education he was prepared to make a concession: 'Let [us] say it would be sufficient to provide lessons for the children on Sundays.' His attitude was typical of a government which attracted foreign capital by modern promotional methods, including a picture of young girls with the caption: 'Inexpensive labour: Thailand's major investment appeal.'[31] Not surprisingly existing laws appear adequate, but are easily evaded because both police and labour inspectors can be bribed and, technically, children getting food and accommodation without wages are not employees. The paltry sums which many in fact earn can go directly to parents without there being any need to keep accounts. Without these remittances most of the parents would be destitute; they live in the north-east, where only one rice crop will grow each year, as opposed to three elsewhere.

Sumanta Banerjee's Thailand report cites specific cases of child exploitation which are disturbing partly because they show the prevalence of widespread police corruption. Provincial police have refused to rescue children from brothels and, when police were persuaded to come from the capital and take the necessary action, brothel keepers were reassured by the local police that all would be well once the visitors had returned to Bangkok. Sex tourism has become a growth industry in the country and is so lucrative to the procurers that the illegality of prostitution is ignored by those with the power to sweep it away. The Thai authorities might be excused from turning a blind eye to child labour in the less objectionable occupations if this could divert children from those which are most injurious. As it is, they do little to curtail a form of slavery which, apart from psychological damage and sexually transmitted diseases, has many horrifying physical consequences. A list of these was compiled from medical reports and read to the United Nations Working Group of Experts on Slavery in August, 1984: 'rectal fissures, lesions, poor sphincter control, lacerated vaginas, foreign bodies in the anus or vagina, perforated anal and vaginal walls, death by asphyxiation, chronic choking from gonorrheal tonsilitis, ruptured uteruses, bodily mutilation, and death in childbirth.'[32]

Apart from innumerable child prostitutes, Thailand has some 10,000 children, many under 10, sold or leased to sweat shops. Conditions vary, but many young workers are permanently confined to unhealthy premises where they sleep communally in the room in which they work. They may be assembling machine parts or batteries, or wrapping toffees or making paper cups as part of the extensive, unregistered and illegal part of the economy. In addition, many are legally employed making glass objects, confectionery, clothing or ornaments. Their pay is minimal, their conditions poor and often dangerous to health; their schooling has ceased. In India the effect of poverty is more general; apart from the multitude of children legitimately engaged within the family in subsistence farming, and abuses echoing those of Thailand in kind, though not in national profitability, there is a greater diversity of exploitation, and often children start younger. In the Tamil Nadu match industry, for instance, the starting age was found to be 5; and, more firmly on the wrong side of the law, self-employed rice smugglers, using the advantage of their size, have been operating at the age of 4. To enforce the law in this case would simply cause starvation.

In both reports Sumanta Banerjee wisely put his emphasis on short-term reforms to bring about real and immediate improvements. In India one urgent need was for a separate child labour inspectorate, not to weed out the young, but to see that they are paid and looked after properly; particularly in the small concerns, a priority is for hours to be shortened and tasks adjusted to suit the age of the worker. In the unorganized self-employed sector trade unions and voluntary organizations have been recommended to draw these irregular child workers into the main stream of employment as far as a guaranteed wage is concerned, and to see that, as far as possible, they are provided with educational opportunities which match their work commitment. Education should be made more vocational and the Minimum Wages Act should be strictly enforced. In Thailand the situation requires consolidation of the existing laws and a drastic increase in the severity of punishment for offences against children. The labour inspectorate should be enlarged and a campaign needs to be launched to make the nation as a whole aware of the false values which have led people at all levels to accept practices which are regarded in many cultures as horrifying. Finally, the law must prescribe, the courts impose and police enforce effectively deterrent punishments for the agents who recruit children into slavery and for those who employ the agents.

Although example countries were chosen to illustrate the intercontinental extent and diversity of the problem of child exploitation, certain characteristics emerge which are common to all. Third World and developed countries alike have shortcomings in their educational provision which predispose many parents and children to believe that the workplace has more to offer than the school. President Nyerere of Tanzania indicated the solution when he said, 'Every school should also be a farm.'[33] Although this may not be true for a substantial proportion of developed countries, the vocational message is clear for all to hear. If the 'also' is suitably stressed, the means to higher aspirations need not be denied to those capable of benefiting from whatever available funds will allow.

One of the effects of child labour has been increased unemployment for adults – leading, in the case of India, to some 15 million extra unemployed who, in turn, are unable to care properly for their children. An apparently obvious solution, birth control, either provokes religious opposition, particularly in Roman Catholic countries, or, where the state tries to impose it, causes riots. To the peasant, offspring are often seen as essential parts of the family work unit, though too easily, like the dependent races of Nazi Germany, they can become disposable assets. This is vividly demonstrated at times of natural disaster when a family, having built up its labour force in order to farm difficult terrain, may find that drought translates assets into liabilities. All may starve, so some of the children must be sold. In the industrial field, the fact that children have no voice and are easily intimidated makes them more attractive to employers than unionized adults; and they are often better than their parents at work requiring dexterity and agility.

Investigations have rightly led to recommendations that short-term reforms should be quickly initiated. Education specific to national and occupational problems is the elusive key, but it is needed at all levels of society, including the level with the necessary power to co-ordinate relevant legislation. Important as the law is, in breadth and detail of treatment, short-term alleviation depends on the effectiveness of the bodies responsible for its enforcement; weak and corrupt inspectorates need to be translated into strong and enlightened organizations, supported by police and informed public opinion. The advice of ILO technical missions for action programmes on child labour, as recommended for India for 1985–7,[34] can help to resolve the apparent dilemmas posed by the rival pressures and claims of school and farm or factory. Long-term solutions, however, await international determination to abolish poverty.

Birth control is an entire category of abuse, exploitation and murder.

CHAPTER 6

EXPLOITATION OF WOMEN

Complete abolition . . . of. . . . Any institution or practice whereby: (i) A woman, without the right to refuse, is promised or given in marriage on payment of a consideration in money or in kind to her parents, guardian, family or any other person or group; or (ii) The husband of a woman, his family, or his clan, has the right to transfer her to another person for value received or otherwise; or (iii) A woman on the death of her husband is liable to be inherited by another person

UNITED NATIONS SUPPLEMENTARY CONVENTION ON THE ABOLITION OF SLAVERY, THE SLAVE TRADE, AND INSTITUTIONS AND PRACTICES SIMILAR TO SLAVERY

From the earliest times the ascendancy of the free man over the slave has had a certain parallel with the ascendancy of the male over the female, though this did not prevent the rise of exceptional individual women or sometimes women of elitist background to the highest level in the state. The widely accepted yet vague view, held by men and seldom openly disputed by women, that the female is inferior to the male has persisted in most societies to the present day and in the Western world has been seriously challenged only in the twentieth century. It makes necessary a constituent of the definition of slavery used by the Anti-Slavery Society: until recently narrowly expressed as a summary of the appropriate section of the United Nations Convention, 'servile forms of marriage', it has been expanded to a deliberately vague reference to 'certain types of abuse and exploitation of women', a wording which can be made to fit whatever iniquity of slave practice is being combated at any particular time. Certainly the United Nations article as it stands is inadequate, for it is often within other male-female bonds than marriage that basic human rights are ignored. Three main areas of exploitation are considered here; all have marital connections, but their ramifications and implications go far beyond the institution of marriage: forced prostitution, female genital mutilation, and enslavement in the name of religion.

Article 1(c) is the part of the Supplementary Convention on the Abolition of Slavery cited at the head of this chapter, but (b), relating to serfdom, has a special relevance for women in so far as it encompasses and helps to define one of the main ways in which women are enslaved today: forced prostitution. Just as in the last chapter a distinction had to be made between child labour *per se* and its exploitation, so here it is necessary to distinguish between two types of prostitution. Article (b) of the Convention addresses itself to the problem of the condition of a person who renders 'some determinate service to such other person, whether for reward or not, and is not free to change his status'; forcing the prostitute to adhere to the trade is what makes it slavery. The distinction between the free and the forced prostitute is a blurred one, however, and is dismissed by the Special Rapporteur appointed by the United Nations to make 'a synthesis of the surveys and studies on the traffic in persons and the exploitation of the prostitution of others'[1] and submit recommendations. Jean Fernand-Laurent states that 'even when prostitution seems to have been chosen freely, it is actually the result of coercion',[2] and he supports his opinion with the views of the prostitutes themselves given to the Congress of Nice in 1981. The reason for taking a narrower definition here is not to take issue with the Special Rapporteur about the social problems which lead women to become prostitutes, but to avoid watering down the concept of slavery. Uncoerced prostitutes, common or rare, are not slaves.

The convention specific to prostitution appeared in 1949 and states have been slow to ratify it. Some states will ratify almost anything and ignore the obligations; and yet, by the time Jean Fernand-Laurent's report was published only fifty-three had done so, including a number quite notorious for blatant activity in this field. Why, as with the Minimum Age Convention (no. 138), are many governments so cautious? In some cases one can see the present futility of such a meaningless gesture. Thailand, for example, can be commended for its lack of hypocrisy; although a shift of investment from urban to rural development could close the economic gap between peasant and brothel keeper upon which the tourist industry depends for the internal migration which sustains its exciting image, the country is moving too rapidly and profitably for government or people to contemplate a quick policy reversal. Greed is unashamedly placed before compassion. Other motives influence wealthy advanced nations like West Germany. The West German underworld has discernible links with Thailand and many Thai girls have been brought to Europe by German pimps. That there is a flourishing market for these immigrants is partly because of the Federal Republic's belief in the legalized brothel. It is argued, by police chiefs among others, that, apart from the obvious benefits of keeping prostitution off the streets and making sure that there are regular medical inspections, the prostitute herself is protected from the man who translates the whole activity into slavery: the procurer.

Article 1 of the 1949 Convention obliges the ratifying nations to punish anyone who, in order 'to gratify the passions of another: (1) Procures, entices or leads away, for purposes of prostitution, another person, even with the consent of that person; (2) Exploits the prostitution of another person, even with the consent of that person.' Although the consent phrase points an accusing finger at several governments, it is article 2, which makes all forms of brothel illegal, that has been the greater obstacle to general acceptance of the Convention. Police chiefs are not the only ones who believe, or pretend to believe, that the brothel which does not need to disguise itself as a massage parlour has somehow been freed from the national or international criminal element traditionally parasitic upon women's sexual earnings. One is apparently supposed to agree that the major investment in Eros centres and the like is simply fulfilling natural laws of demand and supply. Such affected naivety overlooks the harsh facts of recruitment.

According to a West German Ambassador to Thailand,[3] many Germans have gone to Bangkok ostensibly as tourists and have married Thai women in order to introduce them to the trade in Germany. Seen as a one-to-one venture, this seems to be a tortuous way of doing things until one looks closer at the economics of such a marriage. Once on his home ground, the pimp is in a position to drop most pretences and, by a mixture of mock affection and brutality, should be able to appropriate most of his wife's earnings. Nevertheless, looked at from the procurer's standpoint, phoney but efficiently organized marriage bureaux can transform a merely profitable business into a major concern always free from the effects of world recessions. And there are easier ways of luring the gullible than marrying them. Advertising for hostesses and dancers is a well known but still effective method of acquiring inexperienced girls in search of excitement and money;

it works in England, as well as Thailand, and euphemisms for prostitute are multiplying. Among its recent records Interpol has cases of English girls under the heading 'Disguised traffic in persons'; they had answered advertisements for barmaids, receptionists and croupiers in West Germany, Italy, Nigeria and Lebanon.[4]

To those who approach the concept of prostitution simply from a moral or religious point of view, it can be difficult to accept the idea that there are different degrees of evil within or around the profession. Subjective moral condemnation might be justified if casual self-indulgence were ever the sole or prime cause, but researchers who monitor this sphere of human rights agree that overt or subtle pressures are usually found and, once the unsophisticated girl has been removed from her country of origin, they are magnified until she is exposed to cruelties of an altogether different category. Traffic in women is to forced prostitution what the old slave trade was to traditional slavery; in each historical context the uprooting of the victim from the native culture can break the remaining lifelines that could still lead to physical redemption. During the last three years, this has been demonstrated – in one sense inadvertently – by the contrasting emphases of independent research in Thailand and West Germany. One investigation[5] was part of an ILO World Employment Programme project which sought to clarify the role of rural women in the Third World and, appropriately, was financed by West Germany. The other research,[6] published by the Human Rights Group, was primarily concerned with what happens to female citizens of Thailand and many other countries when they enter the European flesh market.

In the ILO enquiry fifty Bangkok masseuses were interviewed in their massage parlours and five northern villages, whence most of them came, were visited. Unlike Banerjee's Anti-Slavery Society investigation, research into child prostitution was not part of the brief; most of the girls in the brothels were over 18 years of age and of the entire sample only three were virgins when they arrived. It was hoped to discover why the girls left their villages, what their experiences were in the massage parlours and how their families reacted to their careers. Predictably nearly all the girls left poor families in search of wealth and glamour. Two-thirds had been married before they took up their new employment and all but six of these had been divorced. Looking at their case histories degrees of coercion can be discerned among the varying shades of grey. Although most of the girls are victims of a tradition which grew out of the poverty in the north-east, some have acquired sufficient wealth and independence to escape the trade. They are not slaves; some actually set themselves up in other occupations. But there is another end to this scale. Distinctions should be made between those who are forced, those who could escape, and those who exist somewhere between the extremes.

In Thailand, although prostitution is technically illegal, there is not the deep-rooted antipathy to the trade that exists elsewhere, and this, though the report does not bring out the point, has to some extent frustrated the activities of traditional procurers within Thai society; in effect these are superfluous to a large section of the trade. Often girls are happy to go to Bangkok simply because they observe the wealth of masseuses who can afford to take early retirement. Sometimes encouraged by parents with no illusions about their daughters' activities, they go to raise the standard of living of the entire family; earnings are such that only a few years' work is necessary to make a dramatic transformation, not only in lifestyle, but in acquisition of real estate; a state of affairs which can only occur while the pimp's influence is diverted into other channels. Families living at or below subsistence level have only to send a daughter or two to the capital for a few years and all financial troubles will cease. Girls barely of marriageable age have become breadwinners and the mainstay of a significant part of Thailand's rural fabric.

That is the accepted, though not altogether acceptable, side of the picture. But one does not have to look very close to see evidence of the coercive pressures to which Jean Fernand-Laurent alluded. Study of individual case histories and analysis of medical statistics can modify the impression greatly. False names are, of course, used in the report, which gives detailed accounts of several girls, whose working lives are seen in the contexts of workplace, family and the wider social and economic environment. Sometimes parents fulfil the role of the pimp, pushed by poverty and not always freed from feelings of guilt by the permissive tradition. But the pimp is not missing from the scene. The small-time pimp, in his guise as employment agent, devotes some of his attention to bonded girls and to satisfying the appetities of the paedophile. More ambitious procurers think in terms of exports to Europe or the Middle East.

The least coerced end of the scale was exemplified by Taew, who may be regarded as typical of the majority. She grew up in a small hut with holes in the roof, while her aunt and elder sisters were helping to satisfy the sexual and domestic needs of United States soldiers at a nearby base. During this period poor rice yields had hardly mattered. Earnings paid for a new house and then another, sold for cash. After the departure of the Americans, however, the family circumstances changed; and when the elder sisters, after a period as barmaids and part-time prostitutes, got married and left, a point of crisis was reached. At the age of 18, Taew was persuaded by her parents to go to Bangkok; they were, in a sense, fulfilling the function of the pimp, but they seem to have deceived themselves about the true nature of their daughter's inevitable destination if she were to be a genuine breadwinner. Despite her background, she avoided the massage parlours at first by labouring on a construction site; but the tedious outdoor work soon induced her to go into poorly paid domestic service and thence to a restaurant where, as a waitress, she was supposed to persuade customers to drink more. She left when she heard that her employer derived most of his income from the export of prostitutes. At that point, while still a virgin, she started at a massage parlour and after a period of caution was persuaded to sell her virginity. Although she only retained a quarter of her fee, by this one act she earned five times her monthly earnings as a domestic servant. She sent the entire sum to her parents who used it to provide the household with drinking water by means of their own well.

The worst cases researched invariably involved the agents. There was 16-year-old Lek who went to Bangkok to work off the sum an agent had lent her parents; she had been formally bonded in accordance with the terms of a promissory note. A physically unattractive girl, she had to work in what was described as 'fifth-grade massage parlour which is actually a whore-house'[7] and about half the thirty other girls there were also bonded. The debt was 1,500 baht[8] (three-quarters of the sum Taew received for the sale of her virginity) and the speed at which it was actually or theoretically paid off depended partly on the number of clients, partly on her rating as one of the uglier bonded girls. On a visit to her parents' house in the north it was discovered that Lek's father had visited the agent and mortgaged her a second time in order to meet additional financial needs.

The more ambitious procurer, as has been mentioned, looks to the international trade. His victims can be purveyed in Hong Kong, which has a flourishing internal market of its own with specialities, particularly in the under-aged sector; or there are equivalent opportunities in other Far Eastern cities. Alternatively he may look to North Africa, the Middle East and the Gulf States. For a high and reliable income, however, he will find it difficult to improve on West Germany. Shares in love-centres there, openly advertised, are said to have a 22.3 per cent yield.[9] The prostitute who receives her clients within the walls of some luxurious establishments may appear to be a volunteer. But foreign girls are commonly relieved of their passports by pimps who instal them and intimidation prevents disclosures about the proportion of earnings earmarked for purchase of protection. And the effectiveness of intimidation is the most frightening aspect of the whole way of life; it becomes the more effective once the girl has borne a child, which is then used as a pawn by the pimp. Time and again psychological domination by the pimp is a feature of court cases;[10] girls and young women will refuse to testify against men who have raped and enslaved them and even subjected them to the cruder forms of physical torture. Particularly when initiation of a young prostitute involved a false declaration of love by a procurer, his victim may go to desperate lengths rather than admit to herself that her affection for her Svengali is in no way reciprocated.

Considering that West Germany hides behind a mask of progressive permissiveness, for which the only excuse is ignorance, the available figures for procurers' offences are remarkably high. A nine-and-a-half-month check on West Berlin[11] showed that 229 procurement crimes were reported. The total for West Germany[12] as a whole for 1980 was 4,158. With so many prostitutes co-operating masochistically with the authors of their destruction, it is difficult to imagine the enormity of the true statistical position throughout the Federal Republic.

As an altogether bogus glamour has developed around the myth of 'the oldest profession', one of the first steps urged towards freeing this type of slave is educational. Presentation in schools and on television and the wireless of the full medical facts should, even without stressing other horrific aspects, deter the party to the crime whose guilt is second only to that of the procurer: the customer. He has long deluded himself that the woman he rents is free to change her occupation. Curbing his self-indulgence may be the only benefit that the venereal diseases and possibly the AIDS virus bring to civilization; so far his ignorance has prevented a falling-off in the demand which creates the procurer's motivation and only a very high-powered message will deter the heterosexual majority. Supplementing an attempt to influence the minds of the clients should be concerted efforts to resolve contradictory attitudes of governments to the 1949

Convention for the Suppression of the Traffic in Persons and of the Exploitation of the Prostitution of Others. The big profits of this particular criminal activity are in the international sphere and only consistent action will defeat the rings of procurers, just as only international co-operation will make Interpol's task feasible.

Seen within the narrower terms of the Thai-German axis, the solutions seem clearer, which is not to say that they will be given a chance. Thailand is not entirely the poor Third World country that she pretends to be; an equitable distribution of wealth, channelling resources to the north and north-east, would stem the tide of migrant girl breadwinners on whom so much of the economy is allowed to depend. Then again, careful licensing and inspection of employment agencies should weed out unscrupulous elements. Censorship in almost any form is always to be feared, but there seems to be a case for police monitoring (or monitoring by a press council) of the sort of advertisement which is meant to lure girls into dangerous activities. German police appear to cultivate self-deception; Thai police are sometimes barefacedly corrupt.

For half a century the Anti-Slavery Society had been inclined to speak of its efforts with regard to female genital mutilation, popularly known as 'female circumcision' (a euphemism for various forms of mutilation), as having had no impact whatsoever. That was how it appeared, and it was not far from the truth; after many disappointments it was decided that African women alone must be seen to wage this war; Europeans could advise and help but must not be seen to participate. Long before the wind of change blew with any strength throughout the colonies, it was thought proper that tribal ritual practices which stopped short of cannibalism or wife burning should as far as possible be left alone, and colonial administrators, who on rare occasions responded to missionaries' appeals to intervene, were faced with serious trouble. The advent of the rapid process of imperial withdrawal tended to reinforce the belief that ethnic integrity was sacrosanct: 'they' or 'we' have always done these things – why should they not continue now that the territory is independent? It was, and still is, argued that humanitarians seeking to prevent parents from amputating or diminishing their daughters' sexual organs are tampering with sacred and eternal freedoms. Freedom to violate has taken over from freedom from violation, and in many rural areas the spontaneous equivalent of the Women's Liberation Movement has supported a woman's right to be maimed in this irreversible way, even though the operation is usually carried out before she herself has reached the minimum age of consent.[13] Suggestions about the daughter having any rights in the matter are brushed aside. She is too young to know what is good for her, and if the operation is delayed until she can appreciate its benefits her physical suffering will be worse.

The operation, sometimes performed with an unsterilized razor blade or penknife, is said by several authorities in this field[14] to take three main forms, and the number of women in Africa today who have experienced one or other of them is probably between 30 and 74 million. The lucky ones will have lost only the prepuce or foreskin of the clitoris; they have been circumcised in much the same way as men may be, except that with men the operation is sometimes necessary. Not so lucky are those who have experienced more extensive excision; they may have lost the prepuce and some or all of the labia minora. Those women who have undergone infibulation as well have been crippled for life. Probably between the ages of 7 and 12, the stage favoured for all the forms of mutilation, they will have lost the entire clitoris, all the labia minora, and a proportion of the labia majora. After amputation of these parts the two sides of the vulva will have been stitched together, or sealed in some other way, leaving a small orifice in order that urination, menstruation and some form of post-marital sexual intercourse can occur. In its most drastic form the operation can be compared with cutting the penis off a man.

Distortions of the male sexual motive are among the reasons for the development of this ritual perversion. Two sorts of male must have been involved when the tradition was developing: there are some who can take blind sexual pleasure although the physical passion is not reciprocated, and others who fear above all the loss of face, should it be thought that an uninfibulated wife might not have been a virgin on marriage. If the root of sexual enjoyment is removed, unfaithfulness is thought to be unlikely and the woman can still be used as a vessel. After centuries of conditioning within ancient male-dominated societies some wives have become so committed to their role that they are now among the most ardent advocates of their own mutilation. In the Sudan, for instance, many will insist that only because they have had the operation are they confident of being sexually attractive to their husbands. The truth is very different; when virile males want reciprocated physical love, they have to look elsewhere for it. Moreover, contrary to the folklore, there is no guarantee that the husband of a mutilated wife will not be cuckolded; nor can he be sure of his new bride's virginity. Possibility of proof has been irreversibly removed.

Attempts to justify genital mutilation in physical terms have long been backed up by other arguments. A powerful impediment to reform, for example, is the widespread belief that it is an Islamic requirement, although it is not recommended in the Koran. But by far the greatest obstacle to emancipation of females from this sort of oppression is misguided reaction against American- or Western-inspired interference. Admittedly much that is contaminating has come from modern civilization; articulate opponents of this particular area of reform, however, have placed themselves in the false position once occupied by white advocates of the old slavery. In 1980 Upper Volta's delegates to the world conference of the United Nations Decade for Women walked out rather than debate this issue; and other African delegates let it be known that other matters, like education and – with astonishing inconsistency – medicine, were more acceptable subjects for discussion.

Fortunately, even before Upper Volta inadvertently gave the anti-mutilation cause some useful publicity, an important initiative was already being taken by some African women. They approached several organizations, including the Anti-Slavery Society, for help and, as a result of their efforts and the support which they received, in 1977 the Sub-Committee on the Status of Women of the non-governmental organization Special Committee on Human Rights in Geneva established what was unfortunately but unavoidably called the Working Group on Female Circumcision. The Anti-Slavery Society representative, Kati David, was first to have the chair and it was soon agreed that as far as possible reforms should be brought about by Africans. Two were already on the committee and a policy of discreet enquiry in Africa was soon under way. By 1979 Isabelle Tevoedjre of Upper Volta was in the chair and Margareta Linnander of Rädda Barnen (Swedish Save the Children) represented the Anti-Slavery Society. Together they visited Mali, Niger and Upper Volta in 1981, and the following year Margareta Linnander and an Ethiopian committee member, Birhane Ras Work, went to Guinea, the Ivory Coast, Liberia, Niger, Senegal and Sierra Leone. They found out about the incidence of female genital mutilation and, equally important, they made contact with organizations well placed to work locally for the eradication of the tradition.

The World Health Organization estimates that about 75 million women have undergone one of the three forms of the operation.[15] It is believed that outside Africa the Middle East[16] has the greatest concentration of women mutilated in this way. Recently, however, the practice has been imported to Europe, where immigrant groups sometimes see it as part of a worthy heritage which must not be allowed to die. In France two incidents involving Malian families dramatically illustrate the need for local legislation to outlaw the operation in specific terms. When Batou Doucara was 3 months old her father removed her clitoris with a penknife; his amateur bungling meant that her life had to be saved by legitimate medical treatment. The professional *exciseuse* responsible for the other clitoridectomy killed Bobo Traoure by her ineptitude and fled the country, leaving the parents to face the consequences.

To many the most disconcerting aspect of these operations was that if they had been successful, judged by the values of the imported culture, nothing would have been heard of them. Even as it was, grounds for prosecution were ill-defined. The Traoure parents were charged with criminal negligence; Doucara was prosecuted for criminal assault, and his arrest prompted demands from a Malian workers' group that the French government should guarantee the right to live according to traditional customs. Had Doucara possessed a medical qualification the case against him would have been still more confused; the primitive manner in which he mutilated his daughter did something to disarm those who have taken the line sometimes adopted by the abortionist lobby that to ban such practices is merely to hand another lucrative trade to the criminal community.

Sweden lost no time in banning the operation. The Swedish law prohibiting female excision has been in force since 1 July 1982 and has the great advantage over the efforts of some other legislators of not being hedged about with nullifying amendments. Under Article 1, 'Operations on the external female sexual organs, designed to mutilate or to cause irreversible change (excision), are prohibited, whether or not consent has been given.' Article 2 outlines the punishments for breaking the law and adds that if excision 'has endangered life, caused grievous bodily harm or serious illness, or has in any other way demonstrated that the offender's behaviour was particularly unscrupulous, the act shall be qualified as an aggravated offence' – for which the penalty is up to ten years' imprisonment. And there are other provisions to cover 'attempted excision'. In Great Britain, until a campaign was orchestrated by Lilian Passmore Sanderson, a member of the Anti-Slavery Society who, having been a headmistress in the Sudan, knew of the worst consequences of the tradition, it was believed by a sizeable proportion of parliamentarians, lawyers, surgeons and laymen that existing law was a sufficient preventive. This was, on the face of it, a perfectly reasonable view, especially as the British Medical Association had brought an action against a qualified surgeon for performing clitoridectomies in London over a century earlier. But, as events were to show, legislation in force until 1985 was failing to deter surgeons from performing the operation for non-medical reasons in London and Cardiff.[17]

As so often happens, agitation for reform expressed in general principles gathered momentum slowly. The concern of public and government needs the added impetus derived from a particular event to concentrate influential minds on the issue. For the United Kingdom the excision which helped the campaign had occurred on 19 March 1981, two years before its disclosure to the general public. Because the surgeon responsible had consulting rooms in Harley Street, his removal of a 28-year-old Nigerian woman's clitoris and labia minora, although she had no medical problems, unsettled some of the more complacent believers in current legal provision. Some reputable lawyers had maintained, and continued to maintain, that the operation was forbidden by the 1861 Offences Against the Persons Act, but sympathy was growing for the idea that specific legislation would have to be passed. One sypathizer was Lord Kennet, who, during 1983 and 1984, navigated the Prohibition of Female Circumcision Bill through the House of Lords. It was a private member's Bill, but if it were ever to get through the House of Commons it had to have government support.

Two Bills have failed: one because a general election intervened, another because the government feared that its wording might prevent surgeons from undertaking necessary operations on the genitalia. At one time in the Lords it looked very much as though the third Bill would go through so amended that it would be wholly ineffective. Arguments about the broader implications of cosmetic surgery brought amendments to allow the operation when it might alleviate 'social and mental distress', a wording which could be used to justify almost any ethnic surgical perversion. By 8 February 1985, when this Bill survived its Second Reading in the Commons, the loophole had been closed to the satisfaction of Lord Kennet and other supporters. Grounds of physical or mental health could still be used to justify excision, but in making this judgment about a patient 'no account shall be taken of the effect on that person of any belief on the part of that or any other person that the operation is required as a matter of custom or ritual'.[18]

Seen in a worldwide context the United Kingdom's introduction of legislation into this field may seem to be insignificant. Its true importance comes not only from seriously attempting to stop the mutilation of women and girls, mainly in immigrant communities, though that would be ample justification, but that African reformers are looking to Great Britain for support in what is to them a problem of frightening proportions, and it is not really convincing to campaign internationally until one has put one's own house in order. Africans have already succeeded in changing the laws of some of their own countries: clitoridectomy is now illegal in Kenya for example; the present need is to win over the minds of the people. The idea of wealthy Africans frustrating their own laws by sending their female dependants to London to be mutilated or of members of the immigrant community having the impression that such actions are not forbidden here has at last been found to be intolerable. It is inconceivable that Commonwealth citizens or any other ethnic minorities resident in Great Britain should be encouraged by ignorance to perpetuate one of the nastiest features of female enslavement.

Women are persecuted for or by their religion. In the Soviet Union it can still be a crime to practise one's religion outside the narrow parameters uneasily agreed by church leaders, a state of affairs which can be a peculiar disability for wives. Constitutionally guaranteed freedom of religion was a reluctantly granted compromise with the will of the people and therefore methods of restriction or intimidation are often justified by oblique irrelevant charges; though Article 142 of the Criminal Code indicates the punishments for 'violation of the laws on the separation of church and state and of school and church' and Article 227 deals with 'Infringement of the person and rights of citizens under the guise of performing religious rituals'. The law is of course equally applicable to men and women, but the circumstances whereby most internees are male led to the formation of an unusual group of women with common awareness both of the true reasons for their husbands' imprisonment and the conditions which had to be endured. Prisoners' wives sometimes unite in democratic societies in order to alleviate the problems of confinement which their husbands suffer; in Russia some wives have two other bonds, the joint effect of which has emboldened them to withstand the tyranny of a powerful state apparatus: not only are their husbands all of one religious persuasion, but they are, by international standards, guilty of no crime.

The Council of Baptist Prisoners' Relatives is a women's organization of particular interest to the Soviet security forces. According to Keston College, the United Kingdom-based centre which monitors the relationship between church and state in Communist countries, the Council is the oldest human rights movement in any Communist country; it is also the source of much of the information received by the West about conditions of imprisonment under Communism for men and women. As much of its energy has been devoted to documenting prison conditions, defending fellow Baptists and printing and circulating a bulletin, all of its leaders have now had first-hand experience of the legal and prison systems which they continually denounce. The regimes to which they are sentenced vary from 'ordinary' to 'strict' and may be imposed within labour camp, prison or psychiatric hospital; concessions to the weaker sex are seldom observed, even when it comes to penal slave labour.

Baptists are the most numerous of the identified Christian prisoners and, apart from their own sufferings, their spouses experience persecution of which the West is continually informed. As well as the Baptists, a wide range of Evangelical Christians have attracted the displeasure of the state; some of them have been observed by sympathizers within their place of restriction. Anna Chertkova was arrested in 1973 for openly practising her religion and disseminating religious literature:[19]

> She is in a prison hospital for the mentally ill. . . . The bulk of the patients are murderers. Anna is among such people. She is held behind seven layers of security. . . . The space between the concrete wall and the barbed wire is patrolled by a soldier with an automatic weapon. . . . All this is administered by the Ministry of Internal Affairs. For exercise there is a concrete pen, which the doctors call the exercise yard. The walls are 5 metres high and it is 11 metres wide by 17 metres long. The floor is cement, with not a blade of grass or a bush, although in the grounds of the hospital there are lawns and fruit trees. But in the pen there is nothing. The women's department, together with this pen, is enclosed by a 2 metre high brick wall. . . . The entrance doors

> to the block housing the women's department are steel. . . . If you talk too much you get an injection of sulphazin, which sends your temperature up to 40 C and you are immobilised. Anna got sulphazin. . . .

It may be said that men and women are equally persecuted for their religion in Russia. That it is not, however, an even-handed arrangement stems from deep-rooted national attitudes to women, reflected in this context in the lack of provision of welfare for dependants of political prisoners, many of whom have been imprisoned solely because they have openly practised their religion. The official stance is also attributable, at least in part, to instinctive and habitual responses to the role of women in general, despite the proud boast of Article 122 of the Soviet Constitution: 'Women in the USSR are accorded all rights on an equal footing with men in all spheres of economic, government, cultural, political, and other social activity'. The same article goes on to speak of 'State aid to mothers of large families and to unmarried mothers', a clause which can, where it suits, be conveniently overlooked. One student of Soviet affairs, looking at the society as a whole, has commented that 'for all intents and purposes, the women are the "workhorses" of the Soviety economy',[20] which, paradoxically, is one reason why the Western world has built up the illusion that sexual equality in the workplace was the one area in which Communism had lived up to its ideals. A closer look at the division of labour gives a different picture. Emancipation is only beginning.

Wives of dissidents are known to live a precarious existence; world opinion is less aware that a believer in any religious faith may be treated in the Soviet Union as a type of criminal every bit as dangerous as one who sympathizes with alien policies. The believer and his family are the cancer within. Prisoners' wives, the virus at large, suffer a kind of apartheid which, though it is not comparable in suffering to the experiences of the prisoner, is discriminatory and in some cases an appendage of slavery (see chapter 10).

Islam is one of the faiths which periodically fall foul of the Russian authorities. While, however, supporters elsewhere of women's rights properly condemn Communist malpractices when these become evident, it is frequently clear that what offends them is a practice contrary to an enlightened interpretation of Communist dogma. The same cannot be said for Islamic practices which, despite modifications made to the legal codes of many Arab countries, are always liable to be brought back to the Shari'a, the fundamental interpretation of the Koran. For about half a century it looked as though the same was true of Karl Marx, but Marxist doctrine has opportunism and expediency at its very core, alongside its archaic elements. The room to manoeuvre that reforms in Islam appeared to indicate has in many important respects proved to be illusory. Those reforms which are at present surviving the current revival of fundamentalist principles are largely superficial and fragile.

Despite its authoritarian character, Islam is to be contrasted with another authoritarian persuasion, Roman Catholicism. While the Pope, when pronouncing on matters of faith or morals and speaking *ex cathedra*, is a source of infallible doctrine, in Islam no such authority exists. One cannot get a ruling which is universally binding; and so one finds different degrees of fundamentalism in different countries within Islam, and different degrees of severity of punishment for the same offences, varying with the ruler, the 'alim' (the religious jurist) or the 'imam' (the guardian of the faithful). Unlike other faiths that are widely practised in the world today, Islam does not contemplate any distinction between secular and religious. Although devout Christians maintain that Christianity pervades all their behaviour, they are under the control of a self-imposed discipline which may or may not bring them into conflict with the laws of their society. Whereas in states whose culture is based on Christianity some actions permissible in civil law are offences in the eyes of the church, in Islamic states all actions are judged by a single code, the Shari'a. Some Arab countries have framed their laws so that at first sight they resemble those of a modern secular state. But in the written constitutions of, for example, Egypt, Iraq, Qatar and Yemen will be found the all-important clause which will effectively prevent departure from Moslem precepts: 'Islamic Shari'a is the source of all laws.' Only rarely, as with polygamy in the Ivory Coast, has the state forced its citizens to conform to a modern interpretation of the Koran.

Apologists for Islam claim that Moslems do not approve of discrimination against women because when the Koran says that 'Men should be favoured above women' the reason given is that men 'are responsible for them'.[21] The hair is split nicely on the implication that responsibility for a woman means that she is protected whether she likes it or not, because the word of Allah says so. Most Moslem women have accepted their lot without question. The few who have stepped out of line have run terrifying risks, especially those who are citizens of states which have no intention of adapting their laws to changing needs.

No effort was made to conceal the brutalities of the recent past in Yemen under the monarchy. In the 1950s the state insisted that a woman was her husband's property: as a punishment for the crime of running away, a court order could ensure that a ring be attached to her wrist. This was achieved not by attaching a shackle around the limb but by driving a bolt through it.[22] The offender was given an anaesthetic and the operation was carried out by a professional surgeon. The consequences of a more serious offence were seen when Shahila, a Sri Lankan-born Moslem who was working in Abu Dhabi, committed adultery.[23] When seven months pregnant during 1984 she was sentenced to be stoned to death two months after her baby was born. Italian women took up her cause and, because of, or despite, their agitation, the sentence was commuted to thirty-five lashes, one year's imprisonment and deportation. Her baby was taken from her at birth. Again, during the 1980s, in Pakistan, after Zarina Bibi was convicted for infanticide (admittedly a crime that none would condone), the court imposed a four-fold sentence – a fine, flogging, seven years' hard labour and death by hanging.[24] During 1984 the Pakistan embassy in London would not respond to enquiries about the result of her appeal.

Although Islam proclaimed its support for the anti-slavery cause at the sixth Moslem world conference in 1964, the continued acceptance of polygamy, consolidated by a host of rules governing the relationship between the husband and his wives and their daughters, means that the custom is perpetuated in many countries for half the faithful. The basis of the Moslem family structure, which can be regarded as the classic 'servile form of marriage', can have repressive elements which take it into the realms of simple ownership of persons. That is the way it has always been and, as only the most sophisticated Islamic rulers can conceive of anything like a reformation, that is the way many intend it to remain for eternity. The educated Moslem who settles for monogamy will joke with his Christian friends that in his wisdom the Prophet Mohammad said that a man might have four wives, provided that he love them equally – knowing full well that that was impossible.[25] And the Shari'a does lay down specific guidelines that, if the woman is astute, are daunting enough to make the thoughtful believer hesitate before embarking on a second marriage, let alone a third or a fourth. Moreover, in educated Moslem society, regardless of the country, married women make such decisions as concern the family and, provided that they observe the strict rules, are kept in subjection rather than in slavery. For the great mass of the rural poor, however, the traditional more oppressive relationship prevails.

Inequalities between the sexes begin with the choice of mate. In many Arab countries – though not Algeria, Iraq, Jordan, Syria or Tunisia – the daughter, whether or not she has come of age, must have the approval of her father or nearest male relative before she can marry. Should she have no male relatives power of decision does not revert to her, but to her female relatives; should she be without relatives altogether consent must be sought from a judge. She will be under pressure to marry a first cousin and, if a Bedouin, would risk death if she were to prefer another. Unlike a man, who may choose his spouse from among Jewish or Christian women, provided that she convert to Islam, the Moslem woman may only marry within the faith. Not Bedu alone, but the generality of Moslem women can be made to marry against their will, but increasingly the forced marriage can be challenged in the courts. However, if there were so much as a whisper of promiscuity on the woman's part, the ruling in, say, the Sudan, might well go against her.

The vulnerability of the Moslem wife is generally felt most keenly against the background of male rights of divorce. For centuries the irresponsible husband was hindered from marrying a new wife at will only by the costs of dowries, half of which were payable before marriage and half, by way of alimony, when the marriage ceased. Bearing in mind these constraints, under the traditional law the husband has only to pronounce the magic word 'bayeen' ('I divorce thee') three times and his obligations cease. The wife has no equivalent reciprocal divorce rights and, although this deficiency has been remedied by the legal reforms of many Islamic states, for which the way had been paved by Turkey under Kemal Atatürk, the new dispensation is held to run counter to accepted religious imperatives. While divorce on demand was, and often still is, the man's prerogative, in some North African countries the woman had old-established ways of gaining her freedom. If her husband was afflicted with impotence, leprosy, venereal disease or insanity, or if he deserted or failed to support her, she could petition for her freedom. These old rights were used as the basis for the legislative reforms of the twentieth century.

According to Islam, a mother's duty is to look after the physical well-being of the children, while all decisions about their future are left to their father. He assumes his authority in this respect when the sons are 7 and the daughters 9, and makes sure that the necessary arrangements are made for their education and religious upbringing. An Arab source[26] states that one of the devices adopted by a Moslem wife, to prevent her husband from marrying again, is to see that she gives birth to many children. By so doing she hopes that his affection for them and his involvement in their educational and religious needs will prevent him from looking elsewhere. Valid or not, the idea reflects the insecurity which undermines a marriage arrangement that has a long, if chequered, history. The more affluent and sophisticated the modern Moslem wife, with increasing access to Western films and television programmes, the less she is likely to be able to accept the fear of being relegated to a demeaning role.

The woman may have other fears. In a male-dominated theocracy it is only to be expected that personal and social assessments of a woman's place in the scheme of things are much the same. The Koran advises the husband that within the family he should chastise his disobedient wife; in the civil sphere it severely limits her rights of inheritance; at the ethical and criminal levels it stones her to death for breaking a law that, where polygamy is still permissible, is applicable only to her sex. Naturally different geographical locations bring different Islamic characteristics to the fore without affecting the basic tenets of the creed. In parts of the Middle East and South Asia, and especially in Bangladesh, *purdah*, which literally means 'the curtain', is still the order of the day for most women. Westerners, who tend to romanticize it in terms of the attractive mystery created by the veil, and echo Moslem praise of the quality of modesty that is preserved, are misled by the obvious external trappings of a form of female seclusion which can amount to imprisonment. A strict interpretation of *purdah* means that the woman must normally remain within her husband's house. In rural areas she is at best a second-class citizen, a fact of life symbolized at her birth; whereas her brothers were welcomed into the world by a call for prayer, she was greeted by silent disappointment.

In Bangladesh puberty brings to a daughter both stricter observance of *purdah* and an arranged marriage, for which the formality of her consent is needed. As one in need of the protection stressed in the Koran, she must disappear from public view, first into her father's house, then, as soon as possible, into her husband's, where, showing due deference to the incumbents, she should take her place in the separate quarters provided for women. If she needs to travel, either she should be veiled from head to foot, or she should be kept out of sight in some other way, according to the means of the family. Her daily duties, unless she is one of the privileged urban few, will be confined to domestic chores and child-bearing.

What has been said here of Islam is an over-simplified description of a past that would not go away and which, under some governments, is coming back with renewed savagery. While it can be observed that exploitation of children the world over occurs because secular laws are not enforced, under Islam exploitation of women is caused by enforcement of religious laws which have been repressively interpreted. Earlier in this century an enlightened process of reform was well under way, despite resistance by those convinced that changes are, by definition, heretical. The reforms were first halted, and then reversed, by vigorous reaction against secularism and decadent Western influences. Renewed commitment to the old ways coincided with, and indeed encouraged, the rapid withdrawal of the imperial powers which followed the Second World War. However, the understandable fears of strict religious conformists that reforms would lower standards and create a gulf, and thereby a conflict, between religious and civil laws could derive little justification from the amendments which were safely carried through before the war; the purpose of change was not to distort Islam. There is evidence that the Prophet would have approved of the modifications.

Polygamy remains a good example of an institution which, like chattel slavery, could be abolished on the basis of Mohammad's pronouncements. Where abolition has already occurred, though, the difficulty of adjusting the relationship between men and women poses a need for more legislation, particularly to curb chastisement carried out in the name of Islam on the pretext that a man's honour has been impugned. It may not be too much to hope that a special world conference, a Moslem equivalent of the Second Vatican Council, will eventually be convened to bring humanitarian benefits that would have repercussions beyond the present boundaries of Islam. Current initiatives for reform are coming from below. It would be far better if organizations such as the newly founded International Working Group on Women and the Family – with autonomous units in a number of countries including Iran, Morocco and Pakistan – could be confident of working within and with the law to change cultural attitudes. At present, under the more violent regimes, simply being a member of an organization which is urging the emancipation of women places one at risk. Moreover there is no forum for dialogue between those who seek change in the name of natural justice and hardliners who believe that the first interpretation of the Koran is the only acceptable one.

It was sufficient for the Communist-supported ruler (since deposed) of the Sudan to proclaim himself an imam for his brand of the Shari'a to come into effect with much jubilation. In 1984, during five months, some forty-two hands were severed for theft, flogging was introduced for many offences including 'suspected intended adultery', and writing pamphlets of protest earned a public execution. So great is the authority of the imams, even those with such doubtful credentials as former President Numeiry, that one looks first to them rather than the ulama, the scholars, for any change that might endure; which is illogical in so far as change will need scholarship if it is to endure. In Islam reform should come from above, and Islamic scholars have no need for casuistry to enable them to achieve this end. They have the power, if they wish to exercise it, to reconcile humane civil law to the Koran and then proclaim its validity. Christianity had to go through a transformation similar to that needed by Islam now. It still gets embroiled in unholy wars, and the reformation is far from complete, but its leaders and theologians have made a conscious effort to shed the habits of the Inquisition and reconcile the contradictions of the scriptures. Christianity no longer deliberately condones slavery.

The spread of female emancipation conditional upon the development of a more merciful Islam would extend reform from the auctioning of wives in West Africa, through the 'honour' killings of Iran to the corrupt uses of bride-price and dowry in Asia and the Pacific. Change throughout so large a part of humanity would help to counter the effects of greed and power lust where poverty is endemic, and could not but influence the standards of other religions which share the same regions. Its contagious effect might not bring an immediate reduction in the wife-burning habits of some Hindu; it would, however alter the global concept of the status of women. The ulama and the imams have only to heed Mohammad's warning: 'If I prescribe something according to my own personal opinions, consider that I am a human being.'[27] It should not be beyond the wit of man to devise a code that is true to the Koran, is true to natural justice, and emancipates without abandoning treasured values. Female modesty or a wife's acceptance of the traditional roles of mother and helpmeet need not be abandoned with the shackle and the lash.

The Roman church still has not repudiated the pronouncements of its scholars in the late 19th century against freedom of conscience, separation of church and state, and persecution of "heretics."

CHAPTER 7

DEBT BONDAGE AND SERFDOM

Debt bondage, that is to say, the status or condition arising from a pledge by a debtor of his personal services or those of a person under his control as security for a debt, if the value of those services as reasonably assessed is not applied towards the liquidation of the debt or the length and nature of those services are not respectively limited and defined;

Serfdom, that is to say, the condition or status of a tenant who is by law, custom or agreement bound to live and labour on land belonging to another person and to render some determinate service to such other person, whether for reward or not, and is not free to change his status.

UNITED NATIONS SUPPLEMENTARY CONVENTION ON THE ABOLITION OF SLAVERY, THE SLAVE TRADE, AND INSTITUTIONS AND PRACTICES SIMILAR TO SLAVERY

Debt bondage and serfdom are sometimes regarded as twin strains of the same malaise and the distinction between them is often blurred because the 'personal services' pledged by the debtor usually oblige him 'to live and labour on land belonging to another person'. Indeed similarities can be so great that one may ask whether there is any point in anyone other than a historian continuing to differentiate between these two forms of slavery. What purpose does the distinction serve, other than to provide academics with endless scope for modifying definitions as they shift their attention from one culture to another? The answer from a practical standpoint is that the separate traditions, although they have overlapped, came into existence for different reasons and against different backgrounds. By analysing what creates and sustains them the way can be paved towards devising effective cures.

Serfdom is notionally the lesser of the two evils, in so far as, technically at least, the serf is less directly the property of his master;

The serf is real estate; the slave is personal property.

custom or agreement compels him to cultivate land for a particular landowner, whom he may or may not know. Any abstract advantages over the debt bondsman, however, are seldom borne out by actual circumstances. He may be tied to the land in perpetuity. He must cultivate it on behalf of his master for a given proportion of the week and may receive no pay. For what remains of the week the land must yield what is necessary to enable him and his family to subsist. He is a disadvantaged share-cropper with no conceivable means of escape; moreover, his share is seldom comparable to that which is normally associated with labourers of this sort, who might from time to time make a profit. Apart from hereditary domestic serfdom, still found in India, serfdom is territorial bondage. The man goes with the land, either because that is the system, or because economic forces prevent his escape. In parts of South America so much are serfs tied to the land that the value of an estate has traditionally been assessed by taking into account the number of serfs on it. The serf's other disadvantages are suggested by the necessarily mysterious phrase in the United Nations definition: 'to render some determinate service to such other person'.

Debt bondage arises from a pledge, usually made under economic duress, of a man's services, or the services of his dependants. He must work until the interest on the debt, and the capital sum, are repaid. Likelihood of rapid repayment is remote, partly because of exorbitant interest rates but also because, the debtor having mortgaged himself completely, on a twenty-four-hours-a-day basis, he will incur further debts for food and, perhaps, for clothing and shelter. He is entirely at the mercy of his master, the moneylender, who by adjusting interest rates, making additional advances, or levying high charges for food, can ensure that the capital sum remains intact. Among the reasons for his enslavement are his illiteracy and his innumeracy. In India, unless he is one of the 18 per cent[1] whose fathers accepted the loan, he will have entered into the arrangement during a time of difficulty in order to obtain food and clothing for his family – over half India's present-day bonded labourers started on their indebtedness in this way, as opposed to a third who sold themselves to pay for a festive occasion which custom obliged them to host. He may be one of the many who will pay interest at a rate of 400 per cent.[2] Not surprisingly, outside intervention is the debt bondsman's best hope of release.

Setting aside the economic pressures which are common to both systems, their origins are historically distinct. It is alleged[3] that debt bondage arises when chattel slaves are set free: on emancipation day the former slave-owner desperately needs a means of maintaining an obedient labour supply, the free worker equally desperately needs to acquire fresh means of survival; therefore both turn to each other and the bond is forged anew. (Straightforward employment is presumably unthinkable.) It is a tidy theory and doubtless there is some truth in it. However, it ignores the fact that chattel slavery and debt bondage existed concurrently in ancient Greece and that Jewish law had to take both institutions into account.[4] More importantly it ignores the power of debt bondage to regenerate itself. Debts are an eternal feature of human existence and there will always be Shylocks of all races to feed on them. Serfdom, too, has shared many centuries with the other systems. Initially the serf was invariably captured in war, along with the land which he tilled; though later in Central and South America the two were often commandeered separately and then united artificially. Unlike the bonded labourer, who saw what was coming and was cornered by economic factors, sometimes partly of his own making, the serf was part of a subjugated race; and when the conquest proved permanent, he became part of a class which deferred to the feudal overlords and their representatives.

The origins of serfdom and debt bondage are still evident in the systems as they can be observed today, and the threads which distinguish them can be discerned even where they overlap in parts of India. There the pattern varies from state to state and is not always simply a matter of exploitation of scheduled castes and tribes by higher-caste Hindu, though that is, admittedly, the general rule. With South American serfdom and debt bondage, more obvious racial differences take precedence over religion as the major difference between master and slave. Both regions have been the subjects of much research, but most recent information on debt bondage has been gleaned in India and that will therefore provide the examples necessary to give an impression of the nature and extent of the problem. The peculiarly Latin American form of the institution, 'peonage', will then be defined and described and some mention made of the parts of the world where similar systems have developed.

A comprehensive survey of the incidence of debt bondage in India took place in 1978, under the aegis of the Gandhi Peace Foundation, two years after the passing of the Bonded Labour System (Abolition) Act.[5] In legal terms the problem had already ceased. The Act lists twenty-nine local versions of forced labour which it identifies as coming within the meaning of the term 'bonded' and declares that, as from 25 October 1975, every bonded labourer stands 'freed and discharged from any obligation to render any bonded labour'.[6] All existing debts were cancelled and all masters were forbidden to 'make any advance under, or in pursuance of, the bonded labour system'.[7] It was a drastic piece of legislation which not only rendered all bonded agreements null and void, but provided for the restoration to the labourers of any property taken from them for repayment of debt. One imaginative clause[8] even went so far as to reverse the advantage and allow the debtor to charge interest on property which the master was slow to return. To prevent a vast increase in homelessness, the title to accommodation which the debtor had occupied in order to fulfil his former obligations to his master passed to the occupant.[9]

Less satisfactory, judged by their consequences, are the chapters of the Act which indicate the measures to be taken to 'try to promote the welfare of the freed bonded labourer . . . so that he may not have any occasion or reason to contract any further bonded debt'.[10] District Magistrates are directed to create Vigilance Committees[11] which shall meet under their chairmanship and take the decisions necessary to ensure that the aims of the Act are achieved. Most members of these committees are nominated by their District Magistrate and are representatives of the scheduled castes and scheduled tribes, social workers and credit institutions. The others, nominated by the state governments, represent rural development agencies. Committee responsibilities are to monitor emancipation in the district, 'to provide for the economic and social rehabilitation of the free bonded labourers',[12] to see that legitimate bodies allow credit in place of that no longer available from the master, and to make sure that masters do not succeed in extracting from former creditors the sums already advanced to them or their families. All of this sounds commendable, but it has proved inadequate for dealing with problems of such magnitude.

Punishment for recruiting bonded labour[13] is up to three years' imprisonment and a fine of up to 2,000 rupees. For failing to return property to debtors, a master can be imprisoned for up to one year; and accessories are held to be equally responsible, and punishable, for any infringement of the Act. These measures seem adequate, but they are ineffective for at least three reasons. By August 1984, although masters had been brought before the courts, they had been fined but not imprisoned; for motives which have rightly led to some suspicion, those presiding over trials decided to disobey the law themselves by not imposing custodial sentences.[14] According to Western logic, unjust acquittals would have been less absurd. Secondly, the Indian government, which has been touchy about the whole issue of bonded labour, has been slow to concede publicly that the problem is widespread. And thirdly, the most serious part of the matter, identification of bonded labourers is a very difficult task. In a poverty-stricken environment a slave need not look any different from a free man. Moreover, since his options are negligible, he often enters into an increased degree of collusion with his master, lest freedom bring starvation. Cancellation of a debt, however large, is not an attractive prospect unless alternative opportunities of survival are guaranteed.

Inevitably, for the Gandhi Peace Foundation's survey the first task was to identify the bonded labourers. Information from the Indian Ministry of Labour and the Report of the Commissioner for Scheduled Castes and Scheduled Tribes for 1975–6 and 1976–77[15] suggested that ten states could be relied upon to produce sufficient data for the position of India as a whole to be assessed. Varying proportions of agricultural workers were believed to be bonded in Andhra Pradesh, Bihar, Gujarat, Karnataka, Madhya Pradesh, Maharashtra, Orissa, Rajasthan, Tamil Nadu and Uttar Pradesh. West Bengal was excluded from the survey on the grounds that it had different problems of serfdom and contract labour. Moreover, it was believed, probably wrongly, that there was no significant incidence of debt bondage in the Punjab and Haryana, because the local people used imported migrant labour instead. Similar convictions about freedom from the institution in the north-eastern states and Jammu and Kashmir led to agreement that the most accurate results would be achieved by concentrating on the ten selected states.

Although all the information gathered was sent to New Delhi for analysis, the administration of the survey was subdivided on a state basis, each state having a co-ordinator who was responsible for recruiting and training his field investigators. Ten to fifteen villages were allotted to each investigator, amounting to 1,000 villages over the survey as a whole. They were selected on a random basis (there being about four and a half million villages in the ten states, every 450th village was selected, starting the count at a different point in each state). Each field investigator had to interview a fifth of the bonded labourers in each of his villages and, having taken great pains that findings would be as statistically accurate as is feasible in so ambitious a study, the importance of care being taken to win the villagers' confidence was recognized. One way of thwarting motives to conceal, and preventing understandable suspicions from being aroused, was never to mention the local word for 'bondage'. The oblique approach meant that the investigator sought out the leading members of the *adivasi* (tribal) or *harijan* (untouchable) communities and asked about living conditions. Village custom would soon generate a group discussion and it would not be long before debt came to the fore. It was then up to the investigator to keep the topic going until he had identified a number of promising subjects for individual interviews.

Next a standard questionnaire was used to gather in the required information. The major goal, identification, had already been achieved; now the co-operative subject began to provide a wealth of valuable detail that could be tapped from no other source. He was asked about his caste, the composition and educational status of his family, and whether any other family members were bonded. Another series of questions explored the terms of the debt, the arrangements for repayment and wages received. The field investigator, who had to complete one form for each labourer in the survey, then asked about the debtor's accommodation and possessions, and restraints on his freedom of movement. From this last topic questions moved naturally to the subject of the master – his occupation, his property and the number of bonded labourers under his control. The investigator's final task was to provide a profile of the village: for this information was sought about the general level of wages and land tenure. He was to find out the amount paid to men, women and children for day labour, the area of land allocated by the masters for subsistence farming by his debtors, and the area of land yielded, permanently or temporarily, by the bonded labourers to the masters.

After the village data had been co-ordinated at state and then all-India level, the findings were published and created a sensation throughout the country. Despite the fact that statistics normally take the life out of any study, it was the overall statistic, the number of bonded labourers located in the ten sample states two years after the passing of the Abolition Act, which shook public opinion. It made no less impact than the more easily sensationalized details of cruel treatment received by many individuals and groups. Partly because a distinction can be drawn, sometimes for useful reasons, between forced labourers and bonded labourers, Indian official figures for debt bondage have always been low. The Gandhi Foundation project discovered well over two and a half million, a figure which was greeted with apparent disbelief at government level. Nor did it help when it was realized that, projected beyond the ten states, and still excluding industry and domestic service, the number would probably double.

The survey cited many individual cases by way of illustration.[16] A 28-year-old man, member of a scheduled tribe, had pledged his services for twelve years when he had borrowed 600 rupees, eight years before the survey. While bonded, he survives and looks after his wife and four children on an allowance of fifteen kilograms of rice a month; and once a year he is given a loincloth and a blanket. He is landless, lives in a hut and has no idea who owns the land on which he works. He entered bondage because otherwise he could find no work. Other cases represent the various divisions and subdivisions within which extant examples of bondage fall. There are two main groupings: the sentimentalized traditional form where there may even be an affectionate relationship between master and debtor, and modern impersonal moneylending, where acquisition of a docile work-force is a far greater incentive to the master than simple usury. Within both these main categories are found inter-generational bondage, multiple (called 'multiplicative') bondage, 'share-cropping-cum-bondage' and widow bondage.

When a father is too old to work his son may have to replace him, an event which usually occurs when the child is aged about 10. Inter-generational bondage may be characterized by its open-ended nature. The example labourer has been bonded since he was 18 and his term of bondage is not fixed. He is paid 260 rupees a year for unlimited domestic and agricultural labour and has no idea why the loan was accepted in the first place. He is a *harijan*, while his master is a Moslem, a social and religious imbalance thought to encourage the survival of the institution. Debts leading to more debts when interest runs out of control may bring the enslavement of additional members of the same family until none is free, as in the survey's example of 'multiplicative' bondage. Here a married, illiterate scheduled caste man of 45 has been driven to mortgage his wife and a son and daughter-in-law, as well as himself. The debt arose because, only two years previously, he had borrowed 400 rupees at 40 per cent to pay for a wedding. Their Brahmin landlord has a dozen bonded labourers in all and has only to provide them with food. No date of emancipation has been fixed.

In share-cropping-cum-bondage, as its cumbersome name suggests, one finds an Indian species of serfdom. As long as the debt lasts the labourer is tied to a parcel of land and works on it, giving to the master about half his produce. Original title to the land may be hard to prove; it may have passed from the labourer to the master or from the master to the labourer. As things are now it hardly matters, unless the Abolition of Bonded Labour Act is rigidly enforced. In the example given some land formerly belonging to the labourer had been sold to a moneylender, the remainder had been mortgaged to the master, who is providing seeds, fertilizer and a tractor. Here there is a contract for payment, but astute masters can engineer arrangements to distance themselves from the work and simply accept 50 per cent of the yield. Finally, there is widow bondage, which often arises to enable the woman to pay for her husband's funeral. Normally she will not receive any sort of remuneration, but will be fed in exchange for her services until she dies. Two examples were given: in one the widow, aged 42, inherited her husband's debt which, at 100 per cent rate of interest, became so enlarged that her daughter had to be bonded as well. In the other a 50-year-old widow was found to be substituting for a dead son. This last example, which is also a confused inter-generational case, usefully demonstrates the complexity of debt bondage in India.

Some findings[17] of the survey were predictable; others were not. Nearly all the bondage agreements were made between wealthy, landowning, propertied Hindu masters and members of the scheduled castes and scheduled tribes; a quarter of those bonded were under 20 years of age, and many were small children. The discovery that nearly three-quarters had three children or less ran counter to the widely held opinion that large families cause the poverty on which moneylending feeds. The poor were getting poorer, so that almost a third of the bonded families had found it necessary to place two or more of their number in bondage. Just under a fifth had never taken a loan themselves; they had acquired their debt by accident of birth. Most masters keep three men in bondage and, although there were ample examples of exorbitant interest rates, the statistical evidence supported the view that the predominant motive for moneylending was the wish to exploit cheap or free labour, not to look upon cumulative repayments as the reward. Although the average period of bondage over India as a whole was shown to be only six years, in Bihar,

Maharashtra and Uttar Pradesh the average term served is over ten years, and it was found that nearly half of those in bondage in 1978 had recently mortgaged themselves for an unspecified period; this was a particularly depressing discovery, coming immediately in the wake of the Abolition Act. Not surprisingly it was found that payment of wages to bonded labourers fell short of the amount needed to repay the capital sum advanced. The investigators noted that in general peasant real estate has no value as security; the labourer has only his labour to pawn and as, when bonded, he is normally forbidden to move out of the village, he cannot try to sell his services elsewhere. He is denied the human right of freedom of movement. Finally, the survey detected that, in addition to debt, social custom and unemployment, there was a fourth factor involved in imposing bondage: the use of brute force.

It was no part of the field investigators' brief to make any distinction between debt bondage and serfdom; the ultimate purpose of the project was to point the way to the permanent emancipation of peasants from their masters. Nevertheless, much of the data was inevitably concerned with land tenure and showed that the physical conquests of ancient history, which ordained the relationship of the poor with land and landowners, have left discernible traces in modern India. Moreover, although more recent, largely economic, forms of conquest have confused the issue, the problem of serfdom is an important constituent of the wider problems relating to debt bondage in India. This is illustrated in Uttar Pradesh where, according to the report,[18] 'once in bondage a person can never succeed in freeing himself again': the average family had lost about four acres to the masters, while somewhere between a third and a half of the bonded labourers received land from their masters for share-cropping or subsistence.[19] Each kind of allocation has merits from the point of view of the master; a comparatively large allotment could yield good profits on a share-cropping basis, a small plot for subsistence can be a loan on which work in lieu of rent can be levied and, at the same time, appear to absolve the owner from the obligation to provide for the physical survival of his debtors.

The dominant tradition of debt bondage in India is superimposed upon a pattern of serfdom long suffered by the *adivasis*, the conquered tribal peoples of the subcontinent. The pattern varies in accordance with the differing histories of the states and, while the tradition retains ancient features, it has been expanded and adapted to meet local conditions and absorb many besides the *adivasis* who subsist at the base of the caste system. Small pockets of the land which had remained in peasant ownership have passed from the peasants to the masters, who then allot them to 'debt-serfs' in exchange for free or cheap labour: 'According to our estimate, half a million acres of land have been robbed away from the bonded labourers by the masters in the last few years due to bondage!'[20] For many Indian peasants the greater struggle has been to retain land, not to escape from being bound to it. An unequal tug-of-war leads to the peasant becoming a serf on what may once have been his own land. When analysing how the peasants had originally entered into their present predicament, other than by taking up a loan, the co-ordinators of the project found that 'bondage through land allotment' was one of the five routes (the others being inheritance, having been given away as a child, customary loyalty and widowhood).[21] A number of those allotted land 'end up as debt-slaves in the farmyard of the landlord to whom they have lost their land.'[22] In short, one is seeing in India today the survival and renewal of a process similar to the one which occurred more dramatically in South America after the Iberian conquest. Bloodshed is rarely evident, but the cruelties of the system are barely hidden behind the screen of pastoral peace.

By focusing appropriate attention on the element of serfdom in pastoral India today, the need for land reform as a means of emancipation becomes clearer. Furthermore, as Sarma Marla, Director of the Gandhi Foundation project, has commented, 'A large part of the rural population has been landless without means of subsistence for several generations now. This landless population is the most vulnerable to the recruitment machinery of bonded labour.'[23] Equitable distribution of land is an important and radical area of reform, and an issue which can be relied upon to stir up resistance among the masters. A completely different step towards freeing individuals on terms acceptable to all is sometimes mooted by Western observers. When Great Britain proposed to free the West Indian slaves, much turned on the difficult question of compensation. Would not some straightforward financial arrangement win the co-operation of the masters? At first sight there is an appealing simplicity about cheque book emancipation; closer inspection of implications and consequences shows that it is quite out of the question. As in the case of Mauritanian slavery, it would probably be possible to side-step the implications of Forced Labour Convention Number 29 (1930) by declaring a brief moratorium while claims were received; then, after a rigidly enforced deadline had been met, existing penalties could be reintroduced. Such a procedure, however, is wholly alien to Indian sensibility about justice; it smacks too much of compromise which is said to contribute to the partition of nations and is instinctively rejected. A policy of compensation also ignores the strength of tradition within Indian village communities; many are the bonded labourers who, like European serfs in feudal times, accept that they occupy a pre-ordained level in the scheme of things, and that they live in communities with a fossilized hierarchy. But the major practical obstacles are financial and administrative. Insufficient funds are forthcoming for rehabilitation of those who have been freed, without burdening the exchequer with well over a million claims, all dependent on the veracity of the claimant.

The Gandhi Foundation researchers strictly limited themselves to investigating agrarian matters, from which they excluded informal agricultural tenancies and the use of migrant labour in farming; but they could not help acquiring accidental information about increases in the use of bonded labour in other fields, and made specific reference[24] in this connection to brickmaking, construction work and quarrying. Much too little attention had been paid to bonded labourers in these non-agricultural occupations, but they have one great advantage over their agricultural counterparts: in 1980 they formed their own union, the Bondhua Mukti Morcha or Bonded Liberation Front. One of the founders of the union, Swami Agnivesh, a member of the General Committee of the Anti-Slavery Society, became its chairman, and has succeeded in getting the truth about debt bondage to a wide audience. At the United Nations he has made the most of his position as a non-governmental organization delegate to persuade the Indian government to face up to the problem.

Partly in his former capacity as a member of the Haryana State Legislative Assembly, Swami Agnivesh has been well placed to bring to light previously neglected aspects of debt bondage, in particular the conditions of 10,000 bonded labourers working in the stone quarries of Faridabad to the south of Delhi. There *jamadars* (middlemen) recruit labourers by making tempting offers of high wages. Before work begins, however, the peasants find that capital is needed to build accommodation for themselves on site, and to purchase drilling equipment; and while they prepare to start, there are all the usual outgoings for day-to-day subsistence. The *jamadars* are only too willing to make cash advances and by the time work begins debts are substantial.

Once inside the system the quarry worker, like the farm labourer, finds it difficult to break out, even though the law is now on his side. His basic disability is his illiteracy; he cannot keep track of his debts, nor is he inclined to explore his legal position. Toiling for a twelve-hour day under the hot sun and often in thick dust, imagining that he is paying off his debts, he is soon in no fit state to make any sort of stand for his rights. His family, whether or not they are bonded with him, live in a nearby hut, often without the statutory water supply. Malaria is common, as are accidents, and expensive medical treatment, if accessible, can only be obtained by increasing the debt. In one quarry a guard patrols the perimeter with a leopard; elsewhere the workers are intimidated by physical assault and persuaded that it is unwise to communicate with researchers. In 1982 the Bonded Liberation Front complained about the Faridabad quarries to the Supreme Court of India, and as a result an enquiry was carried out by the Labour Welfare Department, which declared that the rights of 10,000 workers were being abused. Hitherto it had been practically impossible for workers to prove that it was debt which bound them, but by means of on-the-spot investigations this obstacle was overcome.

Swami Agnivesh's message is not popular with the Indian government. He is accused of making the sort of exaggerations that are 'no doubt attractive to a crusader'[25] and he tends to be classified with the 'Cassandras' of the anti-slavery movement. He is concerned both about the suffering of the bonded labourers and about the response of the Indian authorities to it; it appears to him that all the right judgments are made, but nothing happens. Despite commitment to a policy of identification, release and rehabilitation, if official figures are to be believed, as of 31 March 1985 only 163,245 bonded labourers had been identified and freed, and only 124,904 had been rehabilitated. He asks why there is such a time-lag between release and rehabilitation when a sum of 250 million rupees has been allotted for assisting the freed labourers and only 50 million of it has been used. Another of his complaints is that top officials deny the existence of the problem in their own districts, a reaction which occurred when he raised the issue in the Haryana State Legislative Assembly. The Chief Minister was scornful and declared that there was not one bonded labourer in his entire area; it subsequently transpired that he owned some of the quarries making full use of the system. The position of the female bonded labourers has also been the subject of Swami Agnivesh's concern. They may have accounted for less than 3 per cent of all bonded labourers in the Gandhi Foundation survey, but there are alarming instances which have come to his notice of men selling wives and sisters into prostitution in order to gain their own freedom.

What solutions does he recommend? In the early days of the Bonded Liberation Front direct action was favoured: trucks were driven to the quarries and the more articulate union members attempted to convince the labourers of their rights. Unfortunately few opportunities of employment awaited those who opted for instant freedom and now rescue missions are only used when cruel conditions create sudden emergencies. Instead a broader policy is urged. It is still accepted that identification, release and rehabilitation constitute the essential steps of the programme, but ignorance on the part of the illiterate peasants is a major obstacle in the way of identification and release. Because virtually none of them can read other means of educating them have to be used; a surprisingly large number have access to wirelesses and television sets and it is felt that the government has a duty to make the people aware of their rights and opportunities by means of educational broadcasts. The impact of broadcasting can be reinforced by information disseminated by a government agency, the Directorate of Audio-Visual Publicity. This organization has produced many posters calculated to enlighten illiterates, but none on debt bondage.

Given that masters and bonded labourers are aware of the illegality of their relationship, the next step is to stimulate sufficient political will within each state to implement the Abolition Act (1976). With this end in mind Swami Agnivesh made the imaginative suggestion[26] that the United Nations Working Group of Experts on Slavery should hold its next meeting in Delhi; the principal item on the agenda would be to help the Indian government devise a three-year plan for the eradication of the system. His idea seemed to pass unnoticed, but there should be little difficulty in convening a regional seminar, at which exactly the same non-governmental organizations would be represented, so that experience, expertise and objectivity could be brought to bear on the practicalities of emancipation. Outsiders are better placed to ask awkward questions about what prompts judges to refuse to award mandatory prison sentences to rich neighbours. And the outsiders who form much of the membership of NGO delegations also have sufficient understanding of the host country's problems to realize that the phenomenon is held tightly in a poverty trap. World funds will not be used for compensating the masters for loss of loans, but there is a case for international help for rehabilitation.

The poverty of the people and the greed of the moneylenders made India the ideal environment for the growth of traditional forms of slavery. And as far as old-established rural activities go, Indian examples fit neatly into received opinion about relationships between owners and slaves. If, however, attention is concentrated on the more recent uses to which debt bondage is put, removed from the agrarian setting, another characteristic can be observed which has been more prominent in Western slave-owning societies, old and new. While Lord Acton was right about absolute power corrupting absolutely, it is steadily brought home to students of the institution that when power is concentrated in the hands of those unaccustomed to such responsibility, it is most likely to be abused to an atrocious degree. National Socialist Germany is the outstanding example, encapsulated in a generation; Latin America has been the scene of several examples of cruel repression which have been institutionalized. In both regions conquerors became owners and, by definition, founders of a new order, but in South and Central America the system, which now takes several forms, has survived. The early Spanish and Portuguese conquerers were only too accustomed to power; it has been delegation of excessive authority to a diverse assortment of middlemen, coupled with periodic influxes of adventurers keen to exploit, that has made Iberian debt bondage and serfdom notorious.

By the beginning of the twentieth century, South American countries felt able to claim that slavery was a thing of the past; no Peruvian citizen, for example, was a slave. But, as the Putumayo rubber-gathering atrocities were to show, it all depended on definitions of citizenship and slavery. The world in general only became aware of the existence in the Upper Amazon basin of one of the crueller manifestations of slavery because one of the guilty firms, the Peruvian Amazon Company, had British shareholders, was registered in London and had British directors who might be held culpable. The source of the firm's considerable profits was publicly revealed and, under pressure from the British government, the company sent a commission of enquiry, accompanied by Consul General Roger Casement, who also acted on behalf of the Anti-Slavery Society, to find out the facts. Casement's report, published as a Blue Book,[27] exposed the activities of company officials and, more importantly in the long term, set them against the background of local custom and law. Later a House of Commons Select Committee cross-examined members of the commission and a wide spectrum of witnesses testified about the company's methods, the plight of the Amerindians in particular, and peonage in general.

When the company was still in private local hands it had been encouraged by the Peruvian government to acquire some 12,000 square miles of equatorial forest claimed by Colombia. The political motive was straightforward territorial expansion; the company was attracted by an inferior kind of rubber known as 'sernambi', which would never have been marketed had it not been for the supply of virtually free labour which the forest provided. After the nineteenth-century slave raids had taken their toll, an estimated 50,000 Indians remained in the Putumayo, and 40,000 of these were claimed to be employees when the company's prospectus was published in London. They were basically of four tribes: the Bora, the Andoke, the Ocaina and the Huitoto, not all of which were docile. The timid Huitoto, who numbered about three-quarters of the labour force, lived in the central part of the Putumayo, and Peruvian or Colombian '*caucheros*' had originally induced them to collect rubber by making advance payments to them of simple articles of European manufacture.

The earliest reports of atrocities began to appear in 1907 and the subject matter was probably without precedent in terms of revolting descriptions of torture. Apart from accounts of capture of Indians and brutal exploitation of peons, what jolted the public conscience was the perverted mutilation of men, women and children. It was immediately apparent that the initial motive for torture – to ensure increased rubber yield – had long since given way to an orgy of sadism. It weighed heavily with those who sat in judgment and might have distrusted such information that men trapped in the middle of the rubber-gathering hierarchy were, in their efforts to destroy the system, willing to incriminate themselves. Some were Barbadian British subjects whose presence gave the British consular service right of access to the region, and their evidence helped to show the way the system was applied at the source of the rubber trade. The vast territory of the Putumayo had been divided up and placed under the command of chiefs of sections and '*blancos*'. Below them were the Barbadians, brought in as indentured labourers and then additionally bonded by debts. Next came the '*racionales*', usually of mixed race, who could read and write, and they controlled '*muchachos*', selected Indians whose function it was to discipline the 'wild' Indians.

Members of the Select Committee were shocked to learn that the Indian population stood either within the laws of peonage or outside the law altogether. One expert witness[28] even went so far as to say that in Spanish terminology forest Indians were classed as animals, and there was soon a consensus of opinion that a distinction should be made between a comparatively mild system of peonage, by which a man in debt could be bought or sold, and a much crueller system termed *Correrias*. Peonage was widespread in the mountain area and was embodied in the legal code: a fugitive debtor would be recaptured by the Peruvian authorities and returned to his master. *Correrias* was the slave-raiding system of the lowland forest areas and made full use of expedient aspects of peonage. Debt bondage worked well as a method of recruiting labour and, if objections were raised, its apparent legality could be cited in defence. But while the Indian of the mountains might be legally protected from the greater excesses of slavery, the forest Indian had no such protection. As Sir Roger Casement commented: 'These people have absolutely no human rights, much less civil rights.'[29]

The Peruvian Amazon Company directors, most of whom knew nothing of the rubber-gathering process, were adjudged responsible for the Putumayo atrocities, and suffered the only available punishment: disgrace. Within a year the episode was eclipsed by the European War, during which the high treason of the man knighted for his anti-slavery zeal finally put paid to the British government's reforming role in the Putumayo. Many Huitoto were siphoned off and exploited elsewhere, but meanwhile the rubber seeds which Henry Wickham had smuggled down the Amazon had become the profitable plantations of the Far East and soon burst the wild rubber bubble. Peru agreed that 24 million acres of Putumayo territory, for which it had previously competed forcefully, should come under Colombian sovereignty, and it was to be expected that the South American forests would cease to be of interest to the wild rubber gatherers. Nevertheless the following report appeared in the 1976 edition of the *Anti-Slavery Reporter*:[30]

> In 1974 at the invitation of Survival International the Anti-Slavery Society . . . shared in an operation to free the Andoke, an Amerindian tribe in Colombia, who were working for a rubber merchant to whom they stood in perpetual debt.

The tribe numbers one hundred and twenty persons. These are all that are left of the Andoke nation which in 1905 was estimated at ten thousand and was then enslaved and reduced by The Peruvian Rubber Company Limited. . . .

Under the system operating until December 1973 the men of the tribe collected rubber for the merchant from February to May and from August to December and were paid for the rubber in 'credit'. The rubber area is five days' journey by motor boat or ten days' rowing from the Andoke village where the dependants remained drawing on the credit. The patron – Zumaeta – sold to the Andoke goods in excess of the credit in order to convert credit into debt which was exaggerated and became perpetuated by the low price paid for the rubber and the high price charged for 'white' goods.'

Jean Landaburo, a French anthropologist who had gained the trust of the Andoke and reported their wish to escape, acted as agent for Survival International and the Anti-Slavery Society and with the help of the two organizations was able to pay off part of the debt. Next, realizing that freedom alone would not be enough, he gave them equipment so that they might collect rubber for themselves, and made arrangements for what they harvested to be sold in Bogotá. The habits of a century or more are slow to die, however, and by the end of 1974 most of the tribe had reverted to dependence on their patron; only four independent rubber collectors remained.

The rubber-gathering example, despite the unforeseen intervention of foreign plantation rubber and, later, synthetic products, has ingredients common to many other commercial interests. In a lowland area of Peru, the Gran Pajonal, during the 1960s, the Piro Indians were enticed into domestic service and farm labour by being encouraged to buy expensive commodities on credit.[31] And during the 1970s in the part of Peru next to the Putumayo the Yagua Indians were similarly drawn into indebtedness by timber contractors.[32] Once in the grip of an agreement, which until the Peruvian constitution of 1979 was legally binding, the Yagua had no option but to fell trees and float them down river as instructed. As their debts increased they were made to settle near the rivers where more direct discipline could be imposed. All such practices are now illegal throughout the continent but, as the Indian tribes approach extinction, the system does not die out with them; it seeks its victims from among groups of migrant workers scarcely less vulnerable than their predecessors.

In the forest regions enslavement of Indian tribes which has been traditional throughout the length and breadth of the continent usually followed a routine whereby debt bondage fixed the native to a specific territory and either worked him to death or translated him into a peon or serf; debt bondage was the means, serfdom the end. Elsewhere, in the fertile areas which have been increasingly brought under cultivation since the time of the *conquistadores*, the *latifundia* (large estates) have inherited the earth and those who work upon it. Original rights of conquest gave birth to inter-generational serfdom or peonage, which persisted with few interruptions, other than wars, until the land reforms of this century gave peasants some rights of ownership. Even so, the *enganche* system, whereby debts can be paid off by labouring, continued to thrive, and still does, throughout rural Peru.[33] The advent of minifundia, not so much an alternative to the *latifundia* as the means to off-season subsistence, overlapped in time with other reforms that made it illegal to take possession of a man either by buying the land on which he worked or by accepting responsibility for his debts. Again, as in India, there is a wide gulf between legal freedom and the realities of life. Even if the peasant knows his rights, he is bound by convention and may be enslaved by economic laws. In theory he can sell his labour to the highest bidder. In practice, although his child may run to Lima and search for riches on the rubbish dumps, he will realize that no one is bidding and settle for the familiarity and comparative security of the rural economy. Even if his debts are cancelled by statute, he accepts that indebtedness has its obligations, and there is always the possibility of intimidation.

Governments which have sought to institute land reforms have been faced with a dilemma; only the large estates are economically viable in a permanent sense, but, if peasants are to achieve freedom and security they must acquire title to land. In Ecuador an institution known as *huasipungo* proved to be an unsatisfactory compromise. The peon worked for his patron for half the minimum wage for four days a week, which gave him the right to farm a plot of his own in his own time for profit. The arrangement broke down for a variety of reasons, not least because the peon was paid late and he had no alternative but to build up debt at the *hacienda* store. His condition in the end combined the disadvantages of serfdom with those of the newer forms of debt bondage; his patron was his moneylender and could, if he wished, pay him in vouchers only acceptable at his own store. According to Ecuador's reply to the United Nations Special Rapporteur on Slavery in 1965, these 'unsatisfactory procedures' were amended by the Land Reform and Settlement Act of 1964 and 'agricultural labour has been raised to the level of free contracting'.[34]

The 1964 Act was a radical piece of legislation which included retrospective elements to provide for the transfer of title to a serf who could satisfy a labour inspector that he had worked on his holding for ten years under the *huasipungo* system. Moreover, the value of a plot being assessed at ten years' labour, those who had worked for shorter periods had various options whereby they could pay for the missing years; and for those who had recently inherited their *huasipungo* obligation it was permissible to count the years of service of their forebears. Looking to the future the Act stated unequivocally that 'Agricultural Labour shall be paid for in cash';[35] vouchers, credit or kind ceased to be the legal tender that drew peasants into servitude and kept them there. A major obstacle to complete emancipation, however, is that the two parties negotiating land transfers and establishing a new contractual relationship are separated by the barrier of literacy. The hold of the *haciendado* over the heir to the *huasipungo* system is maintained by his account book, and by his ability to draw up a contract. And in addition his position of strength is fortified by a tradition of deference and by the economics of subsistence farming.

The geographical boundaries of debt bondage and serfdom are not clearly marked. Quite rightly India and Peru are subjected to much criticism for their contravention of the United Nations Slavery Convention, but there are many other countries which are equally guilty. A multitude of local variations of the system are practised throughout South America and extend through Central America to the northern frontiers of Mexico. Most forms have a Spanish vocabulary, because Pope Alexander VI's dividing line, under the Treaty of Tordesillas, of 1494, succeeded in inhibiting the two great Christian imperialist powers from competing for the same spoils, but Portugal's brand of feudalism was equally merciless. In Asia, during the latter part of the twentieth century, feudal practices cross religious and national boundaries with little regard for religious commitment or colonial influence. Both Pakistan and Nepal have distinct cultural traditions, but in each country artificially induced indebtedness is used as a means of enslaving its poorer citizens.

After the partition of India had separated Hindu and Moslem, one might have expected the caste factor to have excluded debt bondage from Pakistan, but this has not been the case. Extensive use has been made of bonded labourers, including children, in the digging of irrigation channels and the building of dams usually on government contracts.[36] Contractors, known as *Kharkars*, are sending agents to remote villages where poverty is endemic and offering employment to the healthier young men if they will come and live in their camps. Cash advances are made to the parents and the recruits are bonded until the debts are repaid. In order to prevent premature repayment or escape by any other means, the Kharkars sell the labourers their food and imprison them within the camps. Armed guards patrol with dogs, ensuring that a twelve-hour day is worked and return to the villages is not contemplated. Should anyone attempt to do so, the penalty is to be bound in chains.

Nepal, with a large population of poor landless peasants, is fertile ground for the growth of debt bondage and the perpetuation of serfdom, and three main types of servitude have developed.[37] In one serfs work a parcel of land for their own subsistence and, in exchange for this privilege, accept that they are the unpaid servants of the master. In another, called *Haruwari*, a landowner lends money to a labourer in exchange for the agricultural and domestic services of the labourer and his family for a prearranged period, its duration depending on the size of the loan; the master accepts the responsibility for providing the bonded family with food and shelter and they will work for between twelve and fourteen hours a day for him. At the bottom of the feudal scale, *Dhakres*, or carriers, are tied to traders in exchange for a series of small loans and are regarded as the most exploited of the country's workers. The overall position in Nepal was not generally appreciated until a seminar on bonded labour and other forms of labour exploitation was held in Kathmandu in May 1984, when those present identified scarcity of employment opportunities as the main cause of the problem. Their report[38] quotes one of the findings of a previous seminar held in India:[39]

> offers to assist a bonded labourer to be liberated from his bondage are often rejected, partly from fear of reprisals and partly from fear that he will be unable to obtain other employment and consequently be reduced to an even worse state of poverty and insecurity.

While it is true that the forms of enslavement to moneylenders and landowners described above are not limited to Latin America and the southern regions of Asia, the temptation to widen unduly the definitions of these forms of slavery should be resisted. Pressures exerted by indebtedness exist in all societies; it is only when they constitute a discernible system in which freedom is lost that they fall within the orbit of slavery, benevolent or malevolent. Africa has many traditions with regard to credit and land tenure, but close acquaintance shows that the balance of responsibility between individuals and tribal groupings is different in kind, and different in psychology, from what might be thought to be corresponding relationships in other continents. The traditional attitude of nomads to land and, in many areas, prolonged dependence on barter, have meant that Africans were not usually disposed to enslave their fellows by sophisticated financial agreements or by debt bondage. Chattel slavery is Africa's form of the institution – where debt bondage has appeared it has usually been communal rather than personal, manifesting itself in the relationship between migrant workers and their dormitory townships or homelands. And different yardsticks are also appropriate for Africa's northern neighbours, where debt bondage traditions, in Sicily for example, have been undermined by the escape routes provided by the work opportunities elsewhere in the European Economic Community. While migration has drawn many Africans away from freedom it has provided numerous landless Sicilians with opportunities to escape from the debt incurred for protection or patronage imposed on them by the *mafiosi*.

Another region rightly associated with slavery, but having a less clear involvement with usury or usufruct, is the Middle East. Since the impact of oil revenues traditional bonds of kinship have given some ground to political patronage; nevertheless, in the majority of cases the relationship between tenant and landlord remains one of shared risk, not debt.[40] Share-cropping is the dominant agricultural arrangement, with the land remaining the property of the wealthy landowner, who has a traditional obligation to see that his tenants do not starve when times are hard. Too much can depend on the character of the landlord, but recent attempts at land reform have been partly frustrated by political upheavals and wars, making the outcome, seen in terms of social justice, difficult to predict. More predictable is cash indebtedness; today, as yesterday, Islam ineffectively prohibits usury.[41]

For serfdom and debt bondage to disappear from the world altogether, a series of steps will have to be taken both within the nations concerned and at the international level. Basic national legislation having already been passed, additional laws are needed mainly to close loopholes and to clarify the action which local officials must take. India was clearly right to concentrate attention on identification, release and rehabilitation, and her experience points the way to the need for an equitable system of land tenancy or distribution – surely one area in which masters might claim compensation without risking the penalties which in other respects they may deserve. As one common denominator of serfs and bonded labourers is passive acceptance of their place in a preordained scheme of things, that is unless abuses become too difficult to bear, universal education is another essential provision. It should be in two stages: first, dispensation of information in ways understandable by illiterates; second, education to abolish illiteracy.

All three first steps – legislation to initiate a programme of reform, changes in land lease or ownership, and education – are useless without an effective inspectorate. An inspector's prime duty will be to ensure that rehabilitation is realistic, and to carry it out he will need the backing of powerful bodies. Ideally, his government will request support from United Nations agencies and invite relevant non-governmental organizations to help, but unfortunately Third World rulers do not always welcome observers who may make adverse criticisms. However, money is another matter, and as poverty lies at the root of the problem, it will have to be made to flow from rich nations to the poor (on grounds that can be shown to be as necessary in the long run as those used to justify relief of a well-publicized famine). And, furthermore, unless the peasant classes of the Third World are going to be delivered into a form of international debt bondage, grants, not loans, must be made. One string should be attached: receipt of rehabilitation grants should be conditional on admission of World Bank or other outside officials to see that the money is actually used to rehabilitate.

CHAPTER 8

PERSECUTION OF TRIBAL MINORITIES

The right of ownership, collective or individual, of the members of the populations concerned over the lands which these populations traditionally occupy shall be recognized.

INTERNATIONAL LABOUR CONVENTION 107, ARTICLE 11

The term 'minorities' in the context of many tribes, persecuted or not, needs some clarification, particularly where there is a secessionist factor at work. In many areas, such as those occupied by the Moros of the Philippines, the inhabitants see themselves as a majority in their own territory, illegally ruled by a powerful neighbour. The Chittagong Hill Tribes of Bangladesh, too, while demanding something which falls short of independence, would not take kindly to the implication that they are a minority in their ancestral land. Nevertheless, within the existing political arrangements, these peoples, who are often heirs to nations with ancient cultural traditions and now aspire to a renewal of their national identity, are minorities; and in so far as they are persecuted their conditions come within the remit of the Anti-Slavery Society.

Since its official foundation in 1839 the Anti-Slavery Society has devoted much of its energy to the emancipation of slaves who were at the same time tribal minorities; but only in 1909, when it merged with the Aborigines Protection Society, founded in 1837, did it assume a specific responsibility for these peoples, even when they were not enslaved. The merger benefited both societies from several points of view, partly because diplomatically it can be useful to have two hats. Changes of name can seem to be purely cosmetic devices, but they also reflect and perhaps encourage changes of policy. The society's old name, the British and Foreign Anti-Slavery Society, identified it with one world power and automatically put rival powers on the defensive. Since 1957, when it became the Anti-Slavery Society for the Protection of Human Rights, incorporating the Aborigines Protection Society, it has, without distancing itself from its heritage, been able to take a more convincingly independent line on international affairs. As an organization dedicated to emancipation it seemed to have to wait until the crime was committed before action could be taken; as a protector of human rights and a protection society for aborigines, it could adjust its priorities so that prevention could take precedence over cure – provided that it could persuade governments to allow access to the peoples under threat.

As has been mentioned, when the crime of genocide was attempted by Germany's National Socialist regime, a vocabulary of euphemisms developed which enabled unspeakable crimes to be spoken about with a minimum of embarrassment so that the 'final solution' could be brought nearer. The language of more recent genocidal campaigns has been less calculated but no less dangerous and, as far as many tribes are concerned, started with misconceptions about the meaning of 'progress'. To some it means giving encouragement to the irresistible force of scientific and commercial development, while to others it means transition from a certain condition to a better condition, and all depends on what is meant by 'better'. Marxists and capitalists alike are guilty of bluntly accepting the supposed inevitability of destructive modernizing trends, and the consequences of capitalism's unacceptable activities were brought home to the Anti-Slavery Society in the 1960s when reports began to come out of Brazil about conflicts of interest between the *civilizados* and many Amerindian tribes. All the familiar causes of slavery were there, often appropriately clothed in euphemistic terminology. Commercial interest, or greed, justified illegal invasion of tribal lands; strategic consideration, or fear, prevented tribal reserves from being preserved where they straddled state boundaries. Poverty, an unmentioned cause, drove the *caboclos*, the peasants of the Brazilian interior, to seek employment with those who sought to exploit Indian territory. Finally, power in the hands of those unaccustomed to it led to the atrocities which alerted the Anti-Slavery Society. Its investigations in Brazil and subsequently in Bangladesh and the Philippines will provide the principal examples of tribal persecution in the non-Communist world. Some consideration will then be given to the treatment of tribal minorities in the Soviet Union, a country which does not encourage non-governmental organizations to carry out enquiries within its national boundaries.

One of the more disillusioning facts about Brazil's culpability, and one that it shares with the Philippines, is that the organization to which the care of the native population had been entrusted was an accessory to the brutal crimes committed against the Indians. Allegations levelled against the Service for the Protection of the Indian were sufficiently serious and consistent for the Brazilian government to be alarmed and, possibly to allay international disquiet, in 1967 it exposed the cruel workings of one of its own departments and identified the officials responsible. Some 300 service officers, having been bribed by multinational corporations which coveted Indian land, were accused of killing the Indians they were paid to protect. The government then allowed the International Red Cross uninhibited access and invited the chairman of the executive of the Primitive People's Fund, Robin Hanbury-Tenison, to come and see for himself. Their respective reports appeared in 1970[1] and 1971.[2] Although the Red Cross was mainly concerned with medical matters, and many Indians had been killed off by diseases such as measles, it could not avoid making mention of wider health issues which affected the Indians' physical welfare; and where the Red Cross left off Hanbury-Tenison, who was accompanied by his wife, began. Next it was generally agreed by all interested parties that the Hanbury-Tenison report, the result of a remarkable tour of enquiry, provoked questions which demanded further investigation, and this led to the Anti-Slavery Society being invited to help the Brazilian government to solve its problems with the tribes, in the hope, presumably, that it would give the lie to any suggestion that it was acquiescing in the extermination of Indians.

The Society had forged sound links with Brazil during Roger Casement's investigations[3] in the Upper Amazon basin and the government evidently had no qualms about inviting it to make similar enquiries on its own territory. Nevertheless the Society thought it prudent to send its team as representatives of the Aborigines Protection Society, a title which can be construed as emphasizing future policy rather than past sins. So urgent was the position of the Amerindians as described by Hanbury-Tenison that the Society broke an unwritten rule that had remained intact since its foundation: it accepted government aid. There was no doubt that without Brazilian government sponsorship the expedition would have been seriously delayed by fund raising. To avoid risk of compromise the Society therefore laid down several conditions about freedom of movement, access to individuals and, above all, freedom to publish, if necessary, a damning report.

These points having been agreed, a four-man team[4] started gathering information in Brasilia on 4 August 1972, and made its first contact with Indians four days later.

Disbandment of the discredited Society for the Protection of the Indians and admission of independent investigators went some way towards exculpating the Brazilian authorities from any further charge of genocide, but it is arguable that inconsistent application of inconsistent policies by FUNAI,[5] the government department now carrying the same responsibilities as its predecessor, will achieve the annihilation of the tribes by other means. The team's first visit[6] was to the Karajá tribe which inhabits what amounts to an inland island between two channels of the river Araguaia. Here a policy of integration had not had the effect on the physical condition and morale of the Indians that had been hoped. Many thousands of head of cattle, some 3,000 the property of FUNAI, were being reared in the park and profits became part of the *Renda Indigena*, the tithe paid by the Indians to the department. Other disconcerting features were the building of a new road across the park and steadily increasing numbers of tourists. Almost inevitably dismissals of many Indian Protection Society staff had meant that FUNAI had had to recruit, without delay, numbers of young and inexperienced staff to take charge of the field posts, and their comparative immaturity meant that they were not always able to make a stand, when necessary, against the divisive and sometimes repressive influence of Christian missions. On this first visit the team was especially alarmed by an apparent indifference on the part of FUNAI to obvious problems which contact with civilization had introduced to the Indians, such as prostitution, begging and alcoholism.

Over the next two months the team visited twenty-seven tribes, but was refused access to the Cintas Largas[7] who had been dynamited and otherwise shot and mutilated in 1963, and whose experiences had been among the more notorious events which stimulated national and international concern. After being connected with the outside world by the construction of a highway, the tribe had come into contact with rubber gatherers of much the same stamp as those attracted to the Putumayo half a century earlier, and valuable evidence could have been obtained had the team been able to compare and contrast the measures employed by FUNAI with those of its predecessor. The grounds for denying access seemed valid enough: visitors must be excluded from areas where relationships with hitherto isolated tribes were still delicately poised; but, although the team accepted the prohibition, it was noted that it was not always applied to others with much less reason to demand access.

Moving from tribe to tribe, it was soon possible to discern general trends of neglect, sometimes partially concealed by paternalism which undermined the Indians' self-reliance. Settlements of naked Indians were thoughtlessly placed by the roadside,[8] for the convenience of FUNAI, attracting the attention of tourists and the viruses that accompany them. Despite constitutional guarantees that Indians have entitlement to their traditional territories, albeit generally vested in FUNAI on their collective behalf, companies and migrant labourers were able to come in and take possession with little hindrance. And then responsibility for physical, educational and spiritual care of Indians who, by one means or another, have been persuaded to settle in specified locations was often left to religious bodies who contradicted each other on matters of dogma and had scant respect for ethnic cultures. Nor was it always appreciated that, while Indians may resemble one another in European eyes, the characteristics of each tribe are different. Some may integrate rapidly and easily with modern Brazilian society; some may need several generations to adapt; others might be best left alone to develop their own form of society, or remain as they are, uninfluenced by alien values.

The Aborigines Protection Society felt that it would be arrogant to make precise recommendations to the Brazilian government, although members of the team had had many years' experience of Amerindian tribes before they undertook this investigation. Instead the report, which was published in 1973, explained the background and aims of the expedition, gave a diary of its movements and activities, analysed the evidence it had gained, drew its conclusions and summarized the overall findings. The verdict on FUNAI, although it gave credit to some well-meaning though disillusioned staff, contained much adverse criticism which, tragically, proved prophetic, as events only a few years later were to show. Whilst clear demarcation of Indian lands was one of the most important functions of FUNAI, time and again the team found that maps were contradictory. How can one protect a boundary if no one knows for sure where the boundary lies? FUNAI's staffing policy was also found to be seriously flawed: new recruits were far too young and often unqualified for their responsibilities; men at the top, including army officers, were conspicuous for their ignorance of Amerindian problems; and, most sinister of all, the organization had not expelled all the individuals implicated in the iniquities of the disgraced Indian Protection Society. Among Brazilians generally attitudes to Indians vary; at worst they are jungle animals, at best they are grown-up children in need of patrons. The FUNAI staff interviewed in 1972 were seen to be trying to rid themselves of such stereotypes, but when it came to practical matters, like acquisition of personal land titles, they resented Indian initiatives which might gain for the grown-up children a degree of independence.

FUNAI was devoid of linguists, an astounding deficiency, and as a result was largely dependent on missionaries for translation of its wishes into practical form. The Summer Institute of Linguistics[9] alone emerges from the report with a clean bill of health, because, although it has a commitment to translate the Bible into every Indian language, it gave the team the impression that it does not impose beliefs on the Indians. Many other missions, Protestant and Roman Catholic, either confuse or divide the tribes with their rival doctrines. Looking at the report with benefit of hindsight it is possible to draw parallels between the religious and secular authorities in their policies towards the tribes and the ways in which policies are distorted in the field. The National Council of Bishops of Brazil is on record as being opposed to 'any form of rapid and intense integration, as has been announced at the high levels of Government'[10] and declared itself to be intent on perfecting rather than destroying cultures. Although professing belief in integration it saw it as a gradual two-way process which encouraged the Indians to develop as self-sufficient nations within the wider community – hardly integration at all, as most would understand the term. By contrast, within the reserves and parks[11] six Christian missions had to be expelled for unspecified unacceptable treatment of Indians, and not all those that remained displayed awareness of the Indians' social, let alone cultural, needs. Beside the inconsistencies of the churches and their missions stands a divided secular approach to the problem. A government wishing to convince the world that desirable humane integration is on the way was prepared to risk admitting an outside body and it may well have regretted doing so. The government had expelled its missions too, but the reborn protection department found it difficult to rid itself of old prejudices.

It was observed that the gulf between *civilizados* and Indians was widened at a purely physical level by problems arising from prejudices about hygiene and clothing.[12] People of European stock are prone to take an unnatural interest in naked bodies, a psychological blemish illustrated by commercial 'Green Hell' tours (now banned) to witness the ceremony of plucking the hair of the virgin at a Tikuna village.[13] And this is one of the several reasons why an increasing number of Indians acquire clothing. Unfortunately they lack the means to keep it clean or in good repair and, despite good habits of personal cleanliness, soon resemble tramps. Worse problems of sanitation arise when Indians who have defecated healthily in their jungle environment during a nomadic existence find themselves confined within a comparatively small space. There is opposition to the installation of latrines, which are considered dangerous to children, and the alternative practice, making use of jungle verges, creates difficulties when larger tribes are involved. This, again, serves to perpetuate the idea that Indians are smelly animals.

It is unfortunate in one way that Indians, and indeed all races, are not easily spoken of as members of the animal kingdom, as in so many cases the causes and cures of problems are to do with habitat and its destruction. When the plight of an endangered species is discussed by the World Wildlife Fund, the preservation of habitat is frequently the prime issue. The investigating team expressed no such thoughts, but they did identify 'the land question as deserving the highest priority and the crucial test of intentions towards the Indians'.[14] They were worried that while the Brazilian constitution guaranteed Indian peoples unqualified, permanent and inviolable ownership of their lands,[15] a 'Statute of the Indian', drafted shortly before the mission arrived in Brazil, stated that 'the lands occupied by the Indians belong to the Union',[16] and FUNAI, as a government department, seemed both powerless and disinclined to fight the statute. In the course of their expedition the team had visited the famous Xingu National Park,[17] described by its opponents as a human zoo; and here they had seen for themselves how even the international prestige of the Villas Boas brothers, the elder statesmen of Indian protection, had failed to prevent serious erosion of established land rights. The self-esteem of tribes so long as they remained cut off from aggressive civilization, and encouraged to lead an autonomous existence, only served to emphasize the danger of seriously reducing their habitat.

It was the penetration of highways that started the rot in the Xingu Park, and national investment in roads poses a threat to tribes generally and to the entire ecosystem known as the Amazon rain forest. Other threats created fears for the prospects of the Yanomami who, numbering well over 10,000, were probably the largest tribe in South America that had not yet been warped by civilization. Their traditional land is divided by the frontier with Venezuela and at the time of the team's visit[18] this artificial problem was to be solved by concentrating them in a part where only about 7 per cent of them would normally be found. The map which the team eventually acquired showed that the new territory excluded every Yanomami village known by FUNAI itself to exist. Moreover, neither the Christian missions nor the FUNAI officials with the tribe had heard of the proposed new park. Plainly at a high level in a government administration anxious to prove its benevolent attitude to Indians someone had taken a decision without seeing fit to consult those charged with their protection. At the time excuses were expressed in terms of national security; the real reasons came to light later.

There were other features of Indian protection which deserved criticism and, it was believed, would not prove too difficult to correct, given the will to do so. Tribal integrity had always been under attack from without by *civilizados* in search of money and power, but two of FUNAI's practices were leading to the same influences undermining from within. Not only was a concealed tax, the *Renda Indigena*, creaming off the profits from Indian work to subsidize FUNAI, but the long-drawn-out process of 'attraction' (or 'pacification' as it had been more realistically termed before the arrival of the team) after contact had been made with a newly discovered tribe had eventually led some Indians into one of Latin America's traditional slave relationships: debt bondage. Endless streams of presents led only too easily to dependence, and FUNAI was already fulfilling the role of master in too many respects. Again, in keeping with the Putumayo system of peonage (though the report does not make this comparison), recruitment of an excessively rewarded disciplinary force[19] from among the Indians had created a privileged elite and upset the natural tribal hierarchies.

After stressing the need to preserve constitutionally guaranteed land rights the team went on to express its views as follows:[20]

> . . . each Indian nation should be treated as a separate case, with its distinct culture, history and problems. Some tribes may never wish to abandon their traditional cultures, and it is of some significance that three of the tribes we visited have been in contact for more than a century yet still show no wish for integration. On the other hand, where the tribe wishes to

integrate and participate in Brazilian economy and culture, it is important that it should be given proper encouragement.

FUNAI was quick to reply[21] to the Society's report and selected sentences can serve to reveal contradictions inherent in a policy which soon led to violation of Indian rights and more bloodshed:

> . . . in Brazil an Indian reservation does not mean a limited area to which the Indian is confined. The Reservation is land guaranteed his own for ever. . . . The Plan for National Integration, which has mobilized the entire Brazilian nation, foresees the opening of an extensive road system throughout the country. Those roads that must, for practical, economic and strategic reasons, be constructed in the middle of the jungle, have to go through regions presumably and actually inhabited by different Indian tribes. . . . There are two valid theses. . . . The first . . . propounds the permanent geographical isolation of the Indian. . . . Thus, their political, social and cultural structures stay intact . . . the maintenance of this geographical isolation is profoundly difficult . . . particularly in a country that is facing a boom such as exists in Brazil today. Pioneers of all kinds are to be found in every corner of Brazilian territory. Each of them is moved by different interests and aims and has a differing reaction to the Indian question. . . . This accounts for the prevalence of the second thesis, i.e. that of gradual and spontaneous integration.

In the event FUNAI opted for neither thesis, the pioneers forced the issue and the Indians were inadequately protected. The Yanomami park proved especially attractive to developers, despite the availability of millions of acres of uninhabited territory in other parts of a vast country, and in 1979 the Anti-Slavery Society had to intervene at the United Nations Sub-Commission on Prevention of Discrimination and Protection of Minorities to prevent it from being divided into twenty-one small pockets intersected by roads. During the same year about thirty Indian leaders were murdered by cattle-ranchers and, while over 100,000 new land titles were granted to colonists, virtually no progress was made in securing the land rights of the tribes. The grown-up children remained minors in the eyes of the law, and official and unofficial attitudes towards them were hardening.

In 1980 FUNAI ceased to be an ambiguous organization. The

investigating team of 1972 had commended aspects of its work and praised individual servants of the department, but what earned praise from outside clearly displeased vested interests. The president of FUNAI, the heads of two of his departments and other occupants of key posts were replaced by officers of the armed forces with experience of intelligence and security matters, and without experience of Indian affairs. The Anti-Slavery Society, which had from time to time noticed Brazil's irritation when outsiders showed what seemed to be a disproportionate amount of concern for 0.1 per cent of its population, felt that its government was alarmed by the extent of support for the Indian cause and intended a clampdown on critical voices. Fears on this score increased with the knowledge that by the latter half of 1980 most of FUNAI's anthropologists had been dismissed and thirty-eight members of the Brazilian Society of Indigenists had been removed from the missions, including the whole of a project team working with the Xavante tribe, whose land had long been coveted by the land owners of Mato Grosso.[22]

The purge of the more enlightened elements of FUNAI's personnel and collaborators coincided with the passing of legislation to decentralize the organization. This meant that henceforth most decisions about the administration of Indian reserves and parks would be taken by the governments of the states in which they were located, and conflicts of interest would therefore be more keenly felt. It was hardly a coincidence that, as these legislative alterations were under way, the general deterioration of relationships accelerated and physical conflict between pioneers and Indians began again. In Maranháo seven members of the previously uncontacted Guajá tribe were poisoned by a gift of flour laced with ant killer, and elsewhere Indians decided to counter-attack. Txukahamaye Indians killed eleven *caboclos* felling trees on their reserve and not long afterwards over 100 Indians attacked a farm and killed twenty more. At this stage one of the original team of investigators commented, 'the curtain has come down again and no one is being given the degree of access we enjoyed in 1972.'[23] The curtain did not, however, inhibit the World Bank when it decided to fund Brazil's programme of road construction, nor did it prevent information from reaching London. 1982 saw the Anti-Slavery Society's Director writing to the Brazilian President about 'recent incursions by miners and prospectors into Yanomami territory'.[24]

Brazil is between four and five times the size of all the European

Common Market countries put together and, as the Indians have dwindled to less than 100,000, it would not be a very great sacrifice to allow them sufficient primeval jungle to develop in their own way. All that is necessary is for Brazilians to abide by their own constitution and the World Bank to invest only in roads which keep well away from the world's last rain forest. Maps should adhere to agreed tribal limits, boundaries should be defended, and the only concession to the twentieth century that needs to be implemented hastily is a vaccination programme. All else should follow if and when tribal councils make their wishes known.

In some respects comparison between the tribes of the Chittagong Hill Tracts and the Amerindians can be sustained. Each group has experienced the effects of hostile government, land theft and irresponsible development; and each is in danger of being destroyed by an alien culture. Like the Amerindians the Chittagong Hill Tribes have been isolated for much of their history and now find that they are threatened by migrants of a different race and religion. But at this point parallels begin to break down and are best abandoned. The 600,000 Chittagong Hill tribesmen occupy what used to be an insignificant portion of north-eastern British India and, in the normal course of imperial advance and withdrawal, had reasonable grounds to expect independence to confirm a degree of autonomy. In 1900 the British granted limited self-government under the local chiefs; in 1935 it was designated an 'excluded area' which separated it still further from the rest of the state of which it formed a part: Bengal. Eventually, when it came to the partition of the subcontinent, it aspired to be a Native State.

The only body which proved able to voice the will of the Hill Tribes at the independence negotiations was the Chittagong Hill Tracts People's Association, and its request that the ancestral lands become part of a secular Indian state was refused. The overwhelming majority of people for whom the Association spoke were Buddhists; the rest were mainly Animists or Christians; only about 60,000 were Hindu. There were no Moslems in the Hill Tracts, and yet, partly because the tribes inhabited only part of an area which included the only major port available to East Pakistan, they found themselves incorporated in a Moslem state. Even so, despite a reputation for pro-Indian sympathies which did not endear them to their new rulers, the tribes could have been content with their lot had the status quo been maintained. They did not seek independence from Pakistan; they sought only the right to continue their traditional way of life and exercise local control over their land and its development. They had been happy with the freedom they had experienced as part of a colony; it seemed unjust that independence from the colonial master should bring repression.

Repression came gradually; it did not begin with the widespread incidence of torture, murder, rape and multiple rape reported to the United Nations Working Group on Indigenous Populations in 1984.[25] The first signs of oppression by central government came with the disbandment of the tribal police force and substitution of Bengali officers after an attempt in 1955 to abolish the Tracts' special status had been defeated by the British district commissioner and tribal chiefs. Next, in 1959, the military government of President Ayub Khan, intent on modernizing administration generally, set in motion the process which led ultimately to the full scale militarization of the Hill Tracts. Many tribesmen fled to India and in 1964 the special status of the region ceased to be recognized. Naturally these political changes had an adverse effect on morale, but the economic consequences of no longer being 'an excluded area' soon affected the physical welfare of the people. And matters could not be expected to improve when, in 1971, civil war split Moslem Pakistan and the Hill Tribes found themselves part of Bangladesh, an Islamic state inclined towards fundamentalism.

Economic repression came suddenly. For many centuries the tribesmen have practised the system of subsistence farming known as shifting cultivation, for which the local name is *jhuming*. An area of forest is cleared and burnt, and mixed crops are sown and harvested over a period not exceeding one year. The cultivators then move on to some other site and leave the old land to lie fallow until it has recovered. Everything depends on a fine balance with nature being achieved and if erosion does begin to take its toll from time to time, the chief or headman must divert the cultivators to some other section of communally owned territory. Above all, the ratio between the population of cultivators (and their dependants) and the acreage of cultivable land must remain constant. It was therefore nothing less than an ecological disaster when the Kaptai dam was built across the Karnaphuli river which flows down to the port of Chittagong from the heart of the Hill Tracts. It was a grandiose scheme, typical of rich Third World oligarchies anxious to make an impression on foreign investors, it took no account of local land rights, and it made few concessions to the plight of the dispossessed.

It is difficult to prevent comparisons with Brazil from springing to mind once again. One can hardly help concluding that the same advisors who persuaded the World Bank to finance the roads which bring death to Amerindians must have been responsible for the bilateral loan from the United States Agency for International Development which paid for the Kaptai dam. Forty per cent of the cultivable land of the Hill Tracts was submerged; 100,000 tribespeople suffered compulsory migration; although compensation and alternative land had been promised, 60,000 received no compensation of any kind; 10,000 migrated to India; 8,000 families who had previously subsisted by *jhuming* on the hillsides were ignored; families stranded in the new lake on islands too small to farm were also left to fend for themselves; and of the sum set aside for rehabilitation only about 5 per cent was paid out, and Bengali settlers were the first to be compensated.[26] Those were the immediate dramatic consequences of a hydro-electric scheme which brought no real benefits to the territory in which it was located. Far more damaging was the effect on shift cultivation throughout the remainder of the region. Reduction of available land without a corresponding drop in the population meant that the essential balance was no longer obtainable. Within three years it became obvious that over-cultivation was transforming the remaining land into desert at such an alarming rate that it was decided to exclude *jhumia* families from certain areas so that afforestation and other measures could be used to prevent erosion. This short-sighted decision repeated an error made by the British in the 1870s, and only served to increase the pressure on land elsewhere. Before long the tribes were forced to look for other means of survival. They tried to adapt, but they found that Bengali immigrants had established themselves in positions of advantage.

Since Bangladesh adopted its constitution in 1972 the Chittagong Hill Tracts have had to contend with fragmentation of their local administrative machinery and a steadily increasing influx of Moslem Bengalis into positions of political and commercial power. The once semi-autonomous region is now reduced to three districts under the deputy commissioner of the Chittagong Hill Tracts, responsible to the commissioner of the Chittagong Division, and only a few junior positions are held by tribesmen. Although lip service is still paid to the idea that tribesmen have some say in local affairs, they are not consulted about crucial matters. When, for instance, it was decided to settle 30,000 Bengali families in the Hill Tracts in 1980,[27] the decision was taken by the commissioner and deputy commissioner at a meeting with the President and the Home Minister which was held in secret. From the first the Bangladeshi leadership had over-reacted against what it imagined were the symptoms of impending secession, a fear which had grown with the knowledge that some hill tribesmen had fought on the side of the Pakistani army during the civil war and led to the massacre of about 400 tribesmen after the major conflict was concluded. A reprisal of this scale heightened the tensions all round and delegations were sent to central government to demand regional autonomy. Such demands, bluntly rejected, only added to the impression that secession was planned and, especially after General Zia's *coup*, the Hill Tracts were increasingly regarded as a rebellious area. The military presence became more numerous and more active, and Bengali immigration was stepped up.

At the conventional political level the government has had to contend with agitation from the Chittagong Hill Tracts People's Solidarity Association, but this has spawned an armed wing known as the Shanti Bahini (Peace Force), which uses guerilla tactics in pursuit of its demands: autonomy under a separate legislature, return of lands taken by Bengalis since 1970, no further Bengali immigration, preservation of Hill Tract culture, freedom of movement and commerce, and freedom from official harassment.[28] Central government at Dacca sought to neutralize this manifesto by appointing a tribal convention which would give a good imitation of regional autonomy,[29] were it not boycotted by many members and were it not administered by the commanding officer at Chittagong. In addition a tribal affairs ministry was also created, under the control of a Bengali, with the right to advise government departments. There is also a secretariat which reports to the President and a regional council to see to the direction of local affairs. Although this was enough to impress the United States Agency for International Development, it is seen locally as a tool of Bengali encroachment and absorption, and a cosmetic device calculated to mislead world opinion.

If non-violent political dialogue were being maintained, one might be inclined to withhold criticism and leave the nation to sort itself out. But, despite the Bangladeshi government's wish to prevent investigators from finding out what its soldiers are doing in the Hill Tracts – and such an attitude invariably indicates guilt – information has been gleaned by the Anti-Slavery Society to the effect that tribal peoples are being persecuted: a crime not far short of genocide is being committed. Since 1976 over 20,000 armed men have occupied the region and although many atrocities have been committed and documented, little has been done to help a people who, despite a massive programme for the immigration of Bengali plainsmen, still constitute a majority in their ancestral land. In 1977 sixty-two villagers were shot, twenty-three women tortured and some villages burnt (the Anti-Slavery Society has all the names).[30] In 1978–79 many more villages were raided – fifty over a two-month period – and in one of them a woman of 71 was burned alive – three 16-year-old boys were hacked to death, two Buddhist priests were murdered and seven villagers were tortured to death. 1979 was a year of many civilian arrests without charge and saw the appearance of a Bangladeshi officer who will not be forgotten. Captain Abul Kalam Mahmud began to make a name for himself on 2 April when he led a raid on the village of Kunungopara and razed it to the ground; he then selected Sindhu Kumar Chakma, Arun Kanti Chakma, Anabil Chakma, and others, shot them and had their bodies burned before their relatives.[31] A year later he ordered tribesmen to assemble in the square of Kankhali Bazar and his men were then commanded to open fire on them. More than fifty were buried in mass graves behind the army camp at the western corner of Poapara High School. It is a racial and a religious war; Buddhist temples are desecrated and the priests assaulted. Inevitably the Shanti Bahini strike back.

The Anti-Slavery Society has appealed to the government of Bangladesh[32] to stop Bengali immigration, reduce the occupying forces, investigate atrocities and allow access to international observers. Its most important recommendation, in the long term, is that discussions be opened with all Hill Tract tribal groups so that a political solution can be found which establishes the land rights of the people and gives them security for the future. For, as with Brazil, land title is the key to the problem. One recommendation is directed elsewhere: international agencies and foreign governments considering investing in the Hill Tracts should insist on discussing projects with the Hill Tribes first.

The final example from the non-Communist world, chosen like Brazil and Bangladesh because it is better documented than other equally vicious cases of tribal persecution, differs from the others because the tribes in question, those of the Philippines, make up a fifth of the rural population: more than six and a half million. Even if it were a valid excuse for riding roughshod over rights, the tribes cannot be described as an insignificant minority blocking the 'progress' of a nation; and yet that is exactly how they were seen by the government of President Marcos, by his relatives in high places, by the multinationals who drive them from the land, and by PANAMIN, the organization responsible for their protection. Viewed from Manila, overall tribal numbers diminish in significance. These people are divided by geography and oppressed by economics; they count for nothing politically. For most of them the great misfortune is to have been of the forests for centuries, and therefore dependent on them for subsistence. Their traditional agricultural methods are similar to those of the Chittagong Hill tribesmen but today, ironically, more erosion of the hillsides is caused by logging companies than by the tribes themselves.

Until it was purged, FUNAI could be said to have had a considerable proportion of staff dedicated to Indian welfare. There has never been anything ambivalent about the role of PANAMIN[33] (the Presidential Association on National Minorities); it has invariably worked ruthlessly against the oppressed ethnic groups of the Philippines. It was established as a private charity in 1968 with a board made up of representatives of the interests that stood to gain everything from exploitation of tribal territory. The tribes were not represented. Before PANAMIN there had been a government agency called the Commission on National Integration, which had been founded in 1957 to respond to many complaints about encroachment on tribal land. The more vociferous representatives of the tribes were brought into this organization which, rather like the Chittagong tribal council, was created to defuse and disarm. For a while the Commission and PANAMIN co-existed, in theory the private and public expression of the same benevolent principle, but when in the 1960s multinational companies extended their activities and the reaction of the tribes was to resist, the Commission was no longer able to act as a forum or as any sort of safety valve. In 1975 it was disbanded and PANAMIN took over its responsibilities; having ceased to be a charity, it became the government agency with all the extra authority that could be derived from serving a military dictatorship. There would be no more nonsense about tribal participation in the protection of tribal rights.

It was in the personal interest of President Marcos and the ruling elite, many of whom are members of his own family, that PANAMIN should ensure that tribal minorities do not stand in the way of the wishes of the World Bank, or of foreign investors, particularly

Americans and Japanese. And there was never a decision which displeased the President. The founder and chairman of the board is Manuel Elizalde, whose family ranks as the fifth richest in the Philippines and has extensive business interests, including a major investment in sugar production. He was able to use his position to his own advantage during the period of martial law, 1972–81, by having seven Manobo families removed from tribal land in Mindanao so that the Bukidnon Sugar Company could move in. Some families decided not to co-operate, but PANAMIN was already defining its role as partly that of an enforcement agency and, with the help of its own staff, the police and company employees, evicted them and destroyed their houses.

Neither the chairman's views nor his financial connections are exceptional. Another member of the board of trustees is Jaime Zobel de Ayala, whose family controls the largest business empire in the Philippines. In partnership with the Japanese Mitsubishi Corporation and the Elizalde family, he is engaged in mining in Mindanao, a tribal region which PANAMIN holds in trust nominally for the benefit of its inhabitants. Other members of the board have similar vested interests. The American chairman of the Paper Industries Corporation of the Philippines must reconcile his loyalties to the industry with his obligation to protect the tribes of Agusan and Surigao provinces from the destruction of their means of subsistence. Sixto Roxas, representative of BANCOM, the largest investment house in the country, has to balance the rival claims of the tribes of Mindanao with the removal of what little remains of the natural forest, and has conflicts of interest in six mining companies and many farms and plantations. Yo Shion Shio combines the pharmaceutical industry's motivations with those of a custodian of tribal welfare, and the rest of the list is a selection from the Who's Who of leading Filipino commerce and industry.

Were it not for the board's record such credentials could be forgiven. In some societies it would be sufficient to declare an interest for it to be forgotten. But PANAMIN rapidly developed into a counter-insurgency organization and, encouraged by American fears of Communist infiltration, saw, or pretended to see, every instance of tribal resistance as evidence of politically inspired unrest. It has, since 1975, recruited military men and organized local militia to act on its behalf, in collaboration with the police and the army. Not surprisingly this has had exactly the opposite effect from the one intended. The

Moslem communities of the south have united behind the Moro United Liberation Front in the quest for complete independence; the heterogeneous tribes of the majority of the islands are giving increasing support to the New People's Army, the fighting arm of the National Democratic Front. Reacting to this PANAMIN supporters have moved towards the idea of building strategic hamlets on the Vietnam model to hinder the rebels. And so the spiral turns. It is as though the authorities are mischievously keeping to an agreed ritual to see if Marxism will arise and do to capitalism what Marx said it would do.

The World Bank's influence here has harmed the tribes because, as in Brazil, loans are intended for road building and the provision of hydro-electric power and irrigation. The actual funds inevitably pass through government hands, giving opportunities for patronage and self-aggrandizement, and little trickles down to the rural poor. Nowhere is the contrast between welfare of the tribes and interests of the construction companies more plainly demonstrated than in the building of dams, and more than forty hydro-electric projects are due for completion by the end of the century. Nearly all of these lucrative contracts are for the development, that is, the alienation of tribal lands and to this end large numbers of settlements and a vast acreage of farmland are being flooded. Compulsory migration is enforced by the National Power Corporation, which has been granted special powers to evacuate tribes forcibly from their ancestral lands. PANAMIN's reaction to compulsory migration has been summed up by one of its officials: 'We resettle the natives on reservation lands which we manage for them. From then on, any company that is interested in the land deals with us.'[34]

The National Power Corporation's special authority to evict is matched by the National Development Corporation's assumed right to allocate tribal land to the lessees of its choice. Presidential decree 472 created an obligation for the lessees of forests and pasture to produce food within the concessions and this opened the door to three multinationals which have virtually taken over fruit production and canning throughout the islands: Castle and Cooke, United Fruits and Del Monte. United Fruits monopolizes the banana trade, operating through the Tagum Agricultural Development Corporation which is owned by Antonio Floirendo, described by the Anti-Slavery Society as a 'close friend'[35] of President Marcos. Tribes sometimes resist the confiscation of their land for use by multinational corporations. When, for instance, United Fruits expanded into the territory of the Ata

Manobo tribe in 1979, to use the land for banana cultivation, one of the tribesmen who resisted was caught and tortured to death, an act which naturally stiffened resistance by the tribe as a whole.[36] Castle and Cooke's plantations are in Mindanao, and in 1981 they were paying their workers about one-thirtieth of the rate which they were paying in Hawaii.[37]

The friends and relatives of former President Marcos were appointed to key commercial and military positions in the state and are, at the same time, the links with the multinational corporations. The chairman of Zamboanga Wood Products, financed and owned by Boise-Cascade, is Simeon Valdez, an uncle of Marcos; the Cellulose Process Company and the Cellophil Resources Corporation, whose appetite for wood is denuding the nation's forests at an alarming rate, are subsidiaries of the Herdis Group of Companies headed by Herminio Disini, related by marriage to Imelda Marcos; the Construction and Development Corporation of the Philippines is controlled by Rodolfo Cuenca, fund raiser for Marcos's presidential campaign – and so on. It may well be argued that at the top of an illiterate state nepotism is unavoidable and even desirable, and, had the position of advantage not been so cruelly abused, there would be nothing very remarkable about it – it has been the rule rather than the exception in most forms of society. The unsavoury truth is that the members of the oligarchy have taken advantage of a ubiquitous fact of tribal life: the occupants of ancestral lands have held those territories by undisputed tradition for centuries and, as has been seen, rarely have registered title. And since by presidential decree lease of lands has been granted to multinational corporations, tribal groups, in Mindanao especially, have found that the only way they can avoid being expelled by the police and PANAMIN is to agree to be tenants on their own farms. That, for the present, is their best hope. Those who do not co-operate suffer the fate of a group farming in Mansaka. Davao Timber wanted the land, and eviction of the community occurred with PANAMIN support.

The Anti-Slavery Society had little confidence that its recommendations for reform would be given serious consideration by the Philippine government and its most practical request is addressed to the external sources of financial support. The American government, the World Bank and the Asian Development Bank are all asked to see that funds for development projects are 'withheld where such projects have been imposed without consultation with and against the wishes and interests of the affected populations'.[38] Whether, now that they are better informed, investors will consider human rights when committing funds remains to be seen. Judged by their past record the outlook is bleak, and similar pessimism was felt about the Society's other recommendations until President Marcos fled the country in February 1986. It called for the release of political prisoners, and for withdrawal of military forces from tribal lands to be followed by an independent international enquiry into military abuses. Most importantly, as a prerequisite to extension of secure land entitlement to the tribes, it has recommended that PANAMIN be abolished; with this obstacle removed, 'open and democratic processes' should be used to plan all future development in tribal territory. These are the bloodless solutions. Recent developments suggest that, if the Society's advice is disregarded, the Communist party of the Philippines will soon be in a position to exert a very different sort of influence on the heirs to the Marcos regime.

As a day seldom goes by without Western commentators referring, perfectly accurately, to Soviet Russia as a single highly centralized political unit, it is only too easy to forget that it is nominally a union of socialist republics. Today the republics are no more than administrative regions; although they may act as safety valves for ethnic identities, they have no autonomy. Where national minorities were concerned, recognition soon after the death of the last Tsar of apparently autonomous or self-governing states within a large federal structure was a clever device of Lenin's to prevent the Russian empire from disintegrating. Among the racial minorities placated in this way were the Crimean Tartars, whose Crimean Autonomous Soviet Socialist Republic was officially established in 1921, and their subsequent history provides an insight into Communist attitudes to tribal minorities.

Even forgetting Lenin's motives for encouraging national minorities to form identifiable parts of a larger whole, the supposed autonomy of the republic had other reasons to wither away: within the administrative area of the Crimea, the Tartars, descendants of the legendary Mogul hordes, were only a quarter of the population, and during their brief period of dominance, when their language and art flourished, they were not popular with the local Bolsheviks from whose revolution they had seemingly profited. But the main cause of their downfall was their commitment to Islam. In 1927 the atheist central government focused its attention on the Moslem republics and stage by stage their objectionable elements were removed. In the Crimea the nationalists who had been politically active before 1917 were the first to go. Then the Moslem leaders were selected for elimination and at the same time thousands of peasants were deported, mainly to Siberia. Had it not been for the intervention of the Second World War, the national identity might have been extinguished.

The present sufferings of the Crimean Tartars are mainly the result of their fathers' behaviour during the war. Stalin's policies had alienated them to such an extent that when the Crimea was invaded, many, though by no means all, were keen to enlist in six German-officered battalions or collaborate in some other way to ensure the defeat of soldiers whom they no longer regarded as fellow-countrymen. They must have known that in the event of Germany's defeat they would be shot, and that is exactly what happened to many of them. What they did not realize was that the entire civilian population would be deported, under conditions similar to those used for the Jews by the SS, to Siberia and other inhospitable localities thousands of miles away. 'It was a journey of lingering death in cattle trucks, crammed with people, like mobile gas chambers' and there was no exemption for loyal service to the Soviet Union: 'They took the Red partisans of the Crimea, the fighters of the Bolshevik underground, and Soviet and Party activists.'[39] It was May 1944 and women, children, invalids and old men formed the bulk of those transported, unsupported by their menfolk who were still away fighting at the front and had to follow later. 'Death mowed down the old, the young and the weak. They died of thirst, suffocation and the stench.' When all the Crimean Tartars had been deported it was found that 46 per cent of them had died en route.[40]

The Crimean Soviet Socialist Republic was abolished and even though, in 1967, after much agitation, Crimean Tartars had the stigma of collective responsibility for collaboration with the Third Reich officially removed, their status was, and is, defined as 'citizen of Tartar nationality formerly resident in the Crimea'. While the ethnically distinct Volga Tartars, numbering about 6 million, have their own Soviet Socialist Republic – for what it is worth – the Crimean Tartars, numbering less than half a million, are denied the homeland to which constitutionally they are entitled. Taking into account the mythical nature of the autonomy which the Soviet Republics enjoy, it may be asked whether it matters very much that Crimean Tartars lack this hypothetical refuge. There are several answers to this question, one of which is that, like the Jews of the Diaspora, these Tartars want a place in which they may exist as a group and want this to be their ancestral land; unlike the Jews they are content to remain within the overall political structure of the Russian Communist state. But other answers are more down to earth. Under Soviet pass laws the Crimean Tartars have too often been denied residence permits for their homeland, by a policy of apartheid in reverse that can only be construed as indicating an authoritarian wish to divide and conquer, to alienate people from the land of their forefathers, or to destroy by assimilation. Of about 6,000 who arrived in the Crimea after a brief relaxation of restrictions in 1967, only three single men and two families succeeded in becoming officially registered. The rest were compelled to leave, some by forceful deportation.

Attempts to return to the ancestral land became more frequent after collective political rehabilitation was decreed[41] in 1967, but by 1975 less than 1 per cent had succeeded in settling legally in the Crimea and about 3,000 who had settled in violation of the pass laws came under pressures ranging from denying their children access to schools to bulldozing their houses. Throughout this period many Crimean Tartar representatives visited Moscow to complain, but several hundred found themselves barred from hotels on account of their nationality. In 1978 events took a turn for the worse: evictions led to protests, protests to trials, and each side fell back on more drastic measures. Two Crimean Tartars killed themselves, one by self-immolation, and wide publicity was given to a cause which had already become part of a wider movement dedicated to democratizing the Soviet Union from within. Two months after the ritual suicide and a demonstrative funeral the USSR Council of Ministers passed a decree banning from the Crimea all who infringed any of the petty regulations connected with the pass laws. It was an unpublished decree, but its details soon became known to Andrei Sakharov, who asked President Brezhnev if it might be repealed. Sakharov described denial of 'the right to residence, based on ethnic identity' as 'the most dangerous form of discrimination' and complained about the way in which the military units responsible for 'mass actions of expulsion of the Crimean Tartars from the Crimea' were carrying out their task:[42]

> During the actions of deportation, staged as war-time punitive expeditions, heart-rending incidents of violence and brutality

> towards the elderly, children, women and the ill take place. The personal property of Crimean Tartar families is often destroyed or ransacked. . . . Houses purchased are destroyed or confiscated. Extremely severe and unjust measures of punishment are used toward those who protest against the above actions, up to long-term imprisonment.

The protests have continued, as have arrests and detentions.

What now? Ukrainian settlement in the Crimea has made a wholesale return of the exiles a difficult practical proposition, but Crimean Tartars would be willing to agree to a phased return. According to current Soviet thinking they have put down firm roots in Uzbekistan where much economic damage would be caused by their withdrawal, but again a gradual approach is all that is needed to prevent existing structures from being undermined. The Soviet authorities also worry about other aspects of the problem, mainly to do with precedents. What applies to Crimean Tartars and the Crimea could apply, though not in terms of a Republic, to the Mesketians and Georgia; and what applies to the freedom of movement or emigration of ethnic groups has relevance to the Volga Germans, who have abandoned the idea of re-establishment of their Republic, and to Jews. But why not?

Always sensitive about the implications of the Helsinki agreement on human rights, the Russians appear to be making errors which correspond to those of the Third World dictators. Their intransigence is driving basically loyal Soviet citizens underground, so that sympathetic responses are sought from outside the Soviet Union. However, although the USSR has not ratified the Indigenous and Tribal Populations Convention, Article 35 of its own constitution guarantees citizens the right to use 'their native language', and in recent years the authorities have had the courage or the prudence to make educational concessions to this effect which have benefited Crimean Tartars in exile in Uzbekistan. Next they might consider implementing Article 13 (i) of the Universal Declaration of Human Rights: 'Everyone has the right to freedom of movement and residence within the borders of each state.' For the Crimean Tartar language and culture to survive it is essential for the people to be allowed to reunite in their ancestral land, and what better Marxist justification could be cited than Lenin's original policy? Re-establishment of the Republic, seen purely from the Russian point of view, would bring back to the faith a disillusioned tribe and need involve no political loss. It is unlikely that an Aborigines

Protection Society team will be invited to check up on what changes, if any, actually occur. And for the Jews and the Volga Germans, non-governmental organizations can do little more than draw attention to the second part of Article 13 of the Universal Declaration of Human Rights: 'Everyone has the right to leave any country, including his own, and to return to his country.'

Chapter 9

Migrant Workers and Forced Labour

Each Member . . . undertakes to apply, without discrimination in respect of nationality, race, religion or sex, to immigrants lawfully within its territory, treatment no less favourable than that which it applies to its own nationals.

ILO MIGRATION FOR EMPLOYMENT CONVENTION (REVISED), 1949 (NO. 97), ARTICLE 6

. . . 'forced or compulsory labour' shall mean all work or service which is exacted from any person under the menace of any penalty and for which the said person has not offered himself voluntarily.

ILO FORCED LABOUR CONVENTION, 1930 (NO. 29), ARTICLE 2

Whilst everyone knows what migrant workers are (though few without personal experience can comprehend the numerous stresses which they may endure), the concept of forced labour, an integral part of all forms of slavery, is not clearly regarded as a specific condition. All labour of chattel slaves is forced, and every other category of slavery considered so far – Nazi disposable, child exploitation, female exploitation, debt bondage and serfdom – has as its basic constituent the exaction of labour from the slave by force. Why does forced labour qualify for separate treatment? The recent decision by the International Labour Organization's library to catalogue debt bondage separately from forced labour provides a clue to a simple difference which might be clarified by saying: all slaves are liable to be used for forced labour, but not all forced labourers are recruited from the various slave groups. Faced with changed circumstances – war, revolution, or a strong economic compulsion – previously free individuals may undergo a period of forced labour to meet a need which is temporary but easily extended. Taking a global view, the main agents and instigators of forced labour phenomena are governments. Nevertheless, powerful economic trends play a considerable part, not only in encouraging governments to adopt drastic measures, but in driving workers, who are not visibly coerced, to submit apparently voluntarily to demeaning conditions of labour. Migrant labourers are often drawn into the forced labour market because world prices of a particular crop have fallen, and they must shift or starve. And because the causes of forced labour, except within established totalitarian societies, are to do with political or economic instability, periods of rigid implementation of the forced labour regime are often temporary or seasonal. Where this is true it is frequently the case that sudden urgent demands of an unstable regime, or recurring needs of an over-simplified economy, are being met.

Whereas the Forced Labour Convention (no. 29) of 1930 aims to eliminate forced labour generally, the 1957 Abolition of Forced Labour Convention (no. 105) requires the removal and prevention of several defined types. It seeks to prevent member states from using forced labour 'as a means of political coercion or education or as a punishment for holding or expressing political views or views ideologically opposed to the established political, social or economic system', and it goes on to forbid its use 'as a method of mobilising and using labour for purposes of economic development' or 'as a means of labour discipline' or 'as a punishment for having participated in strikes' or 'as a means of racial, social, national or religious discrimination'.[1] The ideological use of forced labour is one of the essential features of established totalitarian states which take advantage of an exemption clause in the 1930 Convention allowing forced labour 'as a consequence of a conviction in a court of law'.[2] The crime committed by these nations involves what may be termed 'penal slavery', used as a punishment for illegal strike action or other labour offences, and is certainly a common means of 'racial, social, national or religious discrimination'. As such it is better considered in its own right (see chapter 10). Outside Communist countries and the more stable Fascist dictatorships a common violation of the Conventions is 'mobilising and using labour for purposes of economic development', and when that labour is migrant it can be more vulnerable than the citizens of the host state. One of the worst examples of this type of slavery is to be found in the Dominican Republic; an even more extreme case, with which the Dominican situation will be compared, is that of Equatorial Guinea.

The West Indian island of Hispaniola, after a turbulent history which has bequeathed a population almost entirely descended from West African slaves, is now divided into two countries; the western third is the former French territory of Haiti, the remaining two thirds comprise the Dominican Republic, formerly Spanish. Both countries are poor, but the great profitability of the Dominican sugar plantations is one reason why Dominicans do not suffer conditions quite as appalling as those of their immediate neighbours. Nevertheless what sugar wealth is not absorbed by the seemingly inevitable multinational tends to find its way into the pockets of a small section of plantation owners and politicians or soldiers. Traditionally there is animosity between Haitians and Dominicans and this can easily be manipulated, as it was when, in 1937, the Dominican ruler, Trujillo, ordered a massacre of Haitians living in Dominican territory some 12,000 were killed. Today Dominicans still fulfil a predatory role in their relationship with Haitians, though exploitation is arranged by subtle means, and a sinister aspect of it is the part played by the rulers of Haiti. Such are the grim realities of physical survival in Haiti that citizens of that country imagine that life will be less harsh in the environment of their enemies beyond the frontier.

It is a disillusioning fact that those peoples which have suffered the indignities of slavery can be among the most merciless when an opportunity comes for them to enslave others. Haiti saw the first successful uprising of slaves after the French Revolution, but no lessons were learned from this historical landmark and in the nineteenth century, when Haiti wanted to unify the island of Hispaniola, unenlightened attitudes to the freed slaves of the Dominican Republic were one factor which prevented union. During the twentieth century both countries followed the now familiar road to tyranny; the Dominican Spanish-speaking mixed races suffered under Trujillo and then Balaguer; in Haiti the Duvalier family acquired control of the mainly Creole-speaking black race. Neither population had reason to rejoice when in 1966 the ruling elites of the two countries reached an agreement about provision of Haitian labourers to work on Dominican sugar plantations.

When allegations of forced labour reached London in 1978, the Anti-Slavery Society assembled all the available information and prepared a report which it submitted to the United Nations Working Group on Slavery in 1979. The original source of information was a 'responsible person' who had to remain anonymous, but, despite the reliability of the evidence, the Society was obliged to make its own investigations. It sent Roger Plant, a researcher with appropriate experience and linguistic ability, who made his enquiries during two visits to the island in 1982. He spent seven weeks in the Dominican Republic and ten days in Haiti, and his findings formed the basis of another report which the Anti-Slavery Society put before the Working Group on Slavery in August of the same year. Two months later Plant appeared with other witnesses before a Commission of Enquiry of the International Labour Organization and the Commission itself carried out investigations in both the accused countries in January 1983.

In its 1979 report[3] the society pointed out that the centuries-old differences between the two population groups were being sustained by religious and educational bodies and the press, and that the outcome of all this propaganda was a divided labour force unaware of the need for unity. The workers, who even lacked a common language, were finding it too difficult to resolve their mutual antagonism for effective trade unions to be formed and, consequently, were at the mercy of the Dominican government and the estate owners. The report went on to draw attention to statistics which, translated into visible reality, must generate extreme resentment among Dominicans. Sixty per cent of their population live at a level of poverty that condemns 60 per cent of their children to death before the age of 5. And among these distressed Dominicans must be the 25 per cent of the population who are unemployed, only too aware that 90 per cent of the cane-cutters are Haitians.

Half the nation's revenue comes from the labour of 26,500 Haitian migrants, and most of these (19,000[4]) have come as a result of payments under contract to the Duvalier family of sixty pesos (about seventy dollars in 1982) per head. Many more Haitians, about 12,000, fleeing from oppression and a 65 per cent unemployment rate, enter the Dominican Republic illegally, and some of the contract money is paid to frontier guards so that they will turn a blind eye to illegal migration. The illegal migrant is even more submissive than his officially purchased counterpart and there are few impediments to his exploitation.

In much the same way as Jewish survivors of the Nazi extermination programme speak of slavery as 'a ticket to survival',[5] Haitian illegal migrants justify their willingness to work under Dominican oppression by saying that Haiti is 'even worse'.[6] The report did not express the idea in these terms, but it was noted that Haitians knowingly entering the Dominican system were prepared to bribe guards on both sides of the border for the privilege; the guards were thus beneficiaries from both sides of the transaction. Eagerness of Haitians to enslave themselves is more easily understood when it is appreciated that during the few years before the Anti-Slavery Society's investigations began some 20,000 fellow citizens died of starvation. Once migrants have crossed the border the customary procedure has been for them to be taken in trucks to an enclosure at a staging post, where private landowners or representatives of the State Sugar Council, the Vicini family or Gulf and Western have come and paid ten pesos for each man before taking him by truck to the estate where 'the workers live in camps under conditions of extreme squalor, deprivation and danger to health'.

A direct danger to health was seen to be the result of causing a labourer's pay to fall below the cost of his food. He is paid fortnightly for the amount of cane cut and loaded and, being illiterate, he is unable to check whether the weigher has been crediting him with the correct amounts on his receipt. Moreover, if there is an appreciable delay in the sun before transport is available, because dry cane weighs less than fresh, he will lose some payment anyway and the weigher will have more scope to defraud him. It is seldom possible for him to survive for a fortnight without credit, and so his receipt may have to be sold at a loss of 10 per cent. Five per cent of his pay will go to the Haitian government to hold as an incentive for him to return at the end of the season.

Other complaints were made about arbitrary detention, cruel conditions of transportation and obstruction of unions, before the report summed up the position:[7]

> A high proportion of the 280,000 Haitian immigrant workers and their families in the Dominican Republic suffer from chronic malnutrition, a variety of preventable diseases, high maternal and infant mortality, illiteracy and hopelessness.
>
> This is due to deliberate neglect: neglect by employers and Government alike of housing, sanitation, hygiene, diet, clothing, education, pay, medical and welfare services and of every obligation to their workers prescribed by law and dictated by morality, by common sense and even by self-interest. Most important of all, maternal and child care are virtually unknown.
>
> This workforce is kept in a condition of abject, unprotected

subservience for reasons of private and governmental profit by means of foreign aid which is used *inter alia* to maintain a large force of police.

The basic cause of the conditions described is the same as that of trans-Atlantic slave-trading two centuries ago; namely the profit motive abused, coupled with ignorance and apathy on the part of the consumer who votes with his stomach.

The Anti-Slavery Society then recommended that its report be brought to the attention of the Dominican Republic, Haiti and the United States of America, and to a number of international agencies, of which the International Labour Organization was one. The ILO, armed with the report and other information already in its possession, then set in motion the necessary procedures[8] which, in brief, would establish whether or not the countries concerned stood in violation of the Forced Labour conventions which they had ratified. Both states in Hispaniola were on trial, but the Commission lacked the powers of a court and, should the accused be found guilty, the sentence would be no more than a public rebuke, which might, or might not, benefit the peoples of the island.

Apart from a difference of 5 per cent in each case when assessing the Dominican unemployment rate and the number of Haitian cane-cutters, there was no disagreement between the ILO's and the Anti-Slavery Society's figures, but the resources of the ILO, together with other serious specific complaints received from independent sources, meant that it was better placed to find out the whole truth. Its ultimate findings vindicated the Anti-Slavery Society's summing up, and on the way to that vindication, a composite picture of enslavement of migrant workers for forced labour was steadily built up. Some complainants were better informed than others; they ranged from private individuals to representatives of the churches, trade unions and educational bodies, and their complaints, put together with the Anti-Slavery Society's charges, meant that the Commission had many detailed allegations to investigate.

Despite the diversity of accusations put before the Commission, members did not lose sight of the nub of their brief which was to find out whether Dominicans were purchasing workers from Haiti for use as forced labourers; and from the start it was useful to be hearing evidence from two governments allegedly guilty of the same violation of human rights, but which, apart from the profit motive, have no other basis for a friendly relationship. When, for instance, Haitian government representatives were asked awkward questions about the amount of protection the Haitian embassy could offer Haitian migrants, they were quick to say that complaints were forwarded to the Dominican ministry of external relations.[9] But receipt of such complaints was not admitted by the Dominican representative. And when Haitian officials were asked about the Dominican security forces arresting Haitians legally resident in the Dominican Republic, destroying their identity documents and compelling them to work on the sugar plantations, the officials said that they were unable to deny the allegations.[10] The Dominicans, for their part, 'categorically denied' that such things had occurred.[11] A favourite ploy which, because the Haitian regime had undergone no recent political changes, could only be used by the Dominicans, was to imply, when all other means of explanation had failed, that some irregularities alleged to have happened on their territory could have occurred under a previous administration.

The value of on-the-spot investigations was continually demonstrated. The Commission was able to see for itself that the labourers, particularly on the state-owned plantations, were prisoners. They described 'an extensive system of personnel surveillance'[12] with contingents of uniformed soldiers and policemen installed on site and, in addition, armed rural guards, many of whom were former soldiers, on the staff of the plantations. Some attempt was made by plantation officials to explain away this heavy armed presence by saying that property must be protected, or brawls prevented, but other officials, and the guards themselves, admitted that the purpose was to prevent escapes and to recapture those who ran away at night. Representatives of trade unions pointed out that Haitian inspectors also make sure that the recruited workers are arrested should they try to leave, and this was confirmed by the Dominican Minister of Labour and the state sugar board spokesman, who both argued that under the contract with Haiti no worker had the right to leave his plantation.

Inevitably much of the Commission's time was devoted to making enquiries about the agreements and contracts which have been used to justify delivering the Haitians into conditions which, despite some hastily added paint, were found to be as squalid as the complainants had claimed. The true nature of the inter-governmental agreement was most clearly indicated not by an answer, but by a point-blank refusal to answer on the part of the Haitian Minister of Social Affairs,

Theodore E. Achille. The Commission, after referring to the substantial payments made to the government of Haiti for recruitment expenses, simply wanted to see the accounts. The minister replied that the question was abusive,[13] and spoke of contesting the accusation which had been made by the complainants before the international court of justice. But, as about two and a quarter million American dollars was paid each year and did not appear in the Haitian budget, the Commission could not feel confident that it had all been spent on such a limited area of expenditure. Nor did the minister inspire confidence when it came to discussion of workers' contracts. As it gradually became apparent that for some years the texts of the contracts had not been published, that the labourers had not received copies, that they were in any case written in a language that the labourers did not understand, the minister fell back on the illiteracy of his fellow citizens as his defence. 'No peasant', he remarked, 'can distinguish between a contract and a flower.'[14]

The Commission, having noted with disapproval Mr Achille's opinion that, because the people could not read, the government had a responsibility to conclude a collective contract for 19,000 of them, turned its attention to the other 7,500 who had entered the Dominican Republic illegally. The Dominican authorities had every right to arrest and expel them; instead they imprisoned them within the plantations, where, lacking documents of any sort, they were even more defenceless than the contract workers. Why were they not expelled at a time when 20 to 25 per cent of the Dominican workers were unemployed? The only logical explanation was that they, like their contracted counterparts, would work for a fraction of the minimum wage, and, as was suggested from time to time, would go anywhere to get away from the Duvaliers' semi-official thugs, the Volontiers de Securité Nationale, better known as the 'Tontons Macoutes'. And, better still, the host country was spared the per capita contract fee which worked out at well over 100 US dollars, not counting the cost of transportation.

The Dominican authorities, as the purchasers of the seasonal workers, had made an investment in them and adopted various methods to improve the yield. Encouragement of illegal immigration, permanent and temporary, was one way of lowering the cost of sugar production; another way was to deduct a set proportion of the weight of each load of cane, ostensibly to compensate for theoretical losses on the way to the mill. Weighers admitted to the Commission that they were under instructions to credit the workers' receipts with 150 pounds less than was actually placed on the machine.[15] A further deduction of 10 to 15 per cent could then be made if the receipt, which was negotiable, was exchanged at one of the state sugar board shops, where, to recoup another element of an already low payment, prices of essential foodstuffs were notoriously high.[16] Then there was the vexed question of 'incentive' or deferred pay.[17]

As mentioned above, the Anti-Slavery Society's report had drawn attention to deductions made from the labourers' wages, on the understanding that they would be paid in Haiti after the end of the season. The Commission looked into this practice with some care and soon found that, among other things, the deduction could amount to as much as a quarter of a worker's earnings. Questioned about this the Haitian government claimed that until the 1979–80 harvest, 0.50 pesos was deducted from the total payment of 2.33 pesos for each tonne of cane cut and loaded, and the money was remitted to the Haitian embassy whose reponsibility was to arrange payment as or after the labourers left for Haiti. But the embassy denied receiving the payment and insisted that the state sugar board retained it for distribution at the frontier. In its turn the state sugar board produced receipts signed by the Haitian ambassador for over a third of a million dollars. The date on the 1977 receipt was so long after the workers' repatriation that it gave support to the cane-cutters' insistence that their money never reached them. After the 1980-81 harvest the Dominican Republic ousted Haiti from the position of advantage which it had enjoyed with regard to this aspect of exploitation by substituting a system of vouchers. These, unlike the fortnightly receipts, were not negotiable. They accounted for all deferred wages and the Commission was shown vouchers from the previous year which workers had been unable to cash.

Although, since the Dominican Revolutionary Party had taken over in 1978, there had been less political repression, the unions could still do little or nothing to organize the labour force in its own defence. Contracted Haitians, fearing that the inspectors provided by their own government were Tontons Macoutes sent to spy on them,[18] kept well away from any activity which could be thought to be political, and those living or staying illegally on Dominican territory refrained from joining unions for fear of displeasing their employers and thereby risking deportation.[19] Attempts to form unions within their own country had met with police intimidation and sequestration of funds[20] in violation of the Freedom of Association and Protection of the Right to Organize Convention, 1948 (no. 87), which Haiti had ratified in 1979. But the Commission emphasized that there was nothing unusual in this behaviour. Haitians were used to periodic suspension of constitutional rights;[21] in 1960 'full powers' were granted to the President of the Haitian republic and he had suspended many guarantees. He could legislate by decree for most of the year without reference to the assembly, and his record was only fractionally worse than that of Dominican rulers at least until 1978. Unfortunately, although the new Dominican government had given assurances that reforms were in hand, there was little evidence to show that any real progress was being made.

The Dominican military forces came in for much criticism for their role in the illegal recruitment of sugar workers. It was alleged that they were not subject to civilian control and 'arrested Haitians and decided their fate at will'.[22] In 1979, 1980 and 1981, when cane-cutters were needed the army rounded up resident Haitians at will and transported them under armed guard to the plantations; Haitians caught crossing the frontier illegally were liable to be imprisoned without food for several days and made to part with any money they might be carrying. Moving about the country members of the Commission saw that in the northern region in particular, 'the presence and great influence on everyday life of the military forces were very evident'[23] and they heard from many independent witnesses how the soldiers 'persecuted and exploited the Haitian population in a wholly arbitrary manner'.

The Commission's report was published in 1983 and a summary of its findings and recommendations was heard by the United Nations Working Group on Slavery in July. The complaints were shown to be fully justified by an investigation that had uncovered even more iniquities than had been alleged. Having described the situation as it had found it, the Commission underlined the changes that were needed. It was essential that the agreement between the two governments be replaced by one which could be clearly seen by all to incorporate guarantees for the workers. Texts should be freely available in a language that the people can understand, and individual contracts should be given to each worker in the official language of the country, with a duplicate text in Creole. This prime recommendation may seem to fall short of what anti-slavers might reasonably demand; should not an arrangement which has regularly delivered unprotected people into a system of forced labour be scrapped altogether? Those unfamiliar with the paradoxes of slavery might well be tempted to take this view, but if implemented it would place an even less tolerable burden on the peasants of Haiti. Seasonal migration is not an especially desirable means of earning a living even when conditions are good. For Haitians, however, it provides the only hope of survival until a process of democratization means that foreign investment can benefit the population as a whole.

The Commission went on to say that sums paid to the Dominican government for recruitment should be no more than was actually spent, and should appear in public accounts; and furthermore, steps should be taken by both governments to ensure that recruiting officers could neither demand nor receive bribes from those seeking recruitment. But, as the governments themselves had been guilty of this very crime, it is difficult to imagine them making what the Commission could only describe as 'appropriate arrangements'; and as the Commission continued to make wholly admirable recommendations, the absence of powers of enforcement cast doubt on the validity of the whole procedure. Confiscation of passports should stop; the army and the police should be subject to the law; workers should never be forcibly confined within the plantations, and those who try to confine them should be adequately punished; there should be a new labour code or the old one should be amended; trade union participation should be encouraged; the minimum wage regulations should be enforced, and related to a maximum number of hours worked; it should be possible to cash wage receipts without deductions; incentive payments should be bonuses that are unconnected with basic earnings; labour inspection arrangements should be reformed. And the position of illegal Haitian residents, who form a special class of exploited labour in the Dominican Republic, was the subject of detailed recommendations about 'regularization' of their status: 'it is not legitimate for a State to leave in a status of illegality workers whose employment it accepts as necessary to the functioning of the economy, the more so when they are employed in undertakings belonging to the State itself.'[24] Finally the Commission suggested that the two governments sought the International Labour Organization's help in implementing its recommendations. During 1984 an Anti-Slavery Society source was able to say that the message had been received loud and clear in Washington (in 1977 President Carter had described the Dominican Republic as 'a model for human rights'), and that recently there had been 'some slight improvement in conditions'.[25]

Lest it be thought that the circumstances which have sustained forced labour in Hispaniola are unique and therefore unlikely to provide lessons for environments outside the Caribbean, it is useful to see an example of the extent to which similar patterns can be discerned elsewhere. Across the Atlantic there is a comparable dictatorship that shares the Dominicans' Spanish imperial legacy and which, despite more diverse pressures from rival imperial powers, has almost uncanny parallels with its Caribbean counterpart. In Equatorial Guinea, as in Hispaniola, a country preyed upon the needs of a neighbouring territory's work force, and a system of exploitation grew up that was even more oppressive than that practised by Trujillo's successors.

Equatorial Guinea, one of Africa's smallest countries, is in two parts, of which the better known to European travellers is the island of Fernando Po, a few miles off the coast of Cameroon in the Gulf of Guinea; it is about seventy-five miles from Nigeria and is less than 800 square miles in area. On modern maps it appears either as Macias Nguema, the name of its first post-independence dictator, or since his death, as Bioco. The other part, separated from the island by 100 miles of continental shelf, is Rio Muni, a coastal enclave of about 10,000 square miles sandwiched between Cameroon and Gabon. Spain acquired Fernando Po two centuries ago and subsequently Great Britain negotiated with Spain an agreement giving her naval facilities. A British consul became governor of the island and the Navy was used for, among other things, intercepting slave-traders and annexing what is now Nigeria. For some time Spain's involvement on the island was minimal. In 1858, however, it became clear that the introduction of West Indian cocoa seeds was going to lead to a remarkably profitable trade. As a measure of the greatly increased Spanish interest in this tiny imperial possession a Spanish governor-general was appointed. The African population of the island, the Bubis, soon proved inadequate to meet plantation needs and a reliable mainland source of cheap labour was sought. After a period of negotiation France was persuaded that Spain had a prior claim to the north-western corner of Gabon and in 1900 Rio Muni, part of the ancestral land of the Fang, passed to its new colonial master.

As it happened Rio Muni never did fulfil its intended purpose of providing a work force for Fernando Po's plantations. Apart from the fact that the Spanish did not occupy the interior until the African independence movement was well under way, and the Fang did not prove to be as co-operative as the Bubis, the Spanish plantation owners of Fernando Po had long since made their own arrangements and established a system of forced labour which looked to the north rather than the east for its work force. Nineteenth-century Liberia, the state of the freed American slave, anticipated twentieth-century Haiti by using a contract system that had many identical features of exploitation, and which persisted until the 1930s; Fernando Po was the Dominican Republic of the relationship. The labourers, the 'Krumen' or 'Kruboys' of innumerable Victorian and Edwardian memoirs – and some of later date – were recruited by fellow Liberians who acted as Spanish consuls and received commission on a per capita basis.[26] Payment, after deduction for keep, was by voucher which a returning worker had to present to his consul and, as on the Dominican sugar plantations in the 1980s, there was nothing to prevent the illiterate from being defrauded.

The condition of the Krumen was notoriously degrading and led to much disease which they took back to Liberia. They were misled into believing that they had agreed to work for short periods of time and, once on the plantation, many were kept there against their will for three years, instead of the one year for which they had been contracted. Missionaries and traders were well aware of what was going on, but the climate of the times was such that little notice was taken of exploitation of black labourers who, whatever might be happening to them, had apparently undertaken their current tasks voluntarily. And so it continued until a disappointed candidate[27] for the Liberian presidency of 1927 created a sensation in the United States, where he made a number of complaints about the conduct of Liberian ministers, including the accusation that they kidnapped young men for forced labour in Fernando Po and would not investigate charges of brutality.[28] The immediate outcome of the protest was a request from President King of Liberia that the League of Nations send a commission to carry out an enquiry into what he insisted were false accusations. A commission was appointed and reported in 1930 that:[29]

> a large proportion of the contract labourers shipped to Fernando Po and French Gabon from the southern counties of Liberia have been recruited under conditions of criminal compulsion scarcely distinguishable from slave raiding and slave trading, and frequently by misrepresenting the destination.

Mention of French Gabon was no surprise as Krumen were regarded as fair game along much of the West African coast.

The supply of Liberians to Fernando Po diminished from the moment that the President heard the accusations and the Spanish authorities at once diverted their recruiting activities to the traditionally migrant populations of eastern Nigeria. They did so precipitately and almost immediately the British Nigerian administration had to respond to allegations of improper methods of recruitment and slavery by attempts to regulate migration; but complaints continued to be heard throughout the remaining years of British rule. In so far as the colonial administration in Nigeria had success in this field it lay mainly though inadvertently in influencing Spain to concentrate its attention on the Rio Muni hinterland, which had remained neglected until the late 1920s. But, as the occupation was only completed after the Second World War, there was really no time left to draw the reluctant Fang into the plantation system. They were 'a fiercely independent and tradition-conscious ethnic group'[30] and drew inspiration from the liberation movements of neighbouring territories only too happy after independence to grant them asylum should they wish to escape from the imperial power. Moreover their tribal lands straddled the frontiers of Cameroon and Gabon and, as the Fang of these countries shared in newly acquired freedoms, so the Fang of Rio Muni became increasingly nationalistic. Their aspirations were not lost on the Spanish, who appreciated that if, in the long term, they were to salvage their trade interests, they would have to alter their strategy. The Bubi of Fernando Po were slow to develop nationalistic tendencies and were producing 90 per cent of the cocoa of the country as a whole. If Fang labourers were imported to the island they might jeopardize the entire plantation system; far better to allow them a measure of autonomy and arrange for co-operative Bubis, only 6 per cent of the overall population, to control half the seats in the governing council.

The birth in 1964 of a legislature responsible for internal self-rule was insufficient to stave off demands for complete autonomy and, despite Spain's efforts to engineer Bubi leadership, thereby ensuring continued Spanish influence or, as a good second best, the secession of Fernando Po, a Fang was elected president in 1968, the year of independence. Although Macias Nguema assumed responsibility for one of the least efficient states in Africa, and foreign observers were by this time used to post-independence political upheavals, few can have foreseen the wholesale violation of human rights which was about to take place. By means of a series of decrees[31] set in motion by real or feigned fears of a *coup*, a one-party system was inaugurated and all powers were transferred to the President. He was the sole source of laws and he alone could authorize their implementation. In 1972, in addition to acquiring various ministerial posts, he was proclaimed commander-in-chief of the army and President-for-life. In 1973, by which time his executive authority had given him the power to impose the death penalty for a wide selection of offences which might be interpreted as threats to himself or to the welfare of his country as perceived by him, the independence constitution was abolished and with the help of a new constitution the dictatorship gained a facade of respectability; the President-for-life's powers were in no way diminished by some seemingly democratic clauses. One of these required election of the President by universal suffrage, and was immediately suspended.

Within weeks of independence the usual consequences of rapid concentration of power in the hands of those unaccustomed to it were beginning to be felt. There were rumours of an impending *coup* and the Chief Minister of the pre-independence government was arrested and several suspected plotters, including a former governor of Rio Muni, were murdered in prison without even the pretence of charge or trial. Among those believed to be rebels were Nigerians, members of the race which, because of its crucial contribution to the forced labour economy, outnumbered all other nationalities or tribes on the island of Macias Nguema. A state of emergency was declared, many Spaniards fled the country, and there followed a chain reaction of repressive acts directed at all groups which could conceivably pose a threat to Macias's authority. Bubi leaders suffered terribly: one, a deputy president, died of thirst in prison, another had his eyes gouged out and died of gangrene. Some tortures and murders occurred behind locked doors, others in public.[32]

One of Macias's priorities was the establishment of his own version of the Tontons Macoutes from within the only political party which he allowed to exist. Only one point of view was allowed and, as a result, the educated class of Equatorial Guinea, including more than two-thirds of the government in power at independence, disappeared and will not be seen again. As the normal safeguards of individual human rights were dismantled the Nigerian work force soon began to feel the effects of national degeneration. Nearly 100 Nigerians were killed in 1970–71 for demanding wages. Not long afterwards the

Nigerian government behaved as the Haitian rulers would behave; despite the fact that some 20,000 Nigerians had left the island in 1972, it agreed to supply 15,000 replacements. Not until 1974 did it begin to take heed of reports of cruelty; even then it hesitated before suspending the agreement and, as was happening in Hispaniola, migrants continued to find their way to the plantations illegally. They would still be doing so, no doubt, as recruiting them was a profitable activity, were it not that in 1975 brutality was used not merely on Nigerian plantation labourers but also on embassy staff. This altered official policy instantly and by the end of the year between 10,000 and 20,000 Nigerians had been evacuated, mainly by air. The Nigerian government had realized at last that its citizens were the victims not only of repressive plantation owners but of Macias's personal attitude to labour and power.

Unlike the Haitians, the Nigerians were rescued by their government, albeit late in the day, and Macias reacted as Balaguer was to react in 1978, when the Duvaliers held out for a higher price: he made his own citizens go into the plantations to save the crop. Reports indicate, however, that conditions in Equatorial Guinea were much worse than the Dominicans were to suffer. In March 1976 Macias issued a decree making it compulsory for citizens over the age of 15 to work on government plantations or in government mines as manual labourers, but as during the previous month *The Times* correspondent in Madrid had reported the testimony of exiles who had fled rather than submit, the law was simply legitimizing an existing state of affairs:[33]

> More than 20,000 people are being pressed into slavery to work on cocoa plantations in Equatorial Guinea . . . . [Refugees] claimed that President Macias Nguema had ordered his guards to arrest between 2,000 and 2,500 people in each of the 10 districts of the mainland province of Rio Muni, to be used as unpaid forced labour on the island of Macias Nguema, named after the 'lifetime' President. The order was reportedly issued about two weeks ago at a congress in Bata, capital of the Rio Muni province, of the Workers' National Union Party, the only political party allowed.

Suzanne Cronjé, author of many works on human rights issues, assessed the position in Equatorial Guinea for the Anti-Slavery

Society and her report[34] formed the basis of the Society's submission in August 1976 to the United Nations Sub-Commission on Prevention of Discrimination and Protection of Minorities. Perhaps the most remarkable feature of the report, apart from horrifying details of persecution of potential political rivals, Roman Catholic priests and missionaries of several persuasions, is that it denounces United Nations agencies for silently co-operating with a monstrous regime; and the Society did not shrink from giving full weight to this denunciation at Geneva. The United Nations presence in this comparatively small community is extensive and printed matter[35] issued to its personnel by way of warning reveals intimate acquaintance with the state and its failings. Moreover, United Nations agencies staff members have been witnesses of irregularities and on at least one occasion have themselves been victims of Macias's strong-arm methods. The President believed that the Haitian director of the United Nations Development Programme and some of the staff were plotting against him; he therefore closed down the office and had them beaten up.[36] It is believed that only their passports and the need for continued United Nations assistance saved their lives.

Besides the United Nations many organizations and governments have ignored or profited indirectly from ignoring Equatorial Guinea's forced labour programme, and co-operated with the rule of terror. Suzanne Cronjé pointed out[37] that the Organization of African Unity has only the excuse of non-interference in the domestic affairs of member states to justify silence about inhumane treatment of black Africans by black Africans. No such inhibitions prevent the United Nations from denouncing 'the crime of apartheid' and the Organization of African Unity would only improve its reputation if it were to denounce coercive measures; and it would make a great leap forward if it were to take the additional decision to make human rights reforms a condition of continued membership. It is true that such a move would embarrass other member states, but a valuable precedent would have been set and even Equatorial Guinea would not dismiss an OAU decision as the product of 'Spanish capitalist imperialism', the alleged source of the few unfavourable comments which, before the Anti-Slavery Society report, were made about the way in which it conducts its internal affairs.

Spain must, of course, accept much responsibility for the way in which Equatorial Guinea was inadequately prepared for independence, but the Spanish government is guiltless of the charge of disseminating any sort of adverse propaganda about its former colony. Its guilt derives from the reverse crime of condoning forced labour and other forms of repression in order to maintain a profitable economic relationship. As happened not infrequently when a colony gained autonomy, political control by the imperial power simply gave way to economic control. According to the International Monetary Fund, after Equatorial Guinea achieved independence 90 per cent of its exports continued to go to Spain and 70 per cent of its imports were still Spanish.[38] Faced with the ugly facts of forced labour, Spain prevented by law the publication of any information about Macias's state. Anti-Spanish blustering by the dictator was a small price to pay for economic domination.

Other countries with sufficient vested interests in Equatorial Guinea to make them fully acquainted with the country's human rights violations are China, Cuba, France, USSR, Sweden, Switzerland and, until 1976, the United States of America. As the list indicates, implications go far beyond the cocoa harvest. Funding derived from international sources makes investment in grandiose schemes, such as the Malabo administrative complex and the construction of Bata harbour, attractive to overseas firms, and the French with their nearby Community involvements have been well placed for gaining contracts for these developments and for acquisition of forestry concessions. The Swedes are developing a telecommunications system; the Swiss are operating jointly with the French in Forestry and the Swiss Red Cross has renovated Malabo hospital.[39] While the Chinese, Cubans and Russians all have excuses to be in the region – the Chinese assist with irrigated crops, the Cubans originally had timber interests and the Russians have a deep sea fishing concession – the presence of all three cannot fail to have strategic or political significance, particularly as they arrived at a time when the United States was believed to be gaining influence in West Africa and was rumoured to be in pursuit of local uranium deposits. Relationships between the United States and Equatorial Guinea were broken off in 1976. Nevertheless Suzanne Cronjé feels that 'the possibility of important uranium deposits might supply one answer to the intriguing question about the international silence on Equatorial Guinea in the face of the excesses of the Macias regime'.[40]

In 1976 the Anti-Slavery Society recommended that the United Nations justify the presence of its agencies in Equatorial Guinea or withdraw them immediately. What did happen, but not until after

Macias had been deposed by his nephew and executed in 1979, was an investigation of conditions in Equatorial Guinea, at the invitation of its new leader, by a United Nations Commission on Human Rights mission which reported in 1980. It found that Macias's rule had reduced the people to living on roots and berries, that only one doctor was to be found in the hospitals that remained, the road system was crumbling away and there were no ships in the harbour. A potentially rich country had been desolated. The new government showed no wish to abolish forced labour; on the contrary, it was 'rather inclined to justify it'.[41]

Why did the United Nations help to prop up a regime which it knew – unofficially – to be tyrannical? The answer to this question is likely to lie entangled in a bureaucratic web for ever. There is, however, another pertinent question. The resident representative of the United Nations Development Programme was occupying a privileged vantage point in Equatorial Guinea, supervising the spending of large sums of money extracted from the taxpayers of the world and intended for the deserving poor. Why did he keep silent for eleven years? Unfortunately the answer to this question is too easily found. According to his terms of reference, and those of his colleagues in all other United Nations agencies and funds, he is required by the General Assembly never to engage in any activity without the knowledge and approval of the government of the host country. Speaking out on forced labour or threatening withdrawal of funds might help 20,000 unpaid workers to return to their families, but it would not meet with the approval of those who hold the whip hand at the United Nations. As one observer commented, 'Solzhenitsyn was right to call UN the United Governments Organization.'[42] And sometimes a government is only one man.

The Dominican Republic and Equatorial Guinea are examples of countries which at stages in their recent history have used the workers of adjacent states for forced labour. This has directly or indirectly helped to sustain in each a dictatorial regime. The preference has been for migrant workers who can be lured into an alien society by false promises and then held either by economic necessity or by coercion, but sometimes the country of origin has intervened and removed or withheld the labour force. When this has occurred the poorer citizens of the host states have been hastily conscripted as forced replacements. In North America and Europe, however, it is more difficult to expose coercive practices. Economic pressures alone are enough to bring in foreign workers seeking an improved standard of living or in flight from poverty in, say, Mexico or Turkey. It would be wrong to describe the adult migrants as forced labourers, but in many cases the term is exactly applicable to the children.

Many children of Mexican migrant workers in California, where during the 1960s a quarter of the state's farm workers were minors,[43] were found to be suffering from sunstroke, food poisoning and serious complaints caused by irresponsible use of chemical pesticides. Fruit and vegetable harvesting here, and especially also in the states of Ohio, Oregon, Maine and Washington, have long been dependent on a regular and plentiful supply of seasonal labourers and, as adults are needed for such tasks as cutting and packing, the simpler work is often left to children aged 6 and upwards for whom by comparison it is heavier. In 1971 it was estimated[44] that in Washington state 99 per cent of migrant children over 6 years of age were engaged in agriculture, working long days in temperatures approaching 38 degrees Celsius. Maine made use of Indians and French Canadians who, as family units, worked a ten-hour day picking potatoes; use of chemical sprays on the potato crop caused injury and sometimes death. In Ohio some 30,000 migrant workers included many small children used for the sugar beet and cucumber harvests.

In the United States not all the children abused in this way are migrants, but almost all those who can clearly be described as forced labourers have been introduced to the work by migrant parents. Widespread exploitation in this context has been caused partly by appropriate federal legislation being originally intended for the industrial workplace, partly by local unwillingness to enforce adequate state legislation because profits would fall, and partly by the urgent economic needs of the migrant labourers who, traditionally, have had to commit the family as a whole in order to survive. The parents who so readily coerce their children in the service of a rich host country that has not ratified the relevant ILO conventions are usually themselves the victims of the repressive economics of their own countries of origin.

As in the United States, forced labour by migrant workers in the European Economic Community is limited to children, though exploitation of the guest workers in general is a common phenomenon. In 1983 the Anti-Slavery Society reported[45] to the United Nations Working Group on Slavery on the position of Turkish migrant children in West Germany. The Federal Republic has a bad record for exploitation of the young, as has been seen in the field of prostitution, and child prostitution is one area in which the record is particularly nasty. However, a substantial amount of suffering is inflicted on Turks by Turks; German responsibility lies in allowing the children of immigrants to be forced into unpaid, or poorly paid, labour on German soil, many of them in the open-air markets of Berlin. In defiance of the law which makes it an offence to employ children under the age of 16, many well below this minimum age are required to report for heavy work at 4.30 in the morning, and boys of 9 and 10 years often receive only food in payment. A particularly ugly feature of the practice is the holding of child labour markets each autumn, again early in the morning, when hundreds of children gather and await selection.

While asking the Working Group on Slavery to invite the West German government to take the necessary measures to wipe out this problem, the Anti-Slavery Society emphasized that Turkish children are the victims of sham mining apprenticeships in Belgium and – with Moroccan children – of prostitution in France and Holland. It gave other examples of exploitation of migrant children (in the United Kingdom and, again, France), and stressed the need for 'a coherent international policy' to eradicate the abuse in Western Europe.

A final example is needed to show how a migration can itself be forced within a nation in order that forced labour may be manipulated by a government for its own ends. It also serves to show that politicians of both left and right can be equally vicious when the urge to enslave comes to the fore. In 1980 the Ethiopian government decided to use forced labour to harvest the sesame crop in Humera, part of Western Tigray. As part of a land reform programme owners of large farms in Humera had already been expelled so that a state farm might be created, but by 1980 output was falling and a decision was taken to bring 57,000 hectares under cultivation by sending government employees and town-dwellers to work the land. False promises about pay and conditions were made; nevertheless, despite a wireless announcement that all members of these two groups must go to the sesame fields, too few responded and security officers therefore resorted to brute force. People were beaten with gun butts and 'herded into trucks and transported under the most appalling conditions, with no food, unable to sleep or even urinate, except over the side of the trucks'.[46]

More than 14,000 men, women and children from Addis Ababa

alone were crammed into only 202 trucks to be transported for eight days to the state farm; *en route* the women were made available to the army camp at Sanja and some did not survive. About 900 were brought from other towns. On arrival at Humera it was found that there was no accommodation of any description, and the first task was to find materials and build huts. What followed showed that the followers of Lenin had little to distinguish them in practice from the followers of Hitler:[47]

> According to Ethiopian government supervisors at Humera, 1,626 people died during the whole operation. They included those who died from sickness, persons beaten or tortured to death, those shot whilst trying to escape and those who simply starved. Several hundred people just disappeared, including women who were abducted for sexual purposes. Some, who had demanded to go back to Addis Ababa, were told that they could return and were then rounded up and sent back to the fields.

But some of the forced labourers who survived escaped to the Sudan where they were able to give their testimony. Thanks to their evidence, carefully cross-checked by the Anti-Slavery Society, the few with ears to hear were soon aware of the cruel and counter-productive means adopted by the Ethiopian authorities to further their aims. A few years later the results of the misguided priorities of Ethiopian agricultural policy were seen on the television screens of the world. An agricultural programme which concentrated on exports and the acquisition of foreign currency might have benefited the ruling elite. As everyone knew, even if forced migration and forced labour were morally justifiable and productive, and they are neither, concentration on sesame cultivation, even using urban workers for the purpose, was not compatible with maintenance of minimum subsistence standards elsewhere. The overseers of Humera may be amused that drought has attracted much of the blame for the famine which they did nothing to avert; one can only hope that those responsible for allocation of international aid will not allow official Ethiopian denials of Anti-Slavery Society reports to deceive them into lowering their guard. As a general principle, funding should be conditional on receipt of invitations to inspect the human rights position of the intended beneficiaries.

People separated from their country of origin can be psychologically as well as physically at a disadvantage when it comes to an unexpected application of force by the host country. They are the most easily enslaved element of the population, as Hitler appreciated when he chose to persecute Jews and Gypsies, and much recent history has shown that it is easy to galvanize prejudice to the disadvantage of a supposed 'enemy within'. If, as is usually the case, there is historical evidence of friction between the races, propaganda can be directed against minorities who are cut off from their legitimate protectors and therefore easier to subdue. The Dominican Republic and Equatorial Guinea have both shown their preference for the enslavement of foreigners – Haitians, Liberians, Nigerians – but they, like Ethiopians, have had no compunction about initiating forced migrations of their own citizens. Solutions will have to be varied to help rectify conditions within diverse environments, but, lured by the carrot of aid, access may be granted more frequently to United Nations teams by Third World countries; while in, say, the United States and the European Economic Community, federal legislative development and extension of the powers of courts across the old national boundaries should bring enforcement of ratified international conventions several steps nearer.

CHAPTER 10

POLITICAL/PENAL SLAVERY

Each Member . . . undertakes to suppress and not to make use of any form of forced or compulsory labour . . . as a punishment for holding or expressing political views or views ideologically opposed to the established political, social or economic system.

FROM ABOLITION OF FORCED LABOUR CONVENTION, 1957 (NO. 105), ARTICLE 1

The 'Standard Minimum Rules for the Treatment of Prisoners' adopted in 1955 by the first United Nations Congress on the Prevention of Crime and the Treatment of Prisoners states that 'All prisoners under sentence shall be required to work'.[1] And, given that a serious crime has been committed, most law-abiding citizens would agree that, quite apart from theories of retribution, it is right and proper that a prisoner should work, partly to contribute towards his keep and partly, or principally, for the sake of his own health and self-respect. This is not slavery; it is justice and common sense. Loss of freedom is sufficient for punishment, for deterrence, or for the protection of society, and work is, or should be, a means of rehabilitation given to the prisoner for his own benefit. However, much hinges on whether a crime has actually been committed, on the impartiality of the court and on whether prison conditions are up to a minimum standard suitable for the incarceration of a human being. Where the crime is invented by the security forces or where activities which are encouraged by the Universal Declaration of Human Rights are defined by agents of a government as crimes, people who are not criminals by any stretch of the imagination may find themselves deprived even of the tenuous protection which has sometimes been afforded to those born into slavery. The penal slave works unseen, usually coerced by a petty official of the invisible apparatus of the totalitarian state.

Others, including wholesalers and retailers in Western democracies, profit from the sale of his products. His anonymous master is the ultimate criminal of the case, but there are many others who must take their share of the guilt.

Mention has been made (in chapter 4) of the consequences of inadequate supervision of farm jails in South Africa, a country in which the white rulers are not following the conventional ritual of political disengagement; but penal slavery has been one of the phenomena of the era of precipitate imperial withdrawal and one does not have to look far to find an example of a Third World ruler forcing whole sections of the community into penal servitude. When President Samora Machel took over Mozambique, after the Portuguese were forced to abandon it in 1975, he was impatient to bring about change and soon established re-education centres in remote parts of the country, where thousands of prisoners are still held. There the detainees, many of whom are held for their supposed political beliefs, must labour in order to survive. One of Machel's milder inspirations was to send 1,600 university students and staff to do agricultural or industrial work during their summer vacation, so that they would shake off colonial habits and elitist notions.[2] They were the lucky ones. Many others disappeared at this time and relatives heard nothing of their fate until a 'Legality Offensive' was launched during 1981–82 and scapegoats were punished for negligence. Initially government repression was directed mainly at whites and white women were forced to share prison cells with men and to work in the fields stripped to the waist.[3] Naturally there was a rapid exodus of whites from the country and now the Mozambican ruler, like his neighbouring Third World counterparts, seems content that the strong shall enslave the weak, regardless of colour.

China, a country which has been keeping the fair side out for some time, partly in order to lull the fears of capitalist Hong Kong, has until recently managed to keep Western eyes well away from its 'Reform through Labour' programme. In the north-west provinces are many rehabilitation camps out of sight of ordinary Chinese citizens, let alone foreign observers, and within their confines tens of thousands of inmates underpin the economy of the region while a slow process of brainwashing rids their minds of political or religious deviation. Sentenced to work in factories or farms or mines, suspected deviants are kept on a subsistence diet and gradually persuaded to come round to the orthodox opinion on all matters thought significant by their political masters. In Qinghai province, for example,[4] the governor, Huang Jingbo, who once spent eleven years in prison for apparently doubting the omniscience of Chairman Mao, admits to having about 10,000 prisoners labouring their way to redemption. Some, including Buddhist monks stripped of their robes and forbidden to practise their religion, work under the supervision of armed guards in a local factory making hydro-electric equipment; others cultivate the province's ten prison farms. The adjacent province of Gansu has admitted to 20,000 penal labourers and thanks to their presence the region is beginning to exploit mineral resources to the extent that it can make a significant contribution to the economy of the People's Republic as a whole. Although an amnesty thinned the ranks of the work force in 1979 and 1980, during 1980 it was decreed that young people could be despatched to the camps without trial should local officials regard them as delinquent in any way. It is believed that China's penal labour force runs to hundreds of thousands, rather than tens of thousands, but apart from the above details which came out in August 1984, little reliable information has emerged. To get a more thorough impression of penal slavery today one must turn to the Soviet Union.

In Geneva in 1984 two letters were handed to an Anti-Slavery Society representative[5] who was about to assume the role of Expert, as members of the United Nations Human Rights Sub-commission are termed. Both had been written in Russian and one had been found in a shipment of wood in 1979 and began:[6]

> 'We need your help, people
> We don't know to which country – socialist or free – the production is going to be exported, made by the slave labour of Soviet prisoners. In any case, however, whatever is the political system of the importing country, we address our appeal to the people of the country and to its government on behalf of Soviet political prisoners. . . .'

It was signed N. Akhmetov and V. Mikhalenko. The other, dated 1983, was from the first of these, Nizametdin Akhmetov, who had by this time already served eighteen years and was in Krasnoyarsk penal camp expecting a further sentence of three years for attempting to write a letter to the West, for monitoring the practices of the prison guards, and for having had discussions, presumably political, with fellow prisoners. During this period of detention he was severely beaten up.

When the details of Akhmetov's experiences became known in the West he was adopted as a Prisoner of Conscience by Amnesty International (in the charge of Group 1563: Heidelberg) and the usual attempts were made to bring about his release. Before long his talent as a poet led to membership of PEN clubs and it was the Writers in Prison Committee of International PEN which initiated renewed agitation in Geneva in 1984. Until then, apart from the poetry, there had been nothing very exceptional about Akhmetov; he was just another politically undesirable penal slave, deserving of no more sympathy than countless others for whose welfare Amnesty and like-minded organizations work. But things changed in 1984 when it became known that the prisoner, who was now apparently suffering from thrombosis in both legs as a result of his physical punishment at Krasnoyarsk, had been transferred to Alma-Ata Special Psychiatric Institution, where efforts would be made to modify his implacable opposition to totalitarianism by use of sophisticated drug techniques. PEN International, who appreciated that matters had become much more urgent, feared for both body and mind. Some of the drugs used experimentally for brainwashing and personality modification – Aminazin, Haloperidol and Triftazin – could worsen the thrombosis and make amputation inevitable. PEN also noted, with the opportunism that comes naturally to human rights workers, that 'as he is probably unable to work now, they might let him go'.[7]

The outcome of Akhmetov's plea is not yet known. There is a long-standing invitation for him to go to Heidelberg, where he could settle permanently and have the medical treatment he needs. He is, as PEN International described him, 'very small fry (as compared to Sakharov)',[8] but he is representative of a large population of slaves in a category seldom spoken about at the Working Group on Slavery. In a way they are well known, as latter-day inhabitants of Solzhenitsyn's 'Gulag Archipelago', but a world which imagines that slavery died with William Wilberforce often behaves as though the Gulag died with Joseph Stalin; and it is too easy to forget that those who labour in the many hundreds of camps or prisons dotted about the Soviet Union are not necessarily vicious criminals in need of the good old-fashioned discipline of work. Some are there because they wish to worship God in their own way; some have simply succumbed to a belief in freedom of speech; some are, or were, active dissidents.

Whatever the alleged offence, the innocent will work side by side with the criminal and their joint industry will make an appreciable contribution to the Soviet export market.

Communist autocratic attitudes to work in general, and to political and penal slavery in particular, owe much to Russia's imperial past. The founding fathers of the Soviet Union, those of Russian parentage, had all been born into a society which, as a matter of course, expected that those who departed from the accepted line would be despatched to one of the extensive penal colonies in Siberia. Towards the end of the nineteenth century the number of political prisoners serving their sentences in these colonies was approaching 30,000,[9] but it could not be said that their penal activities furthered the material interests of the Tsar or of the state; they were merely being punished. After 1917 the new rulers lost little time in extending the scope of penal servitude by increasing the criteria of recruitment and translating a comparatively modest punitive scheme (though huge by the standards of its day) into a gargantuan slave labour system. The Bolshevik regime directed its slaves into many ambitious projects including the construction of five major canals and hundreds of miles of roads and railways, the building of towns beyond the Arctic Circle, and the profitable development of coal, iron and gold mines.[10] Although the means were morally indefensible, some of the results were remarkable enough to give the impression to naive visitors that Stalin's methods worked. In humanitarian terms, all that the achievements proved was that descendants of Russian serfs, like the freed slaves of other nationalities, became utterly merciless when possessed of power.

The system of Soviet slavery, which in the middle of the twentieth century reached its highest point in terms of numbers and its lowest level in terms of human physical degradation, owed much to Naftaly Aronovich Frenkel, who after a brief period of collaboration with the GPU (the State Political Administration) had been imprisoned by it. Like so many who co-operated with the autocratic new regime which was already noted for its fickle contradictions, Frenkel, whose loyal services were in a shady area of currency transactions, had earned himself a place in a prison cell. However, unlike many others similarly rewarded, he managed to ingratiate himself with the authorities and in 1927 became a privileged prisoner enjoying a degree of freedom. By 1929 his ideas on the utilization of prison labour were thought sufficiently developed along practical lines compatible with fashionable Bolshevik thinking and he was granted a personal interview with

Stalin, which ensured his future success as an architect of penal administration.

Completely new attitudes to penal servitude had dated from 1918, when it was realized that Marx's well-known view that productive labour is the only means of reforming a prisoner could conveniently serve Lenin's wish to eliminate all opposition. Anticipating Krupp by more than twenty years, it was swiftly appreciated that a combination of Marx and Lenin was best achieved if one took 'correction through labour' to mean 'destruction through labour',[11] and a motley collection of camps had grown up in order to dispose of political prisoners by this means. Such an arrangement seemed satisfactory enough while there was unemployment in the Soviet Union, but by 1928, shortly before Frenkel achieved real authority, the nation was being urged to industrialize; it was bracing itself for the first five-year plan and the party was heavily committed to the liquidation of the comparatively well-to-do peasant class known as *kulaks*. Suddenly there was a need to recruit so many workers that paying them could not be contemplated – nor would it be practicable to allow them to choose their task or place of work. On 26 March 1928, therefore, penal policy was radically altered;[12] it was decreed that, apart from more rigorous treatment of class enemies, and much stricter camp discipline, there should be extensive organization of unpaid forced labour from which the state should profit. The existing camp population was insufficient to meet labour requirements, which meant that new camps would be built and more people arrested. In other words, the prison system was assuming, with its other legitimate and illegitimate responsibilities, the role occupied in Western democracies by the labour exchange.

Frenkel, who soon became famous as works chief of the Belomorsky canal construction project, was not the only architect of the intricate confederation of slave labour camps, but he repeatedly impressed his mark upon it and, after achieving the rank of General in the NKVD (People's Commissariat of Internal Affairs), eventually presided over a part of the empire which had a sort of autonomy. One of his lasting contributions was the division of prisoners into four classes: Group A worked daily throughout the sentence, Group B was responsible for running the camp when not available for other work, Group C comprised all who were ill, and Group D consisted of those restricted to the punishment cells. The net result of Frenkel's classification was that all prisoners physically able to work always did so in one capacity or another. And to ensure that assignments were completed, Frenkel arranged for food allocations to be directly related to production.

The digging of the Belomorsky canal, the first great project which was a proper test of penal labour, was the prototype for many grandiose schemes. A strict time limit was imposed: twenty months were to be allowed to link the Arctic Ocean with the Baltic Sea, a distance of 140 miles, through rocky ground with a gradient necessitating the building of nineteen locks. On this prestige enterprise 100,000 prisoners were occupied using hand tools and horses; they built the dykes of earth, the floodgates of wood. No advance provision was made for accommodation and inevitably many froze to death. Dead workers were easily replaceable, making the estimated toll of 100,000,[13] a number equal to the initial allocation of slaves, not the exaggeration that at first it seems. When completed, the canal was soon redundant; at sixteen feet it was too shallow for the type of vessel which might have found the route useful. But its uselessness can be ascribed to the single error of a vain dictator; it does not invalidate the use of slave labour on economic grounds. A bold project was completed on time, and this was taken as proof that prisoners, lacking capital investment and the benefits of contemporary technology, could move mountains. Henceforth Soviet economic needs could with certainty dictate penal policies. It would not be a case of work being found for prisoners, but prisoners being found for work.

But the Soviets had to have ideological justification for what they did. It was one thing for a wide gulf to yawn between theory and practice, quite another for there to be no theory at all. Consequently, although conditions in the majority of camps from 1918 until 1956 were little better than in the concentration camps of National Socialist Germany (and in some cases no better), there had to be some rationalization. Naturally in a Communist state explanations took the form of justifying a restoration of the required balance between the individual and society: 'All Soviet penal policy is based on a dialectical combination of the principle of repression and compulsion with the principle of persuasion and re-education'[14] and, from the same author, 'With the assistance of revolutionary violence the corrective-labour camps localize and render harmless the criminal elements of the old society.' An economist might express the justification differently: the state, if it is to develop along the lines prescribed by the Party (and ordained by the history of the class war), has material aims which demand an inexhaustible supply of manpower. The best labour force is one which requires no payment for its services, can be moved to any site at any time, has no domestic obligations, and has little or no educational, medical or hygienic needs. All it needs as an incentive is the prospect of increased rations.

Eight years in the camps, starting in 1945, gave Solzhenitsyn experiences which led him at a later date to compare the lot of the post-war political slave labourer with that of a serf of old Russia. The Second World War had for a brief period pushed back the imperial boundaries of the Archipelago, as Solzhenitsyn christened the multitude of penal islands which made up the concentration camp empire, but at the same time it had consolidated Frenkel's grip on a large area of north-eastern Russia which had little else in it but prisoners. Partly with hindsight Solzhenitsyn came to identify Frenkel as the source of much that constituted the new serfdom and even from the perspective of a serf recorded a kind of respect for 'the evil sorcerer' who served 'the evil king'[15] so craftily. Under the Tsars serfs were also divisible into four groups. Corresponding to Frenkel's Group A was the majority whose unpaid labour sustained the estates; Group B was made up of household serfs who ministered to the immediate needs of the estate owners; Group C was limited to serfs too ill to stand; and Group D to those who had broken the rules.

Although there were close similarities, history favoured the pre-revolutionary serfs. The estate owner would whip those who displeased him; under Communism the camp chief made use of a younger tradition of imaginative inhumanity whereby the alleged transgressor was made to suffer in a punishment cell or took his place within a special punishment work regime, where cruelty to the individual took precedence over the individual's opportunities to labour for the state. Either way exposure to insanitary conditions in subzero temperatures on reduced rations was calculated to break the spirit of the strongest detainee. The closest resemblance between the two eras of serfdom, apart from the more squalid environment which the twentieth century prisoner has had to endure, has been in the way of life of the men and women responsible for attending to internal camp tasks. Estate owner or camp chief could help himself to serf or slave of either sex on impulse. But when it came to work, the social objective of penal slavery, the traditional serf had all the advantages and Solzenitsyn wrote[16] with feeling about the denial of customary serf rights to the penal slaves of his generation. From his own experience he knew that a penal slave worked the longer day – he never started or finished in daylight – and that he could never look forward with confidence to a respite on Sunday. The serf could not only depend on the sabbath day being sacrosanct, he could expect many religious holidays in addition to Christmas and Easter and would have a place of his own, a hut, in which to relax. The penal slave, who dreaded the anniversaries of the Revolution which were celebrated by the imposition of a harsher regime, lived in a series of barracks and never knew from one day to the next where he would be based. He could not even rely on having his own bunk.

Serfs wore clothing which was their personal property and had their own primitive equipment and horses to help them with their work. Penal slaves had winter and summer uniforms and no personal possessions whatsoever. Serfs generally lived as families, while separation was the rule in the Gulag; husbands and wives, fathers and sons would be despatched to different camps and accidental reunions meant that one relative must be sent elsewhere as soon as possible. Serfs were tied to one estate, whereas penal slaves were for ever on the move to other camps, suffering extreme privation on the way. It could be argued that a man became a serf by accident of birth; and he was born to a life from which there was no escape. The penal slave, felt that, since he had reached the age of 12, much the same had been true of his destiny; moreover, as during Stalin's time his sentence was infinitely renewable, the likelihood of his achieving manumission seemed no better than the serf's. But above all the serf had a value. However unfeeling his master might be, self-interest dictated that his property should live to work another day. In the camps there was no such reassurance; should the prisoner die he was immediately replaceable, at no cost to the Gulag.

Putting to one side the inhumanity of the Gulag, what have the camps achieved? As the pyramids can still do something for the reputation of some ancient Egyptians, so some Soviet constructions may perpetuate the memory of Stalin, whose attitude to human life closely resembled that of some of the Pharaohs. Apart from this it may be said that the loss of life and the undermining of a sense of pride in national identity did much to postpone a Soviet victory over the Germans. Some individuals will have grown proud and fat on their individual islands, but the cost of administering an institution which has enslaved millions has always exceeded the saving in costs which unpaid labour, now usually deployed secretly, is supposed to bring. The far-flung Archipelago has never been cost-effective. In the short term the camps enjoyed a political success; that is to say that during Stalin's lifetime they destroyed his enemies. But they gave birth to generations to whom the existence of political or penal slavery is an anathema derived from personal experience or the memory of murdered or tortured relatives and friends. It is just possible that, as Hitler's camps gave a great impetus to the foundation of Israel, Stalin's may stimulate the development of democracy within the Soviet Union.

In 1956, after Khrushchev had announced the disbandment of most of the camps, nearly three-quarters of the prisoners were released, but the system proved to be too intimately bound up with the general apparatus of state, and indeed with prevailing ideology, for it to be abandoned altogether. As if by way of reaction, the camps which remained were soon topped up by means of a resurgence of arrests, and the non-criminal prisoners, a minority of the prison population as a whole, still had to be assessed in hundreds of thousands. They were, and are, to be found at different levels of a partially reformed system which has evolved into a carefully differentiated penal hierarchy. As ordinary Russian citizens are compelled by article 60 of the Soviet constitution to do socially useful work, it is hardly surprising to find that the work ethic still permeates an Archipelago which, though shrunken, is probably the most extensive in the world. The law-abiding citizenry must choose to labour at one of a limited choice of occupations; convicted persons, as is laid down by the United Nations Standard Minimum Rules for the Treatment of Prisoners, must undergo a period of labour. However, the emphasis is still on 'corrective' labour, a concept which in the context of the USSR is capable of more than one interpretation. For the criminal intake it can mean either training in useful skills or the purging of wickedness; for 'politicals' the curing of deviant inclinations may be the aim. Both types of prisoner are still used in attempts to satisfy the old Stalinist wish that they yield profits for the state.

For the criminal and 'political' alike (constitutional guarantees of religious freedom mean that religious offenders are often brought to trial on political charges), there are four main penal regimes: general or ordinary, hard, strict, and special. Politicals are assigned to strict and special regime camps as a rule, for such offences as 'slandering' the state (maximum penalty seven years) or possession of banned political literature (maximum penalty seven years, followed by five years' internal exile). Religious offenders are frequently found guilty of the first of these crimes and, during the 1980s, they, together with politicals and criminals, find themselves set increasingly diverse tasks calculated to lower the labour costs on goods destined for sale in the West. Many of the products made by the penal labour of prisoners who have committed no crime by the standards of any civilized state are marketed in Great Britain.

For the purposes of one report, testimony from twenty former prisoners[17] has been used to find out the extent to which old principles of coercion survive and, where possible, to identify the products which contain components made or assembled by prisoners. Although in the Tuva region many prisoners work on military installations, penal labour is no longer squandered on massive schemes of doubtful utility, calculated to impress the international community of Russia's great leap into the modern world. Feelings of inferiority in that department of life have been successfully overcome by many achievements, including those of the space programme. Today the need for low-priced consumer goods to earn foreign currency has meant that different priorities are given to the large obedient work force confined in prisons and camps. One has only to look at the electronics industry to see how penal slavery has been adapted to meet worldwide demand for cheap products which, if normal labour costs were added, would be unable to undercut competitors in the capitalist market.

Manufacture of wireless and television sets by, or rather for, 'Vega' is typical of current penal production methods. Vega's factory at Riga, one of four in the Soviet Union, receives its components from four prison camps, and the Moscow corner of the enterprise depends on Vladimir prison for its supply of resistors. Dr Cronid Lubarsky, after serving five years as a political prisoner, described what actually happens at Vladimir:[18]

> The working conditions are unbelievable and everything is made in cells which, in spite of their ten square metres, contain three men, beds, a w.c. as well as all the equipment and machinery necessary for the work. In the cells the lights are switched on at 5 o'clock in the morning and are not put out until 10 o'clock at night. And only an hour's break is provided for exercise. In order to attain the target of 3,000 resistors a day, it is necessary to work more than eight hours a day. The lighting and ventilation are dreadful and consequently the prisoners' sight and health deteriorate rapidly. The first signs of headaches appear after three months and there is total physical degradation after six months.

And then, as though Frenkel were still alive, Lubarsky goes on to say, 'The daily ration of food is measured according to the volume of production.' Products may have changed, but the new masters are careful to retain much that is fundamental to a coercive system.

Camp OU 85/8 in the Crimea and another camp in Mordovia make the cabinets for the sets; Camp 36 in Perm makes spare parts and electronic elements for cathode ray tubes; and once assembled and exported to Great Britain, the sets are distributed by the Technical and Optical Equipment Company of Edgware Road, London. It is not unknown for a set to be returned to the retailer when the purchaser understands that its manufacture depends to a large extent on the labour of non-criminal prisoners, but this does not deter the Technical and Optical Equipment Company, whose policy has been frankly expressed: 'We have nothing to do with human rights.'[19]

The brand name, Vega, is not limited to electronic apparatus. The word means 'the reliable choice' and is proving to be a handy label for many different products of the modern Archipelago. In addition to cheap refrigerators and tape recorders, miscellaneous wooden items are made by political prisoners said to be working 'under appalling conditions'[20] in Camps 5, 7 and 19 in Mordovia. Cuckoo clock cabinets, chessmen and carved figurines, many destined for the Russian Shop in Holborn, London, all bear the name Vega. One of the reasons that so few people are aware of what is going on – apart from not wanting to know – is that officials of the KGB, anxious to screen off the slave labour end of the production line, have made arrangements for many articles to carry the labels of factories which make no use of prison labour, and to which foreign trade delegations might have access. Several political prisoners of repute, including Yuri Belov and Cronid Lubarsky, have reported that the clocks and chessmen that they made were labelled in this way.

But the industrial empire within the Archipelago is too vast to be hidden for long by such a simple device, and other methods of concealment, such as arranging for products requiring the attention of skilled craftsmen to have the finishing touches applied outside the prison, are also used. The cuckoos made in Camp 19 are sent to Serdobsk, in the Penza region, for painting before the clocks are finally assembled and exported, and horn souvenirs, made in a camp near Grozni, are also finished in ordinary factories. The true origins of the well-known Russian dolls portraying 'Matriochka' (the Old Woman who lived in a Shoe) were revealed by Joseph Lederman,

Abraham Sin and Michael Vais, three of the craftsmen whose task it was to complete work begun by prisoners. All three are dissidents and have testified that the dolls are made in camps in the Sourgout region in the district of Tuymenskaia and in the region of Alam Atinskaia.

As with the illegal employment of children in Italy, one commercial advantage of penal slavery is that the cost of maintaining satisfactory standards of health and safety can often be avoided. Although the antiquated machinery used in the making of clock parts can sever fingers, or even hands, there is no great necessity to go to the trouble or expense of renewing it. Similarly, at the Potma camp glassworks, which produces chandeliers and general glassware for export, and at the women's camp on Lake Baikal and at Roslavl near Smolensk, where vodka bottles are made, the need for masks to protect prisoners from the dangerous effects of the dust was not recognized in 1981, and may not be recognized today. Evidence about the Soviet attitude to the physical welfare of prisoners has come from the personal experiences of Yuri Belov. While an inmate of hard labour Camp 10, in Mordovia, he was a member of a large contingent forced to make wheel cylinders, working in an environment where the temperature was below minus 20 degrees Celsius. The survivors had to sleep fourteen to a dormitory that was three metres square, and food was allocated on the Frenkel principle even under these conditions. Belov was producing 800 cylinders daily, in order that he might qualify for a diet that would just keep him alive.

Using data received from 204 camps, it has been possible to analyse[21] the deployment of penal labourers throughout the Soviet Union. Estimates of the present prison population as a whole vary considerably; the most conservative figure is two and a half million, 1 per cent of all Russian citizens, and this does not include men and women released on parole on the condition that they perform mandatory labour. As might be expected, the largest single category of penal labour is to be found in the timber industry and its subsidiaries. For historical and geographical reasons Siberia is the inhospitable region to which many prisoners are sent and, as trees are a renewable resource, it is likely to remain a principal penal location for some time. It has long been conveniently inaccessible, originally because of poor communications and harsh climate; now there are security reasons for making sure that access is granted only to those whose movements are strictly controlled. Prisoners are therefore used for felling the trees and processing the timber; and within the camps they make pit-props, furniture and prefabricated sections of buildings. Close links between the industry and the prison labour force have meant that, as both expanded to meet political and industrial needs, Siberia ceased to be the only region used for penal labour of this type and prisoners were put to work in the forests of other parts of Russia, especially in the south-west. Now wooden artefacts of various sorts are produced by a large number of camps within and without the timber regions.

The next most widespread form of work for prisoners is in the construction industry and the manufacture of building materials. Almost every camp and prison provides labourers for projects which may be modest in scope or on the scale of hydro-electric power stations. The latter may appear to have Stalinist overtones, but the attractions of cheap energy, not prestige, provide modern motivation. Then, in descending order, come the clothing industry (military and prison wear predominating), mechanical engineering, heavy metal work, manufacture of packing materials, farming, mining, electronics and the chemical industry. Use of prisoners for the construction of the Siberian gas pipeline caused an international scandal, and it is now the practice to restrict prisoners' activities in this field to the concealable tasks, as is done in the camp in Surgut. There inmates make the parts but are not transported to the assembly points, whence their presence might become known to the outside world.

Even when the evocative name 'Siberia' is used, it may be said that there is no reason why the prisoners should not repay their debt to society with some honest toil. It is therefore important to focus attention on the work done there or in any other part of the state by political (or religious) prisoners, and on the inhuman conditions in which many internees – political and criminal – live and labour. In the Perm district, the political detainees of camps 35 and 37 (there are no criminals, as such, in these camps) make drills, taps and various precision-cutting instruments, and Cronid Lubarsky has said[22] that these items are sent to Sverdlovsk tool factory to be stamped with a brand name; other political prisoners in two more camps not far from Sverdlovsk make parts for electric irons. Georgii Davydov, a political prisoner convicted of reproducing and circulating *samizdat* material, has noticed that the Soviet economy makes use of prisoners' labour in virtually every field save one – the food industry. 'This exception can be accounted for by the specific character of the means used to coerce inmates to work, an effective one being hunger.'[23]

Although many religious offenders can find themselves classified as politicals or criminals, they are liable to be arrested for specific religious offences. Apart from infringing the rights of citizens 'under the guise of performing religious rituals',[24] evangelical believers whose churches are unrecognized break the law whenever they teach religion to children, other than their own.[25] Pentecostals and Baptists who have broken away from the officially recognized Baptist church are the prime targets, but most Christian denominations have suffered from their impulse to preach the word, and Buddhists have also transgressed the law. Once the legal machinery is set in motion it moves in a special way for dissidents and believers. Legally, for instance, a person charged with an offence can be imprisoned on remand for up to nine months. However, when it came to Georgi Vins, secretary of the unregistered Baptist Church, he was held beyond the legal limit and then sent to Yakutia in 1975 to serve a ten-year sentence in an area which is inaccessible throughout the winter months. It was not Georgi Vins's first sentence. His manifest patriotism was not broken by a previous term of imprisonment during which, in 1968, he wrote his poem, 'My Love and My Song is Russia'.

According to Yuri Belov,[26] Baptists comprise a majority of the prisoners making wheel rims for Lada Cars (Jigoulis, in Russian), in camps near Gorki, though some workers are politicals. Lada Cars (GB) Limited, of Bridlington, know nothing about the origins of these parts, but two Russian exiles, Nikolai Chtchareguine and Lev Kvartchevsky, have testified that wheel rims are made in Camp 3 at Barachevo, before being sent to the factory with which the British importers make their arrangements. This is in Togliatti on the Volga; and in fact, although some parts are made nearby in prison complex UR-65, an intricate network exists to enable the factory to receive and assemble parts made in a number of widely dispersed camps, which also manufacture parts for other makes of car; Moskvitch, Tchaika and Volga. Some prisoners at Barachevo are engaged in making agricultural vehicles, but it is not known, for certain, that their labour goes into the export models.

Not all British or multinational firms react as Technical and Optical did when faced with the knowledge that they are aiding and abetting a form of slavery, but a disappointing number do. Gowan de Groot, importers of wooden souvenirs, responded with: 'It is not done to question the system. We have our way, they have theirs.'[27] The Razno Company's Marketing Director said that he had visited 'most' of the factories which supply the glassware which was imported, and added, 'prisoners could not make these types of articles.'[28] At Lada Cars, the Public Relations Director said he just did not believe the allegations: 'I can't understand why the dissidents should bring this up again.'[29] International companies are too often the villains when it comes to weighing up the relative merits of profits and human rights, so Rank Xerox's reaction to the discovery that it, too, was receiving the fruits of slavery was reassuring.

Like many other firms Rank Xerox forged its links with penal slavery quite innocently. In the early 1970s negotiations with Soviet trade representatives led to the signing of an agreement whereby copiers and duplicators would be sold to the Soviet Committee for Science and Technology and the Russians would supply electric motors for use in the firm's Gloucestershire factory. At this time Rank Xerox had no means of knowing that the motors were to be made by ordinary and political prisoners in Vladimir prison, where the methods and conditions described by Cronid Lubarsky are ruthlessly applied. The facts only emerged because a request was made for the motors to be modified, and the letter outlining the proposed modifications, forwarded to the officials supervising the work in the prison, was translated by the dissident, Nikolai Chtchareguine. He did not keep his discovery to himself and, as soon as Rank Xerox were aware of the position, the agreement was terminated. The official responsible for the Eastern Bloc Export Division of Rank Xerox reacted in a manner which goes some way towards restoring one's faith in capitalist morality, commenting, 'If we had known, we should never have sanctioned such an operation.'[30]

Other organizations do not seem to want to know. Although much of the Russian timber industry is dependent on camp inmates, the British Woodworking Federation is said to believe that United Kingdom imports are produced under normal working conditions and are 'supplied to us from the west of Russia, from the regions of Murmansk, Archangel and the Kara Sea'.[31] But at Murmansk there are at least seven hard labour camps, and other camps where wooden souvenirs are made are in the other two locations indicated by the Federation. Further south, in the Perm district, one hard labour camp is for women, and they are made to work with saws. Another lucrative British import, and one which traditionally makes use of women prisoners, is red caviar. Although the market is small, the profits are high and nobody, including the customer, seems at all concerned about the circumstances of those who clean, salt and pack the inferior variety of the luxury food. Seven thousand women in penal settlements in Sakhalin and on the Pacific island of Chikotan process this profitable export, while their male counterparts make glass containers for it in a camp at Gouriev. Caviar and containers are then sent to Astrakhan, where ordinary Russian workers otherwise unconnected with the Archipelago make sure that the product enters the market from an apparently respectable source.

Although, judged according to the frequency with which specific types of work are assigned to prisoners, mining occupies a low place on the list, there are other reasons for it to deserve serious attention. Apart from the ten camps which use prisoners for extracting stone for construction purposes, and one where the inmates are reported[32] to be mining uranium, Russia depends on prison labour for what can be its most lucrative source of foreign exchange: gold and diamonds. In 1979, from the largest goldfields in the world, some of which are in the polar regions of Kolyma, the Soviet Union exported 229 tonnes of gold to the West, by courtesy of Switzerland; and at much the same time millions of pounds worth of uncut Russian diamonds were introduced into the London market by De Beers. Kolyma has a reputation for being the coldest inhabited place in the world, and several thousand prisoners are serving their sentences there, mining gold under duress. Nevertheless, although dealers have no illusions about the labour force, which brings them some of their personal wealth, no evidence has come to light that any protest has been made.

The important relationship between the gold mines and the Gulag today reflects a general principle which goes back almost to the Revolution. In 1921 the prisons and camps had to pay their way with the labour of prisoners 'if possible'.[33] From 1922 the self-supporting ideal had given way in some regions to the desirability of making a profit from the sweat of the convicts; then, two years later, the Corrective Labour Code explicitly required all penal institutions to be self-supporting. The following year, 1925, saw the profit motive translated into language which was ideologically more acceptable: the onus was on the camps to make 'reimbursement to the state'. Over the next half century many adjustments were made to take into account, and sometimes disguise, immense losses caused by bureaucracy or ignorance, but the crucial step was taken in 1929, when all prisons and camps were brought into the economic plan. From that year onwards the society was committed to a dependence in some areas of the economy on penal labour. The system has never been profitable overall, but its penetration of the economic structure has been so extensive that disentanglement would present a daunting practical problem.

The economic ramifications of the Soviet network of prisons and camps are so great that care must be taken to keep in mind the ideological aims of current penal practice. Lest the evidence of the more fundamental political commitment be eclipsed by much more obvious commercial exploitation, it is helpful to remember that special psychiatric institutions have been created for the political and religious prisoners, the true penal slaves. Hospitals, such as Alma-Ata, where Akhmetov is being detained, are a drain on the Soviet economy; they contribute nothing that is not believed by the prevailing ideology to be useful. While some attempt has been made to hide the true purpose of these places from the ordinary Russian people – for instance, maintenance is carried out at Sychevka and Volgograd by prisoners who are inmates of penal institutions for the sane – since 1960 the public health laws have ceased to have precise meaning. The opportunity to confine politically inconvenient persons was first provided by deliberately loose drafting[34] of directives, but in 1969 it became legal for police departments to define mental illness[35] and decide what constituted socially dangerous behaviour. Moreover, as they were obliged to prevent such actions from occurring, they could hospitalize people in the belief, or on the pretext, that they might behave dangerously.

The special psychiatric hospitals form the apex of the penal hierarchy and, as they have no commercial aspect, they show that, despite the Soviet obsession with the economic potential of penal servitude, the accepted dogma still dictates that the need for conformity must take precedence over considerations of labour and production. The special hospitals occupy a place in the scheme of things similar to that of the whipping establishments formerly used to instil obedience in negro slaves; they are reserved for obstinate non-conformists, such as Vladimir Khailo, a Baptist, detained since 1980:[36]

> They gave him thirty tablets of haloperidol in one dose after which he swelled up completely and his heart started to fail. His blood pressure rose, his vision deteriorated and he lost consciousness. . . . They told him that they were treating his heart condition and gave him aminazin tablets. They then changed from aminazin and prescribed stilazin . . . his hands refuse to

> function and he cannot lift his right arm . . . now they are giving him triftazin . . . after he has been given these tablets he feels everything in his body contract – his eyes twitch and his mouth twists from side to side.

That is the special treatment for a special category of prisoner, now a sizeable minority, denied the opportunity to work, and for whom labour would be a merciful alternative. It is typical of an area of penal practice, partly devoted to experimentation, which has gained a momentum of its own. The 'patients' are guarded by men who wear military uniforms under their white overalls. Despite the pretence that the building is a hospital, inmates wear prison clothing and all aspects of the regime, including the food, are penal.

The Soviet authorities have taken full advantage of the international instrument stating that 'All prisoners under sentence shall be required to work' and, by an ingenious system of deductions,[37] they have even managed to pay lip service to the rule that 'There shall be a system of equitable remuneration of the work of the prisoners'.[38] There are, however, several 'Minimum Rules' of which they should be reminded. Firstly, 'The precautions laid down to protect the safety and health of free workmen shall be equally observed in institutions';[39] these have been overlooked or ignored in the glassworks, in camps where wooden souvenirs are made, and in a general sense, wherever hours are too long, the climate too cold and the food restricted. Secondly, the system has developed in a way that ignores the principle that 'The interests of the prisoners . . . must not be subordinated to the purpose of making a financial profit from an industry in the institution'.[40] Its evolution was influenced too often by ideas based on the opposite premise. Thirdly, camp administrators should be made to heed the first of the United Nations rules under the heading 'Work': 'Prison labour must not be of an afflictive nature.'[41] And unfortunately, despite the proclamation thirty-six years ago of the Universal Declaration of Human Rights, it is necessary to say again that persons should not be imprisoned because of their religious or political beliefs.

It can come as a shock to an observer to realize that the Soviet penal system is almost a caricature of the ugly face of capitalism; so much of its method and motivation is tied up with desperate attempts to get the better of market forces and become competitive by cutting labour costs. Conversely, looking at the penal situation from the other side of the ideological divide, it can be equally disillusioning to observe that the leading champion of capitalist freedom has a poor record for repressive penal conditions, redeemed only by its concentration on criminals to the exclusion of almost all political offenders. And to make matters more disillusioning, the cruel elements of penal practice in the United States derive their mandate from the thirteenth amendment to the US Constitution: 'Neither slavery nor involuntary servitude, except as a punishment for crime whereof the party shall have been duly convicted, shall exist within the United States.' The penal exception was tested in the courts in 1871, when the prisoner's position was clearly defined: 'He is for the time being the slave of the state.'[42] The Russians, it appears, habitually transgress their own constitution in penal matters; the Americans have sometimes been at their worst when behaving constitutionally.

Putting to one side the degree of hypocrisy of which both major powers are guilty, since Khrushchev the two systems have been barely distinguishable at certain levels in their treatment of prisoners, and during much of the twentieth century there has been little to choose between them in the quest for profits. The United States, however, has been much more diversified because each state has its own penal legislation, and because in many states interpretation of the law has been modified over the years to meet local needs, including those of agriculture and industry.

Until the 1930s it was usual for prisoners to be hired out under contract to private employers who paid the prisons for providing cheap labour. This arrangement had worked to the satisfaction of the prison authorities, but eventually, under sustained pressure from trade unions, employers unable to obtain contract prison labour, humanitarians and prison administrators who were astute enough to see that higher profits could be channelled towards their own activities, the system in general was reversed. Whereas in the old days in, say, California, the prisoners were leased to arable farmers, the new way was for the work to be brought in to the prison or the prison farm. In Texas, 'prison industry', as it was termed, meant that 'The first job every inmate gets . . . if he is able-bodied, is six months on the line – hard, back-bending labour in the fields',[43] while watched over by mounted armed 'bosses'. 'Stoop labour', as this division of prison industry is called today, has been widely used; it has helped to underwrite California's vast agricultural resources and (illegally) in Arkansas it has been the means whereby the destitute have worked off their fines on private farms. As the executive director of the National

Council of Crime and Delinquency said in 1972, the contract labour and prison industry systems 'have exploited the prisoner as a slave worker of the state or federal government.' As in Russia, prisoners are paid, and, as in Russia, there are ways of frustrating payment: 70 per cent of Californian prisoners were receiving no pay at all in the 1970s.[44]

Those who testify against Communist or Western practice in the penal sphere tend to be opponents of one or other social system as a whole, not merely the penal system within it, and whoever sets foot in the minefield of ideologically motivated testimony, unless he has personal experience of what is described, must tread especially carefully. Some anti-Russian evidence is inevitably distorted by the right, as some anti-American evidence is magnified by the left, with the result that history, instead of being analysis of how we are developing, becomes the tool of one partisan or another. But despite these hazards, objective truth is occasionally forced on observers, as was the case when Tom Murton, prison warden authorized to purge corruption from the prisons of Arkansas, disclosed the conditions he found in Tucker and Cummins prison farms. He discovered and revealed the existence of an electrical torture device, known as the Tucker Telephone, found that whipping was the normal means of maintaining discipline, exposed corruption at all levels of the administration, and began to dig up the decapitated remains of some of the prisoners, rumoured to number about 200, who had mysteriously disappeared. His services were dispensed with after the third body had been exhumed.

Are United States prisoners slaves? As their admission to penal institutions, except where there have been miscarriages of justice, was dependent on their having committed crimes, technically they are not. However, once in custody, their physical conditions and the circumstances under which they are often persuaded to do unpaid work can make them temporary slaves in all but name. Furthermore, as they are usually screened off from society at large, they lack the protection which the sympathy of the social environment of a democracy could afford, should their masters be inclined towards sadistic activities seldom far below the surface in a master/slave relationship. Any penitentiary, benevolent or malevolent, can be regarded as the world of slavery in microcosm, and the value of the prison to society is dubious as far as three of its four purposes – punishment, deterrence, rehabilitation and protection of the public – are concerned. The first two are really the same, and the steady growth of the prison population indicates their ineffectiveness; high rates of recidivism show that rehabilitation rarely occurs. Prison is a deterrent to the normally law-abiding citizen who might occasionally be tempted to transgress the law, but for coping with the habitual criminal one is left with protection of the public as the only justification for retaining prisons in any shape or form. Most penal practice is counter-productive; the real cures of crime are economic and educational, and are to be sought outside prison walls.

Given that rehabilitation is still perceived to be the principal aim of most prison services, the career of prison officer should be numbered among the highest callings to which a young man or woman might aspire. That it is not generally seen in this light is, in most countries, partly the result of the ease with which cruelties can be concealed and, especially in the United States, partly the result of responsibility having been transferred from the courts to the prison authorities by means of the indeterminate sentence. The prisoner found guilty is sentenced to serve a term of imprisonment for which a minimum and maximum number of years, as prescribed by law for his offence, are fixed. The amount of time he is actually incarcerated will depend on his prison record as it is presented to the parole board. In theory he is protected from arbitrary sentencing, in practice he is at the mercy of the guards with whom he is in uncomfortably close contact within the oppressive atmosphere of a closed community.

One meets prison officers who are dedicated men with a high sense of vocation. Nevertheless, the peculiar concentration of power within the claustrophobic environment of the prison compound has led to widespread corruption, and the United States has had its full share of penal barbarity. At what might be termed brute level, punishment in Adjustment Centres (which provide America's variations on the theme of solitary confinement) gives opportunities for the straightforward sadist to satisfy his yearnings, but at a higher intellectual, though not moral, level, the scope of the prison system has attracted the same sort of scientist as must be found in the Special Psychiatric Hospitals of the Soviet Union. Patuxent Institution, Maryland, has bare-facedly attempted to modify human behaviour by using brainwashing techniques; as one of the apologists for this sort of experimentation put it, people should not be put off by the fact that Communist forces brainwashed United States prisoners during the Korean war: 'These same techniques in the service of different goals may be quite acceptable to us'[45] or, in other words, 'the end justifies the means.'

Scientists with other priorities play their part in the more typically American form of prisoner exploitation – use of inmates for commercial advantage. The Solano Institute for Medical and Scientific Research has been paying prisoners about one-hundredth of what free employees would receive for performing various technical and clerical tasks, [46] but more alarming has been its use of prisoners as human guinea pigs for medical experiments. Here the Institute has had the enviable commercial advantage of having to keep payments to prisoners to an absolute minimum lest those serving long sentences be given excessive incentives to put their lives at risk. Financial benefits of similar magnitude were obtained by two drug companies, Upjohn and Parke Davis, who, in 1971, did not dispute that they had 'obtained hundreds of thousands of dollars' worth' of free labour by exploiting the skills of inmates who worked a sixteen-hour day.[47] Other less fortunate prisoners were employed by the same firms to test the toxicity of drugs by submitting themselves to increasingly severe doses.

Evidently not enough trouble was taken to conceal from the prisoners themselves the ways in which they were being manipulated in the public and private sectors in order to balance the books of a variety of industrial and agricultural concerns. A typical example of such chicanery was revealed when in 1971 the Supreme Court of California found that in 1967 Governor, later President, Reagan, had violated the state's prohibition against the letting out of convict labour. He had 'authorized the use of prison labour in Merced County to assist in the harvest of figs and prevent a disastrous crop loss'.[48] The wages had been paid to the state and in some cases nearly half of the sum earned on a piecework basis had been deducted by the state as 'expenses incurred', although the prisoners had continued to be accommodated by the prisons throughout the harvest. It may well be argued that it is only just that prisoners should contribute to their upkeep instead of being an unwelcome and heavy burden on honest citizens, but in California, rightly or wrongly, it is illegal to achieve such an end by such a means; and those who have lost their freedom for breaking one law are doubly sensitive about being used by their jailers to break another.

Manipulation by powerful individuals and bodies aggravated the prisoners' growing sense of grievance during the 1960s, but it was the merciless way in which they were put to work, the conditions of day-to-day life inside the prison itself, and above all uncertainty about the duration of their sentences which led to the 1971 prison riots and the famous siege of Attica in which thirty-one prisoners and nine hostages were killed by the forces of law and order.[49] A stage had been reached when prisons, long termed 'universities of crime', were fast becoming 'universities of revolution'. Prisoners admitted for theft eventually emerged as anarchists or members of extremist groups. Since Attica circumstances have changed, but not everywhere for the better. In 1978 the United States Supreme Court ruled that the entire penal system of Arkansas constituted cruel and unusual punishment; prisoners working a ten-hour day on prison farms were disciplined for minor infringements of the rules by being lashed with a wooden-handled leather strap five feet long and four inches wide and by being given imaginatively applied electric shock treatment. In 1983 a prison farm in Tennessee achieved a reputation for the brutal disciplining of prisoners by trigger-happy guards armed with shotguns. In 1985, as the prison population continued to rise, a campaign for conversion of prisons into 'factories with fences' gave new encouragement to those who, like Chief Justice Warren Burger, believe that federal and state laws which restrict the sale of prison-made goods should be repealed; privately owned prisons proliferated and Florida decided to privatize its prison industries.

Prisons will always be needed in advanced societies of all kinds, if only to restrain those who pose a threat to fellow citizens, and presumably there will always be problems arising from excessive concentration of power and cultivation of prison guard mentality, even if standards of recruitment are radically improved. If the United States is to face up to its problems in this field an important first, or early, step must be to remove from the guards much of their influence over the duration of sentences; at the conclusion of a trial, a specific term of imprisonment should be allotted; it should be lengthened for bad behaviour or shortened for good conduct either by means of a truly independent and exhaustive hearing or by normal process of appeal. In the rapidly expanding private sector, where, in theory, responsibility begins and ends with housing and feeding, there is a built-in conflict between the prison manager's wish to achieve profitability and his power to dispense the 'good-time credits' which affect prisoners' chances of earning parole. But it must be admitted that the urge to make a profit has for many years been a characteristic of state penitentiaries. One sweeping reform which could take effect immediately would be to allow uninhibited powers of scrutiny to all responsible persons who wish to see for themselves the true nature of prison conditions. This should at least help to protect prisoners from physical assault. Unfortunately in 1978 the US Supreme Court ruled that independent investigators have no guaranteed rights of admission.

Most forms of slavery will survive for an indefinite period, because they are intimately bound up with human nature, but it can be confidently assumed that penal/political slavery is embarking on a period of dominance. Third World countries have learned little or nothing from the examples of National Socialism and Stalinism, and their new dictators have been quick to unite the talents of the prison service and the security forces in the interests of enslaving sections of the populace. It is a tragic truth that while few societies can preserve freedom without the help of policemen, in authoritarian societies the police themselves are the greatest menace to whatever degree of individual liberty remains. In physical contact, as they frequently are, with the supposed opponents of their leader, they acquire a taste for the abuse of power; furthermore, they often have opportunities to conceal their excesses.

What can be done to turn back the tide of this twentieth-century brand of the old institution? It is common to rich and poor nations alike, and while appealing to old and base human instincts, it thrives on new technology. The International Red Cross comes to mind immediately as a body qualified (by experience, though not mandate) to make regular inspections of penal institutions, until one realizes that, like the Anti-Slavery Society, it was unaware of the very existence of the Nazi concentration and extermination camps until too late. And what could it have done anyway? Again one comes back to United Nations agencies and the problem of access. Would a United Nations police force be the answer, or would it too be corrupted by the unprecedented authority of its mandate? A series of checks and balances which prevented excesses would also curb effective action, and many states – the guilty ones – would refuse to co-operate. A universally acceptable writ of habeas corpus, served by Interpol, would go a long way towards the protection of known individuals, but it would do little for the countless unregistered minority or tribal peoples who are frequently preyed upon by modern slavers. And would a boycott of goods known to be made wholly or partly by penal slaves do more than multiply the methods of disguise used to deceive importers?

Whatever conclusions can be drawn from a consideration of the prevalence of various forms of slavery in the twentieth century will have to lead on to two sorts of solution: prevention and cure. The United Nations has unique opportunities to assist prevention, and it is to be hoped that governmental obstruction will not always be able to frustrate its agencies when the liberation of non-criminal individuals and groups is needed; an essential prerequisite, of course, is that the agencies themselves adopt a more responsive attitude to human rights. Unfortunately they are staffed by government nominees, whose security of tenure is sometimes fragile. As for the causes of slavery, especially the penal variety, Solzhenitsyn's words have a message for believers and non-believers alike:[50]

> . . . to the human being who has faith in some force that holds dominion over all of us, and who is therefore conscious of his own limitations, power is not necessarily fatal. For those, however, who are unaware of any higher sphere, it is a deadly poison. For them there is no antidote.

The greatest slavers of all are Governments. For every one claims to own the labor of every individual within its grasp.

The United States of America, bastion of liberty, uses slave troops, as do or have many other nations.

CHAPTER 11

THE ROLE OF THE UNITED NATIONS

No one shall be held in slavery or servitude: slavery and the slave trade shall be prohibited in all their forms.

UNIVERSAL DECLARATION OF HUMAN RIGHTS, ARTICLE 4

After the passing of the British Emancipation Act in 1834, attempts to eradicate the slave trade and slavery throughout the world found expression in many international agreements; between 1839 and 1890 more than 300 were signed and none was effective. The General Act of the Conference of Berlin (1885), for example, was designed principally to suppress slavery and the slave trade in the Congo basin and had exactly the opposite effect. But the way to genuine progress through the creation of practical machinery was paved by the Brussels Conference of 1890, which, though officially convened by a promoter of slavers, King Leopold II of the Belgians, was a consequence of pressure originating from influential members of the Anti-Slavery Society. The outcome of the conference was the General Act of Brussels,[1] which has been described as 'the most detailed international code against the slave trade ever devised'.[2] As a result of the Act a permanent International Slavery Bureau was set up and, with the unlikely co-operation of such heads of state as the Shah of Persia and the Sultan of Zanzibar, brought the Arabian-African trade virtually to a standstill until the outbreak of the First World War, when the Bureau closed for ever.

The Bureau's successes had been limited to the trade; its only effect on slavery was to limit numbers within given territories. After the war, with no organization to oppose it, the trade revived and slavery persisted in its traditional locations, including Persia and Zanzibar. Unfortunately, preoccupied with the problems of reconstruction, the European powers, instead of re-establishing the Bureau and attempting to modify its terms of reference so as to make possible a start on eliminating slavery itself, decided to make a fresh start. In 1919 the Convention of Saint Germain-en-Laye[3] was signed and, although its theoretical scope exceeded that of all its predecessors – it sought 'to secure the complete suppression of slavery in all its forms and of the slave trade by land and sea'[4] – it was universally assumed until 1956, when the United Kingdom demurred, that it had abrogated the slavery provisions of the Brussels Act. The leaders of the free world knew exactly what had to be done; they had allowed the best means of doing it to slip away.

The Bureau, equipped with a naval patrol based on Zanzibar, had proved itself to be an effective suppressor of the trade from Africa to Arabia and, at a time when the imperial powers could still say confidently that they would 'continue to watch over the preservation of the native populations and to supervise the improvement of the conditions of their moral and material well-being',[5] the problem of access was largely an academic one – except in so far as European transgressions were concerned. A strengthened Bureau, even one sustained by war-weary paternalism, could have penetrated most parts of the world unopposed. But that was not to be. Instead, even when drafting the Covenant of the League of Nations, the only form of slavery its founding fathers took into account, except when they concerned themselves with the welfare of the peoples of the mandated territories, was the traffic in women and children.

But for the mandates, slavery matters would seldom have come before the League. As it was, the Mandates Commission received annual reports on developments in these territories and inevitably there were many references to progress or problems in this field. As early as 1922 the Council of the League decided that it must have further information on the subject and wrote to all fifty-two League members in an attempt to estimate the worldwide incidence of the institution. So inadequate was the response and yet so pressing was the issue that a Temporary Slavery Commission was appointed to assess the situation and make recommendations. At its first meeting members are said to have been startled by the material put before them. Instead of being called upon to deal with the 'dying embers' of the slave traffic, they 'quickly discovered that the slave systems which were in blazing activity in several parts of the world involved several millions of human beings.'[6] In 1925 the Commission recommended that the Bureau be revived and that an international Convention should be drafted; and the same year the British government, which had already had a draft slavery Convention in hand, submitted it to the Assembly. But although the amended Convention that was finally approved in 1926 was an important step for human rights, it was a great disappointment to the membership of a distinguished Commission, particularly to Sir Frederick (later Lord) Lugard, who really knew something about the problem of slavery. Instead of an autonomous, or semi-autonomous, permanent body being entrusted with the task of monitoring compliance with the principal articles of the Convention, signatories were merely required, by article 7, to 'undertake to communicate to each other and to the Secretary-General of the League of Nations any laws and regulations they might enact with a view to the application of the provisions of the present Convention'.[7]

The inadequacy of the Convention, which did not even require signatories to furnish annual reports, as the mandatory powers were obliged to do, was generally apparent by 1929, when the League next discussed slavery. In the forlorn hope that some form of permanent body would be established, a British proposal was made that the Temporary Slavery Commission be revived, and, as the Assembly shelved the issue on that occasion, another attempt was made in 1931. This time the Council of the League agreed to appoint a committee of experts for one year, and part of its brief was to decide whether the League's machinery needed modifying. After holding two sessions in 1932, the Committee, which was horrified by the failure of existing arrangements to produce any significant response from governments and by the total absence of meaningful data, recommended unanimously the establishment of a Standing Advisory Committee of Experts on Slavery, and the Assembly agreed.

The Standing Committee was different from the Bureau, but it just had time to prove its value before it was killed off, like its predecessor, by an outbreak of war. Without consistent regular monitoring of the international position, the League had been able to do little except pigeon-hole information received. Now complaints could be followed up, policies could be co-ordinated, and the Committee had the authority to advise the Council on the validity of requests for financial assistance. During the five years up to and including 1938 the seven members of the Committee, all of different nationalities, assumed responsibility for the documents supplied by governments to the Secretariat, endeavoured to reconcile the contents with the requirements of the Convention and the social system of the countries concerned, and, by means of annual reports, recommended ways in which changes could be made to remove objectionable features. It was still not enough; sources of evidence were limited; there was no means of co-ordinating the resources of voluntary organizations concerned with human rights; supervisory powers were lacking. Then, as now, there was no way of forcing signatories to keep their word. But at least there was an assumption of responsibility on the part of the highest international authority.

The League of Nations was to be born again in another form soon after the Second World War was over, but the Committee, again like the Bureau before it, did not feature as part of the new organization responsible for the promotion of international peace and security. And in another way, in spite of awareness of extensive use of slave labour throughout occupied Europe until only months before the drafting of its Charter, the United Nations got off to a worse start than the League had done, as far as slavery was concerned: the Charter did not mention slavery as such. There was an understandable wish not to repeat the performance of an international association which had failed to prevent war, but in this fundamental area of human rights the League had had successes which should have been built upon, not put out of mind. Despite the omissions of its Covenant, it had, for example, persuaded seven administrations[8] to enact legislation abolishing slavery; in addition it had improved, though not cured, the slavery position in Ethiopia and Liberia, and had done much to curb the flow of slaves to Mecca; and above all, after years of prevarication, it had learned that permanent machinery was needed if further progress was to be made.

In 1946 the responsibilities of the League of Nations shifted to the United Nations Organization, but not until 1953 did the United Nations find itself able to acknowledge its obligations under the Slavery Convention of 1926. During the intervening years recourse had been made to the old, usually unsatisfactory, procedure of – as Lord Lugard had put it in 1933 – appointing 'a temporary committee at intervals of several years with no means of obtaining the information it required, and whose recommendations could be conveniently pigeon-holed. Such committees are mere waste of money and of the time and effort of the people who form them.'[9] However, the *ad hoc* Committee of Experts on Slavery[10] that was appointed in 1949 had wide terms of reference and used the limited time at its disposal to full advantage. In addition to assessing the extent of the problem of slavery and suggesting solutions, it was charged with the task of recommending ways in which the various United Nations agencies could help.

Not surprisingly, a committee consisting of a woman and a man who could speak no English, a man who could speak no French, and only one who could speak both these languages, failed altogether to discover the incidence of slavery in the post-war world. They lacked up-to-date evidence, or the means of receiving it (and they also lacked simultaneous translation equipment). Nevertheless, remarkably, their achievements were to be valuable in the long term. They pointed out that the United Nations should, by special protocol, assume responsibility for the 1926 Convention, and they made the valuable recommendation that a Supplementary Convention was needed; one which would, among other improvements, extend the definition of slavery to include debt bondage, sale of women into marriage and sham adoption. The protocol was approved on 23 October 1953, after a report on slavery had been commissioned by the Economic and Social Council and prepared by Hans Engen of Norway, and the Supplementary Convention, based like its predecessor on a United Kingdom draft, was adopted on 3 April 1956. The scope of international law, or agreements which should have the force of law, was now much improved; the problem of implementation remained. Naturally, in its turn the Committee urged that a permanent Committee of Experts be set up to supervise application of the Conventions.

The Standing Advisory Committee had been asked to consider how the expertise of the bodies which make up the organization of the United Nations might be co-ordinated in order to eradicate slavery. With what sort of apparatus would they be confronted, if they were to receive this instruction today? It is an important question, for ultimately it is in this area of enquiry that the key to the implementation problem is most likely to be found. Perhaps inevitably, like everything else to do with an organization as complicated as the United Nations, the relative importance of its constituent parts and the relationships between them are not precisely fixed, and the Secretariat is careful to dissociate itself from attempts to draft rigid family trees. Nevertheless, in the midst of a daunting number of departments, specialized agencies and other organs, there is a discernible United Nations structure, and a brief outline of it may be helpful at this stage.

Under the Charter, the six principal organs of the United Nations are: the General Assembly, the Security Council, the Economic and Social Council (ECOSOC), the Trusteeship Council, the International Court of Justice and the Secretariat. Of these, the General Assembly, composed of representatives of all member governments, is usually regarded as the decision taker, but the Security Council (one-third permanent members, two-thirds elected by the General Assembly) is the only organ empowered to impose its will on member states in accordance with the Charter. As an important responsibility of the Economic and Social Council is to consult non-governmental organizations which have consultative status (such as the Anti-Slavery Society), it will be considered separately, below. The Trusteeship Council, charged with shepherding trust territories to independence has almost lost its *raison d'être*; the International Court of Justice, as its title suggests, pronounces on matters arising from treaties and conventions; the Secretariat is a body of international civil servants who carry out the day-to-day work of the United Nations independently of the wishes of individual states.

The function of the Economic and Social Council is to co-ordinate the work of specialized agencies and institutions in the furtherance of economic and social aims agreed by simple majority of its fifty-four members. Its subsidiary machinery includes many commissions and committees and one of these is the Commission on Human Rights which has its own subsidiary body, the Sub-Commission on Prevention of Discrimination and Protection of Minorities, to which a number of Working Groups, permanent and sessional, report, and it was at this point in the overall scheme of things that a genuine improvement was to be made. As part of ECOSOC's customary agenda, slavery came up annually and was annually debated until 1966, but to no avail; the world was still not as well equipped to combat the institution as it had been in the 1890s. In 1964, however, there was concerted pressure from non-govermental organizations; this led to a further report being commissioned by ECOSOC, and this time Mohamed Awad, an Egyptian, was appointed Special Rapporteur. He too emphasized that 'the United Nations should establish a committee of experts to deal with the problem of slavery in all its aspects, and to act as an advisory body to the Economic and Social Council'[11] but when ECOSOC debated his report in 1966, although most delegates supported this recommendation, instead of it being adopted it was relegated to the Commission on Human Rights.

The 1966 ECOSOC debate on slavery, though it ended with a

decision to refer the issue to a subordinate body, had revealed to those anxious to achieve a positive result the extent to which many governments feared enquiries in this field. Responses were often instinctive, rather than rational. Although, for instance, no international machinery existed to investigate the incidence of slavery, the Soviet Union objected that to create a new body would add nothing to existing machinery. The United States for its part put forward the wholly uncharacteristic argument that an advisory committee would be expensive. A spokesman from the Third World did his best to hide behind the smoke screen of apartheid, the Tanzanian delegate claiming that it was the only form of slavery which still existed. With some sarcasm, the Peruvian chairman was warned that although there could be no truth in any suggestion that his country harboured serfdom, an advisory committee would be liable to allege that there was; and similarly the Indian and Iranian delegates were taunted with the prospect of reports on imagined slavery in their countries; the United States, Canada and Sweden, it was insinuated, were tacitly supporting apartheid. These emotional reactions – which generally were left to Tanzania to express – concealed, at best, guilty consciences; and from the midst of all the rhetoric there came the beginnings of an uneasy compromise, calculated to save the faces of countries which imagined that some definitions of slavery could have uncomfortable geographical and ideological limitations. Since 1966 the subject of discussion has not been 'slavery' but the 'question of slavery and the slave trade in all their practices and manifestations, including the slavery-like practices of apartheid and colonialism'. Inclusion of colonialism, for no logical reason, has ensured Communist collaboration; mention of apartheid (although it has had machinery specifically devoted to it since 1962) has made it easier for some Third World countries to co-operate.

The Commission on Human Rights debated slavery for the first time in 1967 and arrived at a similar decision to ECOSOC's: on the basis of a resolution proposed by the United States and Egypt, and supported by Third World and Communist delegates, it referred the matter down to its own subordinate body, the Sub-Commission; and at this lower level the entire ritual began to be re-enacted. A new study was proposed and authorized, and Mohamed Awad was again appointed Special Rapporteur – but he lived barely long enough to investigate and present his interim report in 1971. He made two main proposals: one good, but ill-timed, the other ill-conceived. Having seen that many human rights violations which he believed to be within the wider definition of slavery were covered by several different Conventions, he wanted to substitute one comprehensive slavery Convention. Desirable as this might be, it would have meant a delay of several years. His other proposal was for slavery to be combated on a regional basis.

The Sub-Commission then, for no conceivable reason, let matters drift, until the United Kingdom brought pressure to bear in ECOSOC to make the Human Rights Commission instruct its subordinate body to consider the need for establishing permanent machinery. The Sub-Commission complied and, after having considered an alternative proposal that one man should be appointed as a kind of international human rights ombudsman, decided to postpone coming to a decision for a year. In 1973 the Sub-Commission decided to recommend that the United Nations should have permanent machinery for considering slavery in the various forms of the agreed definitions; in 1974 the Human Rights Commission forwarded the recommendation to ECOSOC for approval, which was granted; and in 1975 the United Nations Working Group of Experts on Slavery met in Geneva for the first time. It now functions in parallel with two other Working Groups, the Working Group on Communications and – of direct relevance to the Anti-Slavery Society's other main area of responsibility – the Working Group on Indigenous Populations.

When, after so many delays, a working Group of Experts on Slavery was eventually established, one anti-slaver (who must remain anonymous) was prompted to write to the author:

> It is not without interest, perhaps, that this remarkable advance (establishing as it did the only tiny organ in the great UN in which private individuals, properly sponsored, may provide unsworn evidence of human rights) was only attained by a bit of back-stage horse-dealing. The Russians, after much fighting of a rearguard action, agreed not to oppose the proposal in the Sub-Commission provided that slavery should in future be debated not more than in alternate years in the Sub-Commission. This . . . won't be found in the records.

The Working Group on Slavery which exists today labours under almost as many difficulties and perverse attitudes as were encountered by those who sought to bring it into existence in the first place. After slavery was omitted from the United Nations Charter, it was given great prominence in the Universal Declaration of Human Rights, but this lacked the force of law. Eventually, in 1976, when it appeared as article 8 in the International Covenant on Civil and Political Rights, it entered the mainstream of recognized human rights. No doubt part of the reason for collective reticence about the institution derives from subconscious embarrassment caused by the survival well into the second half of the twentieth century of so much of the old-fashioned chattel slavery. People from all walks of life seem to find that without a considerable effort of will they are unable to face up to the very existence of what they regard as an outrageous anachronism. And, other than in psychological terms, it is difficult to explain why so many educated people will not look at the evidence. What were the reasons, one wonders, that in 1969 at a meeting of the United Nations Administrative Committee on Co-ordination, 'the representatives of all the specialised agencies made it clear to the Secretary-General that they were unwilling to become involved in the question of slavery'?[12] Presumably it was because resident representatives may not engage in any activity without the knowledge and approval of the host country. But it is unfortunate that the proceedings of this Committee are confidential, because one needs to know why opposition was unanimous. Without the co-operation of the specialized agencies the Working Group can achieve nothing, other than give non-governmental organizations the opportunity to influence world opinion through the press and broadcasting.

Seen from the point of view of a slave, how might the present system work? The best hope for the hypothetical example, perhaps a young woman whose sale is accidentally observed by a lost tourist, would be that the Anti-Slavery Society should receive and investigate the details. A telephone call to Geneva would be unlikely to achieve anything unless it was made during August, and even then the only immediate response would be verbal and probably non-committal. Assuming that the government of the state in which the sale occurred responds neither to the Society's initial polite diplomacy, nor to its alternative strategem of publicity, the evidence would be put before the Working Group during the first week of August. (In the meantime the Society would, of course, continue making its own individual representations.) A week later a recommendation would be made to the Sub-Commission that the government of the state concerned should be told the facts and asked to explain what action, as a party to the Supplementary Convention on Slavery (1956), it proposed to take. When the Human Rights Commission had been informed, at best the following March, its permanent staff (the Secretariat of the Centre for Human Rights) would implement the recommendation subject to ECOSOC's approval in May or June. Finally the slave's state would probably issue a denial and a protest, and that would be the end of the affair for the United Nations until the Society raised it again.

Plainly this unproductive circus is unsatisfactory, involving as it does some five tiers of administration, from the non-governmental organization to the Economic and Social Council; the whole edifice is much too cumbersome to have any reasonable chance of achieving specific acts of liberation within an acceptable time-span. The above example is not altogether fanciful (it does, in fact, combine ingredients from actual cases); it is given to show how ineffective the system can be, even when timing is at its best, and assuming an absence of the obstruction which is habitual. A less fraught but more customary failing is that terrible violations of human rights are discussed in general terms and very little positive achievement follows. And yet a Working Group has been seen as the answer to an acute need for over a hundred years. How can it be made to be effective? One way of finding out is to look at areas in which a degree of United Nations anti-slavery success has been achieved.

For all its shortcomings, the new machinery helped to set one valuable precedent: for the first time a United Nations mission has visited a country to investigate allegations made by a non-governmental organization. But nothing could have been achieved without the co-operation of the Mauritanian rulers who, had they themselves been accused, might not have been so amenable. It is the governments which are frequently the subjects of complaints about human rights violations, and are therefore unlikely to extend invitations to teams of investigation. Moreover, as one-party states proliferate and power is increasingly concentrated in the hands of a few men, or one man, fewer doors will open. The Working Group has never been able to rely on other countries reacting in a Mauritanian manner. There may, however, be other means of gaining access.

The International Labour Organization's procedures may repay examination. It has long been associated with slavery committees – and in 1951 played a useful part in reconciling viewpoints within the *ad hoc* Committee of Experts which came out so strongly in favour of establishing permanent United Nations machinery. It has its own well-tried methods of gaining admission to member states, and these have not only been used to enable investigations to be carried out in the Dominican Republic and Equatorial Guinea. Depending on the nature of the complaint one of three types of on-the-spot investigation is used: fact-finding missions by independent bodies, direct contacts or special missions of enquiry. For the first of these the Governing Body of the ILO usually selects a panel of three; 'independent persons of the highest standing' are 'appointed in their personal capacity'[13] and they start by holding preliminary hearings in Geneva. This procedure, as in the case of the Dominican enquiry, is in accordance with article 26 of the ILO's constitution, and usually follows representations from individuals or groups with grounds for complaint, or from governments which have ratified the relevant Convention.

The first on-the-spot visit under the article 26 procedure followed a complaint from the Ghanaian government in 1961 about Portugal's use of forced labour in its African colonies, and a commission of enquiry visited Angola and Mozambique later the same year. Other countries visited by ILO commissions include Chile, Lesotho, Japan and Puerto Rico. A country's consent is not needed to allow the constitutional procedure to be set in motion, and proceedings can take place without the participation of the government concerned. But, as the ILO would find it impossible to carry out an on-the-spot investigation without the government's co-operation, careful diplomacy smoothes relationships in advance and almost always the required facilities are granted. All officials at the ILO have to be discreet and impartial, and possess appropriate technical skills; the senior officials have acquired diplomatic skills which are probably unequalled, and among their tasks is the preparation of on-the-spot visits so that a minimum of opposition is encountered. Obviously only permanent officials can attain this level of expertise.

It can be seen that the ILO's methods, although characterized by high standards of efficiency, depend in the end on the integrity of individuals in key positions. Like every other large organization it has human error to content with, and it is reasonable to ask why it, more than other international agencies, may have some means of improving the anti-slavery machinery. There are intangible as well as tangible reasons for this, to do with both its birth and its early development. Since its foundation as an autonomous agency in 1919, the ILO has developed its own independent tradition, and this – though it is associated with the United Nations system – has allowed it to distance itself from the international jostling which inevitably occurs within the larger and more complex organization. It soon acquired a reputation for objectivity, which stood it in good stead when, in 1968, it embarked on its second method of on-the-spot investigation: direct contacts. In especially urgent cases, instead of a three-man commission, an individual of exceptional calibre is sent to look into serious complaints. His responsibilities approximate to those of the international ombudsman whose appointment was considered at the 1972 Sub-Commission debate, except, of course, that direct contact representatives are appointed for specific visits; there is no continuity. Over thirty countries have had direct contact investigations by the ILO.

In especially delicate and urgent situations the ILO has, during the last twenty-five years, sent special missions to make urgent on-the-spot enquiries in several countries including Argentina, Chile, Israel and Poland. And another type of special mission, entirely composed of independent members, was sent to Spain (in 1969), at the request of the Spanish government, to make a study of the general labour position and trade unions, before the freedom of association conventions were ratified.

The more one looks at the performance of the International Labour Organization, the more one becomes aware of the extent to which its aims coincide with those of the Working Group on Slavery. Would that the same could be said of methods, or the opportunity to put them into practice. Most forms of slavery are abuses of labour, though some involve a motive additional to that of profit. Should not, therefore, a constitutional bridge be built between the International Labour Organization and the Working Group on Slavery? In theory it already exists; in practice the Working Group, like a May fly, is born only to die. Surely what it needs are its own offices within (or adjacent to) the ILO building, a permanent staff, and opportunities for day-to-day liaison with non-governmental organizations. Admittedly such proposals would stimulate fierce opposition from governments and individuals with entrenched positions to defend. Nevertheless both bodies derive their moral authority from the ratification of Conventions, and they should co-operate closely as the recipients of the segments of sovereignty willingly sacrificed by member states. An excellent first step would be for a senior ILO official always to be one of the Experts (a sixth).

At present the Working Group on Slavery is sustained by the

commitment of a nucleus of non-governmental organizations and the good fortune that its chairman has been elected for another term. Otherwise the Experts come and go and a consistent approach is not maintained. Nevertheless, if a permanent anti-slavery secretariat were to be established, preferably in collaboration with the ILO, it would be important for the annual sessions in the Palais des Nations to continue. Even given the advantages that continuous existence would bring, the sessions of the Working Group of Experts can still provide a valuable forum within which representatives of states can be put under direct attack for human rights violations committed by their governments or on their national territory. Moreover, official proceedings in this most fundamental realm of human rights need to be open to scrutiny at regular intervals.

Another reason for strengthening and supplementing the present system rather than replacing it is that one of the other groups which reports to the Sub-Commission is the Working Group on Indigenous Populations, which held its first session in 1981. It is essential for persecuted minorities that efforts in these closely related fields are co-ordinated, and the Sub-Commission should provide the means to this end. There is, however, no question of merging the two Working Groups. Although the Groups are equally political in the sense that they repeatedly attack governments and national institutions, the Indigenous Populations Group frequently spends time discussing devolution, transfers of sovereignty and the redrawing of boundaries. The Working Group on Slavery should not interest itself in these matters *per se* – only when they impinge on ownership of one human being by another. The Anti-Slavery Society, which submits evidence to both Groups, does so because it is also the Aborigines Protection Society.

The problem of access to sovereign territories and of enforcing compliance with ratified Conventions would be eased in the anti-slavery field by the adoption of ILO methods by a permanent staff with their own facilities; in making the constitutional changes, however, care would have to be taken to see that, although closely associated with the ILO, the 'Bureau', under its own Director, had sufficient autonomy to initiate enquiries. The Director would report annually to the Sub-Commission and, once the Working Group had achieved a permanent footing within the United Nations system, it is hoped that enhanced status would enable it to attract support from the only agencies which tyrannical governments respect – those with funds to allocate. Just as the Anti-Slavery Society has recently been successful in gaining assurances that Commonwealth Development Corporation loans to the Philippines will be dependent on improvements in human rights, so there should be a permanent body at the United Nations influencing, where possible, a distribution of international money which takes slavery into account.

A permanent presence at the United Nations would make possible the co-ordination of many bodies, such as the Food and Agricultural Organization and the United Nations Development Programme, whose help is needed in the difficult time after chattel slaves, debt bondsmen or serfs are liberated. And on the other side of anti-slavery work there could be improved use of the International Criminal Police Organization (INTERPOL), notwithstanding the clauses in its constitution which forbid the undertaking of political, military, religious or racial functions, and its failure to establish meaningful links with Communist countries. It can only operate when a crime involves at least two countries and it has no right of access to the sovereign territory of member states; nevertheless, as the official, if not very strong, right arm of a United Nations slavery 'bureau' it could use its skills with extradition treaties to full advantage against traffickers in women and children. The day of the international writ of habeas corpus would have come a little nearer.

However the Working Group on Slavery evolves, one thing is certain: its continued success will depend on the non-governmental organizations. Regrettably, they had their enemies, and some of these are powerfully placed. The official record of the 1977 ECOSOC debate on 'Non-Governmental Organizations in Consultative Status' states that the Soviet delegate said that some NGOs 'systematically abused their consultative status in order to slander socialist countries'. Amnesty International and the International League for Human Rights were named, and the report goes on to say that 'Mention should also be made of the Anti-Slavery Society, which had slandered certain Member States in the Sub-Commission on Prevention of Discrimination and Protection of Minorities'. Were it not that serious efforts are made from time to time to silence the critics of repressive regimes, such words could be ignored. But the animosity is not confined to rhetoric. In 1983 an attempt was made in the Fifth Committee of the General Assembly to abolish the Working Group on Slavery. That, and other anti-NGO moves, some emanating from the Human Rights Centre itself, prompted a response from the Anti-

Slavery Society which took the form of a direct complaint to the Secretary-General, Perez de Cuellar:[14]

> It is governments who wage war, who imprison the innocent, who torture, who abuse minorities and generally flout the provisions of the instruments designed to secure peace and harmony both nationally and internationally. As a consequence an organization of governments – which is what the United Nations is – will often have difficulty in dealing effectively with abuses which may be built into the policies of certain governments: torture in Chile, perhaps, disappearances in Argentina, the use of children by Iran in the war with Iraq, or the virtually universal exploitation of children and their labour. It follows that only exceptionally will states draw attention to the abuses in which they and their fellow states are implicated. The NGOs, on the other hand, exist precisely to apply pressures tending to alleviate or abolish all contraventions of the United Nations guiding principles . . . they can say things which governments cannot and they can help in the ventilation of grievances which might otherwise never come to light.

Unless the NGOs are allowed to fulfil their role, it is argued, detractors of the United Nations will be able to say, with truth, that 'far from being a game keeper in the international forest, it is now a trade union of poachers'.[15]

As the various forms of slavery outlined in the preceding chapters show, there are few common solutions to the complex problems which face the NGOs and the Working Group of Experts on Slavery. Responsibility for dealing at the United Nations with the complaints of tribal minorities is naturally best left to the Working Group on Indigenous Populations, and apartheid is a tribal problem. Although the Committee Against Apartheid pays scant attention to the wishes of non-violent ethnic minorities, one hesitates before suggesting that this additional problem be passed to this Working Group. But what other forum is there for the weaker tribes? Nothing can now be done about the slaves of National Socialism, other than maintain vigilance lest the mistakes of the League of Nations, partly caused by the absence of investigative powers, be repeated by its successor. The other forms of slavery, however – chattel, exploitation of children, exploitation of women, debt bondage and serfdom, forced labour (especially of migrant workers) and penal slavery – all need continuous specialist attention to cope with the diversity of problems which surface daily, or emancipation will barely keep pace with enslavement.

Chattel slavery, despite the simplicity of its definition, continues to call upon whatever co-ordinating expertise the United Nations has at its disposal. Mauritania is only the most clearly visible part of a larger problem in North Africa, and yet the United Nations mission felt it necessary to suggest that seven major international agencies consider offering assistance: the United Nations Educational, Scientific and Cultural Organization, the United Nations Development Programme, the Food and Agricultural Organization of the United Nations, the International Fund for Agricultural Development, the International Labour Organization, the United Nations Children's Fund and the United Nations Fund for Population Activities. The Expert, Marc Bossuyt, commented, 'It would undoubtedly be a very great disappointment for Mauritania if the international community were to shirk its duty of solidarity in this field.'[16] And it would be helpful for all concerned if the Working Group had the authority to make sure that there is no shirking.

Child slavery will always be the most difficult form of the institution to diminish, let alone eradicate, because of the child's inescapable dependence on the parent. Nevertheless, as national legislation becomes more detailed and compulsory education more widespread, one can take a more optimistic view about responses to representations made to or by the Working Group about exploitation. If the United Nations has the machinery to rebuke countries, increasingly the countries will have enforceable laws to rectify the situation; and if the Working Group were to be allowed some say in equitable distribution of funds, steps could be taken advisedly towards provision of universal compulsory education, with a distinctly vocational bias, in the Third World countries where children are most at risk. It will be up to the non-governmental organizations, helped by local police and sometimes by INTERPOL, to reduce the incidence of sophisticated child slavery in the richer nations of the world.

The Working Group's efforts to reduce the incidence of adult female slavery is likely to continue to be limited mainly to protests about forced prostitution, about which it can do very little, and female genital mutilation, against which it is usefully outspoken. But although it will always seek to improve the lot of women born into a condition of slavery believed to be sanctioned by religion, not much will be achieved until the religious leaders can be persuaded to make a more humane interpretation of sacred writings. At the present stage of religious evolution, repressive husbands have three-fold protection from United Nations interference: the sovereignty of the state in which they live, the religion in which they, and their wives, believe, and local custom. If the Working Group were to acquire permanent status, it would be to individual influential religious leaders that it would have to address its appeal.

Debt bondage, serfdom and forced labour all fall within the ambit of the International Labour Organization and, at the same time, form much of the common ground on which a strong, permanent anti-slavery bureau could be built. International Conventions, for the most part matched by adequate internal state legislation, should, when slavery is alleged, open doors for on-the-spot investigations, and in this way there might arise the beginnings of an international human rights inspectorate. All three forms of slavery depend on the existence of a poverty-stricken labour force, and the reports of investigating teams, while sometimes apportioning blame to individuals or groups, would frequently recommend a co-ordinated response from United Nations agencies. The permanent Working Group should decide what sort of help should be offered and should seek to supervise the implementation of recommendations 'on-the-spot'. As with ILO visits in the past, a successful outcome would depend on the personal integrity and diplomatic ability of a rare breed of official. For a time a slavery bureau would have to learn from its more experienced partner.

The present Working Group procedures provide the opportunity for virtually all that can be done for penal slaves, and this gives added strength to the view that an annual open session with the five (or six) Experts should be retained regardless of any other changes which may be made. Because, unless Amnesty International or some like-minded organization knows about them, penal slaves are indistinguishable from the criminals among whom they work, and because they may be made to labour in otherwise uninhabited areas, they are generally beyond the reach of the various missions or commissions which seek to emancipate other types of slave. Probably their only hope of help from the outside world lies in the sensitivity of their government to world opinion, and should information emerge from, say, a Communist country (which it seldom does), there would invariably be a

Communist Expert to sense which way the wind was blowing. Selection of Experts from the five geographical and ideological divisions of the world is one of the merits of an arrangement which can easily be dismissed as a mere talking shop.

Unfortunately it has to be admitted that there are no United Nations plans to upgrade the Working Group on Slavery, or to grant it permanent facilities. The Experts meet briefly once a year to hear evidence and prepare a report. That is the beginning and the end of their power and considerable dissatisfaction stems from the apparent futility of much of the five days' work. As the recent Anti-Slavery Society complaint[17] emphasized, an 'enormous body of information ... has been acquired, often at great cost and sacrifice, recounting terrible human abuses. ... Some way should be found for the United Nations to react – and to be seen to react – to the reports in all their detail. All too often it would seem that such reports end up in the files and are never heard of again.'

Those terrible human abuses, the prerogative of no race or colour, occur under all religions and where there is no religion. They are the products of greed, lust and love of power which feed on poverty and all forms of weakness. To experience the joys of uninhibited power one must own another human being; to satisfy deeper cravings one must torture him. In short the universality of the tendency to enslave others leads to the conclusion that the urge is fundamental to human nature. This was no less true in Wilberforce's day, but he was able to divert the course of imperial history by parliamentary means, towards a humanitarian conclusion, showing as he did so that the urge to emancipate is also fundamental to the human spirit. A century and a half later Wilberforce's successors are striving, by all available United Nations means, to see that the process of emancipation has no territorial limitations.

NOTES AND REFERENCES

ABBREVIATIONS

CHR United Nations Commission on Human Rights
ECOSOC United Nations Economic and Social Council
ICRC International Committee of the Red Cross
ILO International Labour Organization
ND Nuremberg Documents
NEB New English Bible
NIK Nuremberg Industrial Krupp
PRO FO Public Record Office, London, Foreign Office
RCE Report of the Committee of Experts on the Application of Conventions and Recommendations
SUB-COMMISSION United Nations Sub-Commission on Protection of Human Rights and Protection of Minorities
UNA United Nations Association of Great Britain and Northern Ireland
UNDP United Nations Development Programme
WHO World Health Organization

CHAPTER 1 INTRODUCTION: DEFINITIONS AND THEIR ORIGINS

1 Genesis, chapter 3, verse 16 (NEB: 'he shall be your master').
2 Aristotle, *Politics*, L.I., c. 5.
3 For example, J. R. Dummelow (ed.), *A Commentary on the Holy Bible*, p. 69: 'Among the Hebrews, however, slavery was by no means the degrading and oppressive thing that it was among other nations.'
4 Exodus, chapter 21, verses 4–6 (NEB: 'If his master gives him a wife, and she bears him sons or daughters, the woman and her children shall belong to her master, and the man shall go away alone. But if the slave shall say, "I love my master, my wife, and

my children; I will not go free", then his master shall bring him to God: he shall bring him to the door or the door-post, and his master shall pierce his ear with an awl, and the man shall be his slave for life').

5 Leviticus, chapter 25, verse 43 (NEB: 'You shall not drive him with ruthless severity').

6 Jeremiah, chapter 34, verse 14 (NEB: ' "Within seven years each of you shall set free any Hebrew who has sold himself to you as a slave and has served you for six years; you shall set him free." Your forefathers did not listen to me or obey me').

7 Galatians, chapter 3, verse 28 (NEB: 'There is no such thing as . . . slave and freeman').

8 I Peter, chapter 2, verse 18 (NEB: '. . . accept the authority of your masters with all due submission').

9 J. R. P. Montgomery, 'Some common questions answered', a paper printed and circulated by the Anti-Slavery Society for the Protection of Human Rights, p. 1.

10 Ibid.

CHAPTER 2 CHATTEL SLAVERY

1 PRO FO 369/51.

2 J. Laffin, 'The Arabs as slavers', in *Case Studies on Human Rights and Fundamental Freedoms: A World Survey*, vol. 4, p. 458; and Anti-Slavery Society, private communications to author, 1985.

3 J. R. P. Montgomery to author, 30 April 1984.

4 Jacob Oliel.

5 André Chalard.

6 M. Awad (Special Rapporteur on Slavery), *Report on Slavery*, pp. 167–8, paragraph 600.

7 J. Mercer, *Spanish Sahara* and *The Sahrawis of Western Sahara.*

8 J. Mercer, tape-recording played at the Anti-Slavery Society annual general meeting, 8 December 1980.

9 J. Mercer, *Slavery in Mauritania Today*, pp. 35–7.

10 *New York Times*, 10 September 1981.

11 Mercer, ibid., p. 25.

12 Ibid., pp. 10–11.

13 Ibid., p. 11.

14 Recommended by the Sub-Commission, resolution 16 (XXXIV)

adopted on 10 September 1981, decided by CHR in resolution 1982/20 adopted on 10 March 1982.

15 ECOSOC, E/CN.4/Sub.2/1984/25 p. 5, paragraph 22.

16 Forced Labour Convention, 1930 (no. 29), article 25. Jacob Oliel was the independent French witness who made this intervention.

17 ECOSOC, *Report of the Mission to Mauritania*, E/CN.4/Sub.2/ 1984/23, 2 July 1984.

18 B. Whitaker (Special Rapporteur on Slavery), *Slavery*, E/CN.4/ Sub2/1982/20/Rev. 1, p. 19, paragraph 80.

19 J. Challis and D. Elliman, *Child Workers Today*, pp. 111–14.

20 ECOSOC, Sub-Commission, 27th session, 20 August 1974. R. Arens, statement on behalf of the Anti-Slavery Society: Agenda item 8.

21 M. Münzel, *The Aché Indians: Genocide in Paraguay*, pp. 20–2.

22 N. Lewis, 'Manhunt', *The Sunday Times Magazine*, 26 January 1976.

23 M. Münzel to author, 2 April 1985.

CHAPTER 3 THE SLAVE AS A DISPOSABLE ASSET

1 A. Hitler, *Mein Kampf*, p. 248.

2 Ibid., p. 570.

3 Ibid., p. 250.

4 Ibid., p. 249.

5 Ibid., p. 562.

6 Ibid., p. 352.

7 Ibid., p. 256.

8 Ibid., p. 257.

9 Ibid.

10 Ibid., p. 580.

11 T. Friedman in *Jerusalem Post*, 19 May 1970 (cited by A. Speer, *The Slave State*, p. 291).

12 B. Helfgott (Jewish slave labourer throughout the Second World War), tape-recorded interview with author, 23 January 1985.

13 Speer, op. cit., p. 4.

14 H. Himmler to Oswald Pohl, 31 January 1942.

15 NIK-4728; NIK-11977, -2877.

16 ND D-288.

17 *Trials of War Criminals Before the Nuremberg Military Tribunals*

Under Control Council Law No. 10, Nuremberg October 1946–April 1949, vol. IX, 116, 1409.

18 Dr Gerhard Wiele.

19 ND D-283.

20 Hitler, op. cit., p. 574.

21 ND 3040-PS.

22 Quoted by Franz Neumann in *Behemoth* (2nd edn), pp. 462–3.

23 J. F. Maxwell, *Slavery and the Catholic Church*, p. 124.

24 *Gaudium et Spes*, para 27.

CHAPTER 4 APARTHEID

1 M. Awad, *Report on Slavery*, E/CN.4/Sub.2/322, paragraph 167.

2 B. Whitaker, *Slavery*, E/CN.4/Sub.2/1982/20/Rev. 1, paragraph 33.

3 ECOSOC Sub-Commission, 37th session, Agenda item 12, *Report of the Working Group on Slavery on its Tenth Session*, E/CN.4/Sub.2/1984/25, paragraph 75.

4 *South Africa 1984*, Official Yearbook of the Republic of South Africa, p. 51.

5 *Collins Westminster Dictionary*.

6 The Batswana, for instance, are credited with fifth-century settlements in the Zeerust and Hartebeespoort areas.

7 Forced Labour Convention, 1930 (no. 29), article 2, paragraph 2(c).

8 RCE, 1955, p.43; general survey of 1968, paragraph 79; RCE, 1974, pp. 68–9.

9 Affidavit signed and sworn by James Musa Sadika at Johannesburg, 6 May 1959, quoted in A. Cook. *Akin to Slavery: Prison Labour in South Africa*, pp. 67–73.

10 Cook, op. cit., pp. 34–5. Reminiscent of trigger finger stories of the world wars, if this is not an exaggeration it must be explained in terms of mass hysteria.

11 Excerpts from transcript of tape-recorded interview with field worker for South African Council of Churches, November 1984. The interrogation described occurred in Pietermaritzburg in 1976. The former prisoner now lives in Bophuthatswana.

12 *Terrorism Act*, no. 83 of 1967.

13 *Further Correspondence Respecting the Affairs of Bechuanaland and Adjacent Territories*, PP 1890 (C.5918) li, 389.

14 Ibid.
15 Ben Helfgott, a Polish Jew who survived the Nazi concentration camps because, as he puts it, 'Slavery was a ticket to survival', visited South Africa after the war. There were too many reminders of National Socialism for him to stay long. He was the 'Master' now, and all around him was the apparatus of selection: signs marked 'Whites' or 'Non-Whites' at every turn. (They are less obvious now.)

CHAPTER 5 EXPLOITATION OF CHILDREN

1 ILO, *Report of the Director-General*, International Labour Conference, 69th session, p. 12.
2 Ibid., p. 3.
3 Minimum Age Convention, 1973 (no. 138), article 2, paragraph 3.
4 Ibid., paragraph 4.
5 *Minimum Age*, General Survey of the Reports relating to Convention no. 138 and Recommendation no. 146 concerning Minimum Age, paragraph 75.
6 The Black Labour Act (no. 67) of 1964, Section 3(c).
7 Anti-Slavery Society, copy of 'Special permit to recruit underaged Bantu'.
8 Factories, Machinery and Building Works Act (no. 22) of 1941 (amended 1960, 1963, 1967, 1968); The Wages Act (no. 5) of 1957; the Children's Act (no. 33) of 1960; the Shops and Offices Act (no. 75) of 1974.
9 Anti-Slavery Society, *Child Labour in South Africa* (Child Labour Series: no. 7), pp. 29–38.
10 Ibid., p. 32.
11 *Sunday Times*, Johannesburg, 29 July 1979.
12 Anti-Slavery Society, *Child Labour in South Africa* (Child Labour Series: no. 7), p. 28.
13 *Cape Times*, Cape Town, 23 February 1982.
14 B. Rose and R. Turner (eds), *Documents in South African Education*.
15 *Observer*, London, 30 October 1983.
16 Dahir (Moroccan legal decree) of 2 July 1947 (Minimum Age) and application number 2.77.52 of 28 December 1976, i.e. after the first Anti-Slavery Society visit (Minimum Wages).

17 In March 1975 and March 1977.
18 Anti-Slavery Society, *Child Labour in Morocco's Carpet Industry*.
19 J. Challis and D. Elliman, in association with the Anti-Slavery Society, pp. 103–4 (quotation from report made by the Anti-Slavery Society team which visited Morocco in 1975).
20 S. Searight, for Anti-Slavery Society, *Child Labour in Spain* (Child Labour Series no. 3).
21 M. Valcarenghi for Anti-Slavery Society, *Child Labour in Italy*, (Child Labour Series no. 5).
22 Ibid., p. 51.
23 Decreto, 4 gennaio 1971, n. 36, art. 1(1)(c).
24 Anti-Slavery Society, *Child Labour in Colombia*: Report for 1979 to the United Nations Working Group of Experts on Slavery.
25 Ibid., p. 3.
26 J. Fernand-Laurent (Special Rapporteur on the suppression of the traffic in persons and the exploitation of the prostitution of others), *Activities for the Advancement of Women: Equality, Development and Peace*, E/1983/7 17 March 1983, p. 43, paragraph 118.
27 Anti-Slavery Society, *Child Labour on Plantations*, statement of 1984 to the United Nations Working Group of Experts on Slavery.
28 *Report and Special Report from the Select Committee on Putumayo*, Proceedings, Minutes of Evidence, 1913 (H. of C. Paper 148), XIV.
29 S. Banerjee, for Anti-Slavery Society, *Child Labour in India* (Child Labour Series no. 2) and *Child Labour in Thailand* (Child Labour Series no. 4).
30 Banerjee, *Child Labour in Thailand*, p. 31 (from a wireless interview).
31 Ibid., quotation from *Thailand Investment Handbook*, produced by the Board of Investment, Royal Thai Government, 1978.
32 Anti-Slavery Society, 'Sexual exploitation of children', statement of 1984 to the United Nations Working Group of Experts on Slavery.
33 Challis and Elliman, op. cit., p. 154.
34 ILO, *Towards an Action Programme on Child Labour*, Report to the Government of India of an ILO Technical Mission.

CHAPTER 6 EXPLOITATION OF WOMEN

1 J. Fernand-Laurent (Special Rapporteur on the suppression of the traffic in persons and the exploitation of the prostitution of others), *Activities for the Advancement of Women: Equality, Development and Peace*, E/1983/7, 17 March 1983, p. 3, paragraph 1.
2 Ibid., p. 8, paragraph 23.
3 U. Ohse, *Forced Prostitution and Traffic in Women in West Germany*, p.12 (quotation from a statement by Edgar Schmidt-Pauli in an article 'Ehe zum Zweck der Prostitution', *Frankfurter Allgemeine Zeitung*, 1 September 1977).
4 Ibid., p. 22 (quotation from Interpol Report, 'Traffic in women: recent trends', l.c., p. 4, compiled for United Nations Human Rights Commission, 1974).
5 P. Phongpaichit, *From Peasant Girls to Bangkok Masseuses* (International Labour Organization Paper, Women, Work and Development, 2).
6 Ohse, op. cit.
7 Phongpaichit, op. cit., p. 56.
8 At the time of the research the rate of exchange was about 45 bahts to the pound sterling. However, changes have been so dramatic that generally here comparisons have been preferred to figures.
9 Ohse, op. cit, p. 66.
10 Ibid., pp. 46–8.
11 Ibid., p. 49.
12 Ibid.
13 R. B. Cullen and T. Nater, 'A sexual rite on trial', *Newsweek*, Washington, 1982.
14 Anti-Slavery Society and Rädda Barnen (Swedish Save the Children), *Female Circumcision*, p. 1. The range of practice is, in fact, wide: see L. P. Sanderson, *Against the Mutilation of Women*, pp. 13–25.
15 Cullen and Nater, op. cit., verbal information from WHO officials.
16 Ibid.
17 S. Bhatia, 'New evidence on female mutilation', *Observer*, 27 February 1983. There was wide newspaper coverage of genital mutilation in the United Kingdom during 1983; and on 7 February 1984, during the second reading of the Prohibition of Female Circumcision Bill, in the House of Lords, Baroness Masham of

Ilton said that she had heard about the operation being performed at the London Clinic, and in Tower Hamlets and Cardiff.

18 L. P. Sanderson to author, 27 February 1985. When this letter was received the Bill was about to enter the committee stage and it was felt that this clause would bridge the gap between the female genital mutilation abolitionists and the government.

19 Keston College, *Christian Prisoners in the USSR 1983/4*, p. 15. The place of confinement was Tashkent Special Psychiatric Hospital. It is believed that Anna Chertkova is still there.

20 W. Dushnyck, 'Discrimination and abuse of power in the USSR', in *Case Studies on Human Rights and Fundamental Freedoms: A World Survey*, vol. 2, p. 528.

21 Sura IV, verse 35.

22 J. R. P. Montgomery to author, private communication, 1985.

23 R. Bahar, of the International Working Group on Women and the Family, to author, 7 February 1985. A file on Shahila is kept by Amnesty International.

24 UNA to J. R. P. Montgomery, 19 March 1984.

25 Sura IV, verse 129.

26 Costa Luca, 'Discrimination in the Arab Middle East', in *Case Studies on Human Rights and Fundamental Freedoms: A World Survey*, vol. 1, p. 224.

27 From the Hadith, quoted by Clemens Amelunxen, 'Marriage and women in Islamic countries', in *Case Histories on Human Rights and Fundamental Freedoms: A World Survey*, vol. 2, p. 98.

CHAPTER 7 DEBT BONDAGE AND SERFDOM

1 S. Marla, *Bonded Labour in India*, p. 24.

2 Ibid., p. 21.

3 'Debt bondage – a survey', *Anti-Slavery Reporter*, series VII, vol. 13, no. 1, p. 12.

4 J. Ennew, *Debt Bondage: A Survey*, Anti-Slavery Society Research Report, p. 63.

5 The Bonded Labour System (Abolition) Act, 1976, no. 19 of 1976.

6 Ibid., chapter 2, Abolition of Bonded Labour System, 4(1).

7 Ibid., chapter 2, Abolition of Bonded Labour System, 4(2).

8 Ibid., chapter 3, Extinguishment of Liability to Repay Bonded

Debt, Property of bonded labourer to be freed from mortgage, etc., 7(2).

9 Ibid., chapter 3, Extinguishment of Liability to Repay Bonded Debt, Freed bonded labourer not to be evicted from homestead, etc., 8(1) and (2).

10 Ibid., chapter 4, Implementing Authorities, Duty of District Magistrate and other officers to ensure credit (11).

11 Ibid., chapter 5, Vigilance Committees.

12 Ibid., chapter 5, Vigilance Committees, Functions of Vigilance Committees, 14(b).

13 Ibid., chapter 6, Offences and Procedure for Trial.

14 Swami Agnivesh, statement to United Nations Working Group of Experts on Slavery, Geneva, August 1984.

15 Cited by Marla, op. cit., p. 10.

16 Marla, op. cit. pp. 1 and 134–41.

17 Ibid., pp. 144–7.

18 Ibid., p. 123.

19 Ibid., p. 130.

20 Ibid., p. 37.

21 Ibid., pp. 19–20.

22 Ibid., p. 50.

23 Ibid., p. 60.

24 Ibid., p. 146.

25 Representative of the Indian government, addressing the United Nations Working Group of Experts on Slavery, Geneva, August 1984.

26 Swami Agnevish, statement to United Nations Working Group of Experts on Slavery, Geneva, August 1984.

27 *Correspondence Respecting the Treatment of British Colonial Subjects and Native Indians Employed in the Collection of Rubber in the Putumayo District*, PP 1912–13 (Cd 6266) LXVIII. Casement was chosen because of his exposure of similar atrocities committed in the Congo basin in 1903.

28 *Report and Special Report from the Select Committee on Putumayo, Proceedings, Minutes of Evidence* 1913 (H. of C. Paper 148) XIV Q 12269.

29 Ibid., Q 2845 (part of Sir Roger Casement's answer to a question put to him by Sir Thomas Esmonde).

30 'Debt bondage – the Andoke Indians of Colombia', *The Anti-Slavery Reporter*, series VI, vol. 12, no. 5, p. 8. The 1974 patron

of the Andoke – Zumaeta – has the same name as one of the four original owners of the Peruvian Amazon Rubber Company.

31 M. Huxley and C. Capa, *Farewell to Eden*, pp. 161–4.

32 A. Seiler-Baldinger, 'Indians and the pioneer front in the north-east Amazon', in F. Barbira-Scazzocchio (ed.), *Land, People and Planning in Contemporary Amazonia*, p. 246.

33 Anti-Slavery Society, 'Bonded and forced labour in Peru and India', E/CN.4/Sub.2/AC.2/1984/NGO.1) statement of 1984 to the United Nations Working Group of Experts on Slavery, pp. 2–3.

34 M. Awad (Special Rapporteur on slavery), *Report on Slavery*, p. 56 (from Ecuador's reply to Slavery questionnaire).

35 Ibid., p. 56. Ecuador cites Land Reform and Settlement Act, 1964, article 65.

36 Memorandum Prepared by the International Commission of Jurists, ECOSOC, E/CN.4/Sub.2/AC.2/1984/NGO.3, pp. 3–4.

37 Ibid., pp. 3–5.

38 Ibid., Report of Seminar on 'Bonded labour and other forms of labour exploitation in South Asia', Kathmandu, Nepal, May 1984.

39 Ibid., p. 5. It was an International Commission of Jurists' seminar on Rural Development and Human Rights in South Asia, and was held in Lucknow, India in 1982.

40 Ennew, op. cit., p. 41.

41 Ibid., p. 44.

CHAPTER 8 PERSECUTION OF TRIBAL MINORITIES

1 ICRC, *Report of the ICRC Medical Mission to the Brazilian Amazon Region*.

2 R. Hanbury-Tenison, *Report of a Visit to the Indians of Brazil*.

3 *Correspondence Respecting the treatment of British Colonial Subjects and Native Indians Employed in the Collection of Rubber in the Putumayo District* PP 1912–13 (Cd 6266) LXVIII; and *Report and Special Report from the Select Committee on Putumayo, Proceedings, Minutes of Evidence* 1913 (H. of C. Paper 148) XIV.

4 Edwin Brooks (leader of the mission), then 42; Senior Lecturer in Geography, University of Liverpool; first president, the Conservation Society, 1967; investigated Amerindian conditions in Guyana, 1969 on behalf of Amnesty, the United Nations Associ-

ation and the Aborigines Protection Society. Now Dean of Business and Liberal Studies, Riverina College of Advanced Education, New South Wales. Rene Fuerst, then 40, ethnologist; engaged in Brazilian Amerindian research, 1961–69; technical adviser to International Red Cross medical mission to Brazil, 1970. John Hemming, then 37; Iriri River Expedition 1961, supported by the Royal Geographical Society and the Instituto Brasileiro de Geografia e Estatistica; spent most of 1971 in Brazil on a Miranda Scholarship, visiting twenty-two tribes in preparation for a history of relations with Brazilian Indians; member of Council of Anglo-Brazilian Society for 1963 and of Royal Geographical Society (of which he is now Director and Secretary) from 1966; author of *The Conquest of the Incas* and other prize-winning books on Amerindians. Francis Huxley, then 48; social anthropologist; research fellow of St Catherine's College, Oxford, co-founder of Survival International; had worked in Brazil; author of several relevant anthropological works.

5 Fundacao Nacional do Indio (National Foundation of the Indian) – a department of the Brazilian Ministry of the Interior responsible for Indian affairs.

6 E. Brooks (ed.), *Tribes of the Amazon Basin in Brazil 1972*, p. 23.

7 Ibid., pp. 44–5.

8 Ibid., p. 46.

9 Since publication of the Anti-Slavery Society's report, *Tribes of the Amazon Basin in Brazil 1972*, the Summer Institute of Linguistics has been discovered by members of Survival International and other independent observers to be one of the worst of the missions to the Amerindians. It has imposed alien ideas and practices on the tribes to an irresponsible degree.

10 From the third study meeting on the *Pastoral Indigena* held in Brasilia by the National Council of Bishops of Brazil during April 1972, quoted in Brooks (ed.), op. cit., p. 14.

11 A reserve is an area set aside for one tribe, a park is for more than one tribe.

12 Brooks (ed.), op. cit., p. 139.

13 Ibid., p. 51.

14 Ibid., p. 146.

15 Federal Constitution of Brazil (1969), article 198.

16 Statute of the Indian, draft law (1970), article 22.

17 Brooks (ed.), op. cit., pp. 97–8

18 Ibid., pp. 58–65.
19 *Guardas Rurais Indigenas Nacionais*.
20 Brooks (ed.), op. cit., p. 148.
21 O. J. Bandeira de Mello, President, *Observations on the Report Presented by the Aborigines Protection Society*, Brasilia, 21 December 1972.
22 The Anti-Slavery Society attempted to bring the changes affecting FUNAI and their consequences to the attention of the United Nations Sub-Commission on Prevention of Discrimination and Protection of Minorities on 10 September 1980, in a debate on 'Racial discrimination against indigenous populations'. It was refused permission because of lack of time and, instead, released the information to the press.
23 J. Hemming, 'The last colonial frontier: the plight of the Brazilian Indians', p. iv.
24 R. P. H. Davies to Exmo. Sr. General João Figueiredo, 14 June 1982.
25 ECOSOC Working Group in Indigenous Populations, E/CN.4/Sub.2/A.C.4/1984/4/Add.I, p. 8.
26 Anti-Slavery Society, *The Chittagong Hill Tracts*, Indigenous Peoples and Development Series (no. 2), p. 33.
27 Ibid., p. 23.
28 Ibid., p. 51.
29 Ibid., p. 50.
30 'Hillmen of the Chittagong Hill Tracts', *Anti-Slavery Reporter*, series VII, vol. 13, no. 1, p. 3.
31 Anti-Slavery Society, *The Chittagong Hill Tracts*, p. 59.
32 Ibid., p.70.
33 Anti-Slavery Society, *The Philippines*, Indigenous Peoples and Development Series (no. 1), pp. 120–9.
34 Ibid., p. 129.
35 Ibid., p. 145.
36 'Memorandum on the Philippines', *Anti-Slavery Reporter*, series VII, vol. 13, no.1, p.7.
37 Ibid.
38 Anti-Slavery Society, *The Philippines*, p. 167.
39 Arkhiv Samizdata, Radio Liberty, 'Open letter from the Russian friends of the Crimean Tartars'.
40 A. Sheehy and B. Nahaylo, *The Crimean Tartars, Volga Germans*

and Meskhetians: Soviet treatment of some national minorities (3rd edn), p. 8.

41 Ibid., p.13.

42 A. Sakharov to President Leonid Brezhnev, 10 April 1979.

CHAPTER 9 MIGRANT WORKERS AND FORCED LABOUR

1 ILO, Abolition of Forced Labour Convention (no. 105), 1957, article 1.

2 ILO, Forced Labour Convention (no. 29), 1930, article 2(c).

3 Anti-Slavery Society, *Migrant Workers in the Dominican Republic* Report for 1979 to the United Nations Working Group of Experts on Slavery.

4 ILO Commission of Inquiry figure, published in Official Bulletin Special Supplement, Series B, vol. LXVI, 1983, p. 34.

5 B. Helfgott to author.

6 ILO, op. cit., p. 123, paragraph 430.

7 Anti-Slavery Society, op. cit., pp. 9–10.

8 ECOSOC, Working Group on Slavery, *Review of Developments in the Field of Slavery and the Slave Trade in all their Practices and Manifestations*. E/CN.4/Sub.2/AC.2/1983/6/Add.1 28 July 1983, p. 2, note I: '. . . under Article 26 of the Constitution of the International Labour Organisation to examine the observance of certain international labour conventions. . . .'

9 ILO, op. cit., p. 52, paragraph 174.

10 Ibid.

11 Ibid., p. 53, paragraph 176.

12 Ibid., p. 101, paragraph 375.

13 Ibid., p. 20, paragraph 64.

14 Ibid., p. 54, paragraph 181.

15 Ibid., p. 64, paragraph 218.

16 Ibid., p. 66, paragraph 227.

17 Ibid., pp. 145–8, paragraphs 494–501.

18 Ibid., p. 93, paragraph 345.

19 Ibid., p. 104, paragraph 386.

20 Ibid., p. 31, paragraph 98.

21 Ibid., p. 30, paragraph 96.

22 Ibid., p. 58, paragraph 197.

23 Ibid., p. 59, paragraph 199.

24 ECOSOC, op. cit., E/CN.4/Sub.2/AC.2/1983/6/Add.1 28 July 1983, paragraph 13.

25 J. R. P. Montgomery, 'A task unfinished', *Chronicle*, vol. 4, no. 1, January 1984, p. 26.

26 R. West, *Back to Africa*, p. 302.

27 Thomas J. Faulkner, a black American.

28 West, op. cit., p. 303.

29 League of Nations Document C.568M.272, Commission's Report, quoted by S. Cronjé in *Equatorial Guinea: The Forgotten Dictatorship*, Anti-Slavery Society Research Report, p. 16.

30 Cronjé, op. cit., p. 9.

31 Ibid., p. 13.

32 Ibid., p. 22.

33 N. Debelius, 'Equatorial Guinea accused of slavery', *The Times*, 6 February 1976 (report dated 5 February 1976).

34 Cronjé, op. cit.

35 United Nations Development Programme, *Living Conditions in Equatorial Guinea*, UNDP/ADM/POST/EQD/Rev. 3, 11 August 1975.

36 *Africa*, no. 34, June 1974, p. 21.

37 Cronjé, op. cit., p. 30.

38 International Monetary Fund, *Etudes Generales sur les Economies Africaines*, p. 326.

39 United Nations Development Programme, Assistance requested by the Government of Equatorial Guinea for the period 1974–1978. Country and Intercountry Programming, Governing Council, 19th session, 15–31 January 1975, Agenda item 4, DP/GC/EQG/R.I, 23 October 1974, p. 38.

40 Cronjé, op. cit., p. 36.

41 F. V. Jiménez (Special Rapporteur), *Study of the Human Rights Situation in Equatorial Guinea*, E/CN.4/1371, 12 February 1980.

42 Montgomery, op. cit., p. 27.

43 J. Challis and D. Elliman, *Child Workers Today*, p. 73.

44 Ibid., pp. 70–1.

45 Anti-Slavery Society, 'Turkish migrant children in Germany', Report for 1983 to the United Nations Working Group on Slavery.

46 'Forced labour in Humera', *Anti-Slavery Reporter*, Series VII, vol. 13, no. 1, p. 21. The report was put before the Working Group on Slavery and printed in ECOSOC E/CN.4/Sub.2/486.

47 Ibid., p. 23.

CHAPTER 10 POLITICAL/PENAL SLAVERY

1 Protection of Persons Subjected to Detention or Imprisonment: Standard Minimum Rules for the Treatment of Prisoners, Adopted by the First United Nations Congress on the Prevention of Crime and the Treatment of Offenders, held at Geneva in 1955, and approved by ECOSOC by its resolutions 663 C(XXIV) of 31 July 1957 and 2076 (LXII) of 13 May 1977, paragraph 71(2).
2 J. Leguebe, 'Mozambique under Frelimo rule', in *Case Studies on Human Rights and Fundamental Freedoms: A World Survey*, vol. 4, p. 26.
3 Ibid., p. 12, quoting *Tempo*, Lisbon, February 1976.
4 M. O'Callaghan, 'The labour camps of People's China', *Guardian*, London, 29 August 1984.
5 Colonel J. R. P. Montgomery, Secretary of the Anti-Slavery Society 1963–80.
6 N. Akhmetov and V. Mikhalenko, 'Open letter', October 1978.
7 K. Simson, Secretary, Writers in Prison Committee, to J. R. P. Montgomery, 24 July 1984.
8 Ibid.
9 W. Dushnyck, 'Discrimination and abuse of power in the USSR', in *Case Studies on Human Rights and Fundamental Freedoms: A World Survey*, vol. 2, p. 532.
10 A. Shifrin, 'Human cost of Communism', delivered during a panel of the 7th Annual Conference of the World Anti-Communist League, April 8–11, 1974, Washington, DC, p. 1.
11 A. Solzhenitsyn, *The Gulag Archipelago*, vol. 2, pp. 13, 17 and 75–6.
12 Ibid., p. 71.
13 Ibid., p. 98.
14 A. Y. Vyshinsky, in preface to I. L. Averbakh, *Ot Prestupleniya k Trudu* (*From Crime to Labour*), p. vi.
15 Solzhenitsyn, op. cit., vol. 2, p. 139.
16 Ibid., pp. 151–4.
17 C. Verpoorten (ed.), 'Made in Goulag', *L'Eventail Special*, January 1981, English translation printed and distributed by the Wilberforce Council for Human Rights.
18 Ibid., p. 1.

19 Ibid., p. 2. The comment is attributed to the Sales Director of the Technical and Optical Equipment Company.
20 Ibid., p. 2.
21 G. Davydov, 'Compulsory labor in the Soviet economy', Radio Liberty Research, (RL 50/83), 26 January 1983, p. 2.
22 Verpoorten (ed.), op. cit., p. 3.
23 Davydov, op. cit., p. 5.
24 Criminal Code of the RSFSR (Russian Republic), article 227.
25 Ibid., article 142.
26 Verpoorten (ed.), op. cit., p. 3.
27 Ibid., p. 2. The comment is attributed to the Commercial Director of Cowan de Groot.
28 Ibid.
29 Ibid., p. 4.
30 Ibid., p. 3.
31 Ibid., p. 4.
32 Davydov, op. cit., p. 4.
33 Solzhenitsyn, op. cit., vol. 2, p. 581.
34 Public Health Directive no. 04.14 (32), October 1961.
35 Public Health Directive no. 345–209, May 1969.
36 Keston College, *Christian Prisoners in the USSR 1983/84* p. 14.
37 Dushnyck, op. cit., pp. 537–8.
38 Protection of Persons Subjected to Detention or Imprisonment: Standard Minimum Rules for the Treatment of Prisoners, paragraph 76(1).
39 Ibid., paragraph 74(1).
40 Ibid., paragraph 72(2).
41 Ibid., paragraph 71(1).
42 *Ruffin v. Commonwealth*, 62 Va. (21 Gratt.) 790 (1871).
43 J. Waugh, 'Prisons: changing a system that doesn't work', *The Christian Science Monitor*, 16 December 1971.
44 J. Mitford, *The American Prison Business*, p. 190.
45 E. H. Schein, 'Man against man: brainwashing', *Corrective Psychiatry and Journal of Social Change*, vol. 8, no. 2 (second quarter, 1962).
46 Mitford, op. cit., p. 161.
47 *Calvin Sims et al. v. Parke Davis & Co. et al.*, DC, 334 F. Supp. 774 (1971).
48 *Pitts v. Reagan*, 14 CA 3d 112 (1971).

49 The significance of the Attica uprising is considered by Howard Zinn in *A People's History of the United States*, pp. 510–13.
50 Solzhenitsyn, op. cit., vol. 1, p. 147.

CHAPTER 11 THE ROLE OF THE UNITED NATIONS

1 *General Act of the Brussels Conference Relative to the African Slave Trade*, signed at Brussels, 2 July 1890.
2 C. W. W. Greenidge, *Slavery*, p. 178.
3 *Convention Revising the General Act of Berlin, February 26 1885, and the General Act and Declaration of Brussels, July 2 1890*, signed at Saint Germain-en-Laye, 10 September 1919.
4 Ibid., article 11(1).
5 Ibid.
6 Lady Simon, *Slavery*, p. 248.
7 *Slavery Convention*, signed at Geneva, 25 September 1926, article 7.
8 Afghanistan, Bahrein, Iraq, Kelat, Nepal, Persia and Transjordania.
9 F. Lugard, 'Slavery in all its forms', in *Africa*, January 1933, quoted by Greenidge, op. cit., p. 186.
10 Appointed by the Secretary-General in December 1949, the *ad hoc* Committee of Experts on Slavery consisted of Professor Moises Poblete Troncoso (Chile), Madame Jane Vialle (France), Bruno Lasker (United States) and C. W. W. Greenidge (United Kingdom). Professor Poblete Troncoso was elected chairman; C. W. W. Greenidge, who was the Secretary of the Anti-Slavery Society, was nominated rapporteur. The committee members were not appointed as national representatives.
11 M. Awad (Special Rapporteur on slavery), *Report on Slavery*, paragraph 1625, p. 307.
12 J. R. P. Montgomery, 'Background to the present situation at the United Nations concerning slavery', United Nations paper, p. 4.
13 G. von Potobsky, 'On-the-spot visits: an important cog in the ILO's supervisory machinery', *International Labour Review*, vol. 120, no. 5, September-October, 1981, p. 584. This chapter owes much to Potobsky's article, and I thank Klaus Samson, of the International Labour Office, for drawing my attention to it.
14 R. P. H. Davies, Director of the Anti-Slavery Society, to

Secretary-General of the United Nations Organization, 18 January, 1985, pp. 1–2.

15 Ibid.

16 ECOSOC, *Report of the Mission to Mauritania*, E/CN.4/Sub.2/1984/23, 2 July 1984, p. 16, paragraph 85.

17 Davies, op. cit., pp. 5–6.

Bibliography

ANTI-SLAVERY PUBLICATIONS AND PAPERS

(published or privately printed in London, unless otherwise stated)

(a) Publications

Anti-Slavery Reporter and Aborigines' Friend, Series V: 29–31 (1939–42) and 32–34 (1942–45), Klaus Reprint, 1969; Series VI: November 1976, vol. 12, no. 5, November 1979, vol. 12, no. 6 and November 1980, vol. 12, no. 7; Series VII: December 1981, vol. 13, no. 1.

Anti-Slavery Society Annual Report for years ended 31 March 1972, 1973, 1974, 1975, 1976, 1977, 1978, 1981, 1982, 1983 and 1984.

Child Labour Series:
- *Child Labour in Morocco's Carpet Industry*, 1978.
- Banerjee, S., *Child Labour in India*, 1979.
- Banerjee, S., *Child Labour in Thailand*, 1980.
- Searight, S., *Child Labour in Spain*, 1980.
- Valcarenghi, M., *Child Labour in Italy*, 1981.
- *Child Labour in South Africa*, 1983.

Indigenous Peoples and Development Series:
- *The Philippines*, 1983.
- *The Chittagong Hill Tracts*, 1984.

Research Reports:
- Cronjé, S., *Equatorial Guinea: The Forgotten Dictatorship*, 1976.
- Ennew, J., *Debt Bondage: A Survey*, 1981.
- Gretton, J., *Western Sahara: The Fight for Self-Determination*, 1976.
- Pool, D., *Eritrea: Africa's Longest War* (revised edition), 1982.
- With Rädda Barnen (Swedish Save the Children), *Female Circumcision*, Geneva, 1982.

(b) Submissions to the United Nations Working Group of Experts on Slavery

Cronjé, S., 'The wall of silence: forced labour and political murder in Equatorial Guinea', 1976.

'Child labour in Colombia', 1979.

'Child labour in Hong Kong', 1979.

'Child labour in India', 1979.

'The exploitation of child labour', oral intervention by Leah Levin, 1979.

'Migrant workers in the Dominican Republic', 1979.

'Child labour in Sivakasi', 1983.

'Turkish migrant children in Germany', 1983.

'Bonded and forced labour in Peru and India', 1984.

'Child domestic workers in Latin America', 1984.

'Child labour on plantations', 1984.

'Sexual exploitation of children', 1984.

(c) Papers with limited circulation

Arens, R., Statement made to Sub-Commission, 20 August 1974.

Davies, R. P. H., Note to Secretary-General of United Nations, 18 January 1985.

Hemming, J., 'The last colonial frontier: the plight of the Brazilian Indians', 1982.

Montgomery, J. R. P., 'Background to the present situation at the United Nations concerning slavery', September 1974.

'Non-governmental organizations in consultative status', Report of Debate held in New York on 2 May 1977.

Montgomery, J. R. P., 'Some common questions answered', n.d.

'Slavery', Statement made to Sub-Commission, 25 August 1976.

Swift, J., Statement on behalf of the Anti-Slavery Society to Sub-Commission, 1973.

PARLIAMENTARY PAPERS

Further Correspondence Respecting the Affairs of Bechuanaland and Adjacent Territories, PP 1890 (C.5918) li, 389.

Correspondence Respecting the Treatment of British Colonial Subjects and Native Indians Employed in the Collection of Rubber in the Putumayo District, PP 1912–13 (Cd 6266) LXVIII.

Report and Special Report from the Select Committee on Putumayo, Proceedings, Minutes of Evidence, 1913 (H. of C. Paper 148) XIV.

UNITED NATIONS PUBLICATIONS AND PAPERS

(published in Geneva, unless otherwise stated)

Basic Facts about the United Nations, New York, 1984.

Human Rights: A Compilation of International Instruments, New York, 1978.

The United Nations and Human Rights, New York, 1984.

Economic and Social Council

(excluding Anti-Slavery Society interventions listed above)

Anti-Slavery Society report to Working Group on Indigenous Populations, E/CN.4/Sub.2/AC.4/1984/4/Add.2, 16 July, 1984, reference Bangladesh, Guatemala, the Philippines and West Papua.

Anti-Slavery Society statement on the Report of the Sub-Commission, 28 February 1985.

Awad, M. (Special Rapporteur), *Report on Slavery*, E/4168/Rev.1, New York, 1966.

Bouhdiba, A. (Special Rapporteur), *Exploitation of Child Labour*, E/CN.4/Sub.2/479/Rev.1, New York, 1982.

Developments in the Field of Slavery and the Slave Trade in all their Practices and Manifestations, E/CN.4/Sub.2/AC.2/1983/6/Add.1, 28 July 1983. Fernand-Laurent, J. (Special Rapporteur on the suppression of the traffic in persons and the exploitation of the prostitution of others), *Activities for the Advancement of Women: Equality, Development and Peace*, report E/1983/7, 17 March 1983.

Four Directions Council to Working Group on Indigenous Populations, Statement on the Recognition and Protection of Indigenous Peoples' Right to Land, E/CN.4/Sub.2/AC.4/1984/NGO/1, 30 July 1984.

Information submitted by the International Criminal Police Organization (INTERPOL) to the Working Group of Experts on Slavery, E/CN.4/Sub.2/AC.2/1984/7, 14 May 1984.

Memorandum prepared by the International Commission of Jurists for the United Nations Working Group on Slavery, E/CN.4/Sub.2/1984/NGO.3, 30 July 1984.

Report of the Mission to Mauritania (Marc Bossuyt), E/CN.4/Sub.2/1984/23, 2 July 1984.

Report of the Working Group on Slavery on its Tenth Session, E/CN.4/Sub.2/15 August 1984.

Study of the Human Rights Situation in Equatorial Guinea (Fernando Volio Jiménez), E/CN.4/1371, 12 February 1980.

Whitaker, B. (Special Rapporteur), *Slavery*, E/CN.4/Sub.2/1982/20/Rev.1, New York, 1984.

International Labour Organization

Abolition of Forced Labour, General Survey of the Reports relating to the Forced Labour Convention, 1930 (no. 29), and the Abolition of Forced Labour Convention, 1957 (no. 105), 1979.

Application of Conventions and Recommendations. Report of the Committee of Experts, 1984.

Migrant Workers, General Survey of the Reports relating to Conventions nos. 97 and 143 and Recommendations nos. 86 and 151 concerning Migrant Workers, 1980.

Minimum Age, General Survey of the Reports relating to Convention no. 138 and Recommendation no. 146 concerning Minimum Age, 1981.

Official Bulletin, Special Supplement, Series B, vol. LXVI, 1983: Report of the Commission of Enquiry appointed under article 26 of the Constitution of the ILO to examine the observance of certain international labour Conventions by the Dominican Republic and Haiti.

Phongpaichit, P., *From Peasant Girls to Bangkok Masseuses* (Women, Work and Development, 2), 1982.

Potobsky, G. von, 'On-the-spot visits: an important cog in the ILO's supervisory machinery', *International Labour Review*, vol. 120, no. 5, September-October 1981.

Report of the Director-General, 1983.

Towards an Action Programme on Child Labour, Report to the Government of India of an ILO Technical Mission, 1984.

United Nations Development Programme

Assistance Requested by the Government of Equatorial Guinea for the period 1974–1978. Country and Intercountry Programming. Governing Council. DP/GC/EQG/R.1, 23.

UNDP to Sub-Commission, E/CN.4/Sub.2/1984/24, 29 June 1984.

OTHER SECONDARY SOURCES

Africa, London, no. 34, June 1974, ref. UNDP in Equatorial Guinea.

Amnesty International, *Human Rights Violations in Namibia*, AI Index. Index: AFR 42/13/82, London, Amnesty International briefing of 28 September 1982.

Amnesty International Report 1983, London, 1983.

Aristotle, *Politics* (translated by Ernest Barker), Oxford, Clarendon Press, 1946.

Averbakh, I. L. (ed. by Vyshinsky, A. Y.), *Ot Prestupleniya k Trudu* (*From Crime to Labour*), Moscow, Soviet Legislation Publishers, 1936.

Bhatia, S., 'New evidence on female mutilation', London, *Observer*, 27 February 1983.

Brooks, E., *Tribes of the Amazon Basin in Brazil 1972*, London, Charles Knight & Co. Ltd, 1973.

Bullock, A., *Hitler: A Study in Tyranny*, London, Odhams Press, 1952.

Case Studies on Human Rights and Fundamental Freedoms: A World Survey, The Hague, Martinus Nijhoff for the Foundation for the Study of Plural Societies, (Editor-in-Chief: Willem A. Veenhoven), vols 1–2, 1975, vols 3–5, 1976:

Amelunxen, C., 'Marriage and women in Islamic countries', in vol. 2.

Dushnyck, W., 'Discrimination and abuse of power in the USSR', in vol. 2.

Laffin, J., 'The Arabs as slavers', in vol. 4.

Leguebe, J., 'Mozambique under Frelimo rule', in vol. 4.

Luca, C., 'Discrimination in the Arab Middle East', in vol. 1.

Possony, S. T., 'From Gulag to Guitk: political prisons in the USSR today', in vol. 1.

Challis, J. and Elliman, D., *Child Workers Today*, Sunbury, Quartermaine House, 1979.

Cook, A., *Akin to Slavery: Prison Labour in South Africa*, London, International Defence and Aid Fund, 1982.

Davies, R. P. H. to Exmo. Sr General João Figueiredo, 14 June 1982, in Hemming, *The Last Colonial Frontier: The Plight of the Brazilian Indian*.

Davydov, G., 'Compulsory labor in the Soviet economy', Munich, Radio Liberty Research (RL 50/83), 26 January 1983.

Debelius, H., 'Equatorial Guinea accused of slavery', London, *The Times*, 6 February 1976.

de Mello, O. J. Bandeiro, 'Observations on the Report presented by the Aborigines Protection Society', in Brooks, *Tribes of the Amazon Basin in Brazil 1972*.

Dummelow, J. R. (ed.), *A Commentary on the Holy Bible*, London, Macmillan, 1952.

Furneaux, R., *William Wilberforce*, London, Hamish Hamilton, 1974.

Greenidge, C. W. W., *Slavery*, London, Allen & Unwin, 1958.

Hanbury-Tenison, R., *Report of a Visit to the Indians of Brazil*, London, Primitive People's Fund/Survival International, 1971.

Haffner, S., *The Meaning of Hitler* (English translation by Ewald Osers), London, Weidenfeld & Nicolson, 1979.

Henshaw, D., 'William Wilberforce's work goes on – 150 years later', *The Listener*, vol. 109, no. 2803.

Hitler, A., *Mein Kampf*, London, Hutchinson, with Hurst & Blackett, 1940.

Humana, C., *World Human Rights Guide*, London, Hutchinson, 1983.

Huxley, M. and Capa, C., *Farewell to Eden*, London, Chatto & Windus, 1965.

ICRC, *Report of the International Committee of the Red Cross Medical Mission to the Brazilian Amazon Region*, Geneva, ICRC, 1970.

International Monetary Fund, *Etudes Generales sur les Economies Africaines*, Washington, IMF, 1973.

Karunatilleke, K., 'Some aspects of the role of Interpol in the prevention and suppression of the traffic in women and children', paper submitted to the 28th Congress of the International Abolitionist Federation, Vienna, ICPO (Interpol), 1984.

Keston College Staff Study, *Christian Prisoners in the USSR 1983/4*, Keston College, 1983.

Krige, E. J., *The Social System of the Zulus*, London, Longmans, Green & Co, 1936.

League of Nations Document C.568M.272. Report of the Commission which investigated allegations of forced labour in Equatorial Guinea, Geneva, 1930.

Leistner, G. M. E., *Southern Crucible: South Africa – Future World in Microcosm*, Pretoria, Africa Institute of South Africa, 1980.

Lewis, N., 'Manhunt', London, *The Sunday Times Magazine*, 26 January 1976.

Lugard, Sir Frederick, *The Dual Mandate in British Tropical Africa*, London, William Blackwood, 1922.

Mackenzie, J., *Austral Africa: Losing it or Ruling it*, 2 vols, New York, Negro Universities Press, 1887.

Manchester, W., *The Arms of Krupp 1587–1968*, London, Michael Joseph, 1969.

Marla, S., *Bonded Labour in India*, National Survey on the incidence of Bonded Labour, Final Report, New Delhi, Biblia Impex Private, 1981.

Maxwell, J. F., *Slavery and the Catholic Church: The History of Catholic Teaching Concerning the Moral Legitimacy of the Institution of Slavery*, Chichester and London, Barry Rose Publishers in association with the Anti-Slavery Society, 1975.

Mercer, J., *Spanish Sahara*, London, Allen & Unwin, 1976.

Mercer, J., *The Sahrawis of Western Sahara*, London, Minority Rights Group, 1979.

Mercer, J., *Slavery in Mauritania Today*, Edinburgh, Human Rights Group, 1982.

Minority Rights Group, *Violence Against Women*, submission to the Working Group of Experts on Slavery, 1984.

Mitford, J., *The American Prison Business*, London, Allen & Unwin, 1974.

Mohammad, *The Koran*, (English translation by J. M. Rodwell), London, J. M. Dent, 1909.

Montgomery, J. R. P., 'A task unfinished', *Chronicle*, vol. 4, no. 1, January 1984.

Multilateral Co-operation in Southern Africa 1983, Pretoria, RSA Department of Foreign Affairs and Information Service, 1983.

Münzel, M., *The Aché Indians: Genocide in Paraguay*, Copenhagen, International Work Group for Indigenous Affairs, 1973.

Münzel, M., *The Aché: Genocide Continues in Paraguay*, Copenhagen, International Work Group for Indigenous Affairs, 1974.

Neumann, F., *Behemoth* (2nd edn), Oxford, Oxford University Press, 1944.

O'Callaghan, M., 'The labour camps of People's China', *Guardian*, London, 29 August 1984.

Ohse, U., *Forced Prostitution and Traffic in Women in West Germany*, Edinburgh, Human Rights Group, 8 Scotland Street, 1984.

'Open letter from the Russian friends of the Crimean Tartars', *Arkhiv Samizdata*, Munich Radio Liberty Research, cited by Sheehy, A.

and Nahaylo, B., in *The Crimean Tartars, Volga Germans and Mesketians.*

Revue Abolitionniste, abolir l'exploitation de la prostitution, Paris, Fédération Abolitionniste Internationale, Nouvelle Serie, no. 4, Deuxième Semestre 1984.

Rose, B. and Turner, R. (eds), *Documents in South African Education*, Johannesburg, A. D. Donker, 1975.

Sanderson, L. P., *Against the Mutilation of Women*, London, Ithaca Press, 1981.

Sawyer, R., *Casement: The Flawed Hero*, London, Routledge & Kegan Paul, 1984.

Scheir, E. H. 'Man against man: brainwashing', Corrective Psychiatry and Journal of Social Change (now Corrective and Social Psychiatry/ The Journal of Behavioural Technology Methods and Therapy), Martin Psychiatric Research Foundation, Olathe, Kansas, vol. 8, no. 2 (second quarter), 1962.

Seiler-Baldinger, A., 'Indians and the pioneer front in the north-east Amazon', in F. Barbira-Scazzocchio (ed.), *Land, People and Planning in Contemporary Amazonia*, Cambridge, Centre of Latin American Studies Occasional Publication no. 3, 1980.

Sheehy, A. and Nahaylo, B., *The Crimean Tartars, Volga Germans and Mesketians: Soviet Treatment of Some National Minorities* (3rd edn), London, Minority Rights Group, 1980.

Shirer, W. L., *The Rise and Fall of the Third Reich: A History of Nazi Germany*, London, Secker & Warburg, 1959.

Sillery, A., *The Bechuanaland Protectorate*, London, Oxford University Press, 1952.

Simon, Lady, *Slavery*, London, Hodder & Stoughton, 1929.

Solzhenitsyn, A. I., *The Gulag Archipelago*, London, Collins, vol. 1, 1974, vol. 2, 1975, vol. 3, 1978.

South Africa 1984, Official Yearbook of the Republic of South Africa, Johannesburg, Chris van Rensburg Publications, 1984.

Spandau, A., *Southern Africa and the Western World (with Special Reference to South Africa)*, London, Middlesex Polytechnic (as part of Institute for European Economic Studies), 1984.

Speer, A., *The Slave State: Heinrich Himmler's Masterplan for SS Supremacy*, London, Weidenfeld & Nicolson 1981.

Temperley, H., *British Anti-Slavery 1833–1870*, London, Longmans, 1972.

Towards a Constellation of States in Southern Africa, Pretoria, Information Service of South Africa, 1980.

United States Department of State, *Country Reports on Human Rights Practices for 1983 Report*, Washington, 1984.

Verpoorten, C. (ed.), 'Made in Goulag', *L'Eventail Special*, Rush Productions, English translation printed and distributed by the Wilberforce Council for Human Rights, January 1981.

Waugh, J., 'Prisons: changing a system that doesn't work', *The Christian Science Monitor*, Boston, 16 December 1971.

West, R., *Back to Africa*, London, Jonathan Cape, 1970.

Zinn, H., *A People's History of the United States*, London, Longmans, 1980.

INDEX

Abolition Act, *see* Bonded Labour System
Aborigines Protection Society (later merged with Anti-Slavery Society), 9, 144–5, 146, 148
Abu Dhabi, 116
accidents: to children, 78, 89, 97; and debt bondage, 133; *see also* cruelty
Aché Indians of Paraguay, 28–31
Achille, Theodore E., 175
Acton, First Baron, 1, 135
Acts, *see* legislation
adivasis (indigenous tribes of India), 130–1
adoption, *see under* children
advertising for prostitution, 102–3
Africa: chattel slavery in, 14–27, 31, 37, 131, 232; children exploited in, 79–85, 98; colonialism in, 4, 8, 17–19, 55–8, 179, 181, 184–5, 192, 227; debt bondage in, 142; migrant and forced labour in, 169, 179–86, 188–90, 220; political/penal slavery in, 192; women exploited in, 103, 105, 107–10, 112, 115, 117, 120; *see also* apartheid *and individual countries*
Afrikaners, 54, 57, 58
age, minimum, for child labour, 78–9, 80, 81, 84
Agnivesh, Swami, 132–4
agriculture: child exploitation in, 81–2, 92, 93; debt bondage and, 126–33, 138–42; migrant/forced labour in, 40, 63–5, 73, 170–86; political/penal slaves in, 192, 193, 204, 210–11; and tribal minorities persecution, 147, 160–2
Ahmed, Mahmoud Dahane Ould, 21
aid, foreign: role in persecution of tribal minorities, 153–4, 155–6, 157, 159, 161, 230
air transport of slaves, 13
Akhmetov, Nizametdin, 193–4, 208
Alexander VI, Pope, 140
Amazon basin, 8; *see also* Brazil; Peru
ameliorated slavery, 4, 145–54 *passim*
Amerindians, 4
see also under Latin America
Amnesty International, 23, 69, 194, 230, 233
Andoke people of Amazon basin, 136, 137–8
Angola, 75, 227
animals, Amerindians seen as, 94, 137, 149
Anti-Slavery Society for Protection of Human Rights, 8–9, 54, 217; and apartheid, 56, 57, 81–2; and chattel slavery, 15, 23–5, 29; and

child exploitation, 77, 81–2, 84–5, 86, 88, 90; and debt bondage, 132, 137–8; definitions, 9–11; and migrant/forced labour, 170, 172–3, 176, 178, 183–5, 187, 189; and political/penal slaves, 193; and tribal minorities, 144–7, 152–3, 157–8, 162; and United Nations, 225, 229–31; and women, exploitation of, 100, 107, 109
anti-semitism, *see* Jews
Antisthenes, 2
apartheid, 10, 53–76, 238–9; child exploitation and, 80–2; defined, 53; *see also* tribal minorities
apprenticeships, sham, 188
Arab countries, *see* Middle East
Argentina, 68, 223, 231
Aristotle, 1, 2, 6, 33
armaments industry, *see* Krupp
Armando (child slave), 92
Aryan master race concept, 32–3, 34–5 *see also Volk*
Asia: and Africa, 72, 185; children exploited in, 79, 94–8, 99; colonialism in, 5–6, 8; debt bondage/serfdom in, 5, 7, 123–34, 140–1, 143; political/penal slavery in, 192–3; tribal minorities persecuted in, 144, 145, 146, 154–63; women exploited in, 101–7, 116, 118–21; *see also individual countries*
Asian Development Bank, 162
Ata Manobo tribe in Philippines, 161–2
Atar demonstration (Mauritania), 23
Atatürk, Kemal, 117
Auschwitz concentration camp, 36, 40–1
Australasia, 79
Awad, Mohamed, 222, 223–4
Ayala, Jaime Zobel, 160

Balaguer, ruler of Dominican Republic, 170, 183
Banerjee, Sumanta, 94, 96, 97, 103
Bangladesh: tribal minorities persecuted in, 144, 145, 154–8; women exploited in, 118–19
Bantu people of South Africa, 60, 61, 73, 80
Barbadian people in Amazon basin, 136
Basutoland (now Lesotho), 57
Batswana (Bechuana) people of southern Africa, 71–2, 74
Bechuanaland, 57
Bechuanaland Protectorate (now Botswana), 57, 71
beggars, children as, 85, 92
Belgium, 8, 188
forced labour from, 36, 39
Belomorsky canal project, 196–7
Belov, Yuri, 202, 203, 205
Berber people of Mauritania, 17, 18
Bibi, Zarina, 116
Bioco island, *see* Fernando Po
birth control, 98
Blail, M'Barka mint, 19
Bodin, Jean, 6
Boers, 56
Bolivia, 49
Bolshevism, 47
Bonded Labour System (Abolition) Act (India–1976), 124–5, 127, 129–30, 134
Bonded Liberation Front (India – Bondhua Mukti Morcha), 132–4
Bophuthatswana, 50, 60, 65, 71, 72, 73–4
Bora people of Amazon basin, 136
Bormann, Martin, 45
Bossuyt, Marc, 24, 26, 232
Botswana, 71; *see also* Bechuanaland Protectorate
Brazil: children exploited in, 93–4; tribal minorities persecuted in, 145–54
Brezhnev, Leonid, 165
brick industry: children exploited in, 94–5; debt bondage in, 132
Britain, Great: children exploited in, 188; colonialism, 5–7, 13, 56–8, 131, 179, 181; import of goods

made by Russian prisoners, 201–2, 205, 206; legislation, 7, 111–12, 217; migrant labour in, 188; women exploited in 103, 110–11, 241–2
British Bechuanaland, 71
British Emancipation Act (1834), 7, 127
British and Foreign Anti-Slavery Society (later Anti-Slavery Society), 8, 9, 144
brutality, *see* cruelty/torture
Bubi people of Equatorial Guinea, 179–81, 182
Buchenwald concentration camp, 36
Buddhism, 154; child exploitation and, 95; priests persecuted, 158, 195, 205
Burger, Warren, 214
Burkina Faso, *see* Upper Volta
Bushmen of South Africa, 54–5
Buxton, Sir Thomas Fowell, 8

Canada, 187, 223; *see also* North America
canal construction using political/penal slaves, 195, 196–7
captives, war, 8; *see also* disposable asset
Caribbean, *see* Central America
carpet making industry, child exploitation in, 83
Carter, J., President of USA, 178
Casement, Sir Roger, 8, 94, 135, 137, 146
castration, 13, 20; *see also* cruelty
caviar industry, political/penal slaves in, 206–7
Central America and West Indies: debt bondage and serfdom in, 124, 140; emancipation in, 7, 131; migrant and forced labour in, 169–79, 180, 183, 190, 227; South African interests of, 75, 185; United Nations and, 227
Chad, 15
Chakma people of Chittagong Hill Tracts, 158
chattel slavery, 1–4, 8, 9, 12–31, 232, 236–7; and debt bondage, 124, 142; defined, 12; in Mauritania, 15–27; in Middle East, 13–15; in Paraguay, 28–31; *see also* disposable asset; political/penal
chemical industry, political/penal slaves in 204
Chertkova, Anna, 113–14
children, exploitation of, 4, 10, 42, 77–99, 232, 239–40; 'adopted', 10, 92, 93–4; in Brazil, 93–4; in Colombia, 90–3; in debt bondage, 128–9, 141; defined, 9, 77; in India and Thailand, 94–8; in Italy, 86–90; kidnapped, 19; as migrant/forced labour, 187–8; in Morocco, 82–5; as prostitutes, 78, 86, 90, 93–7, 188; of slaves, 14, 30, 44, 78; sold, 19, 20, 23, 27–8, 92, 98; in South Africa, 80–2; in Spain, 85–6
children of Moslem women, 118
Chile, 227, 228, 231
China, 7, 185, 192–3
Chittagong Hill Tribes (Bangladesh), persecution of, 145, 154–8
Choggar revolt (Mauritania – 1977), 22
Christianity and slavery, 3–4, 6–7, 30; imprisonment for practising, 194, 204, 208; and prevention of totalitarianism, 50–1; and tribal minorities, 147, 149, 151; *see also* religion
Chtchareguine, Nikolai, 205, 206
Cintas Largas tribe in Brazil, 147
'circumcision, female', *see* genital mutilation
Ciskei, 70, 74
'Clapham Sect', 7
coal industry, child exploitation in, 91
cocoa plantations, migrant/forced labour on, 179–86

Colombia, 90–3; debt bondage, 136, 137
colonialism, 4–5; Christianity rejected after, 51; *see also under* Europe; *individual countries and continents*
Commission on Human Rights, *see* United Nations, human rights
communications, *see* media
Communism, 11, 47; in South Africa, 68; USA and, 160; *see also* Eastern Europe; political/penal slavery; Soviet Union
concentration camps: in Nazi Germany, 36, 40–1, 44; *see also* Gulag Archipelago
construction industry: debt bondage in, 132; political/penal slaves in, 195
Correrias (slave-raiding system), 137
Council of Baptists Prisoners' Relatives, 113
coups d'état, see military.
crime, prisoners not guilty of, 191
Crimean Tartars, persecuted, 49, 163–7
criminals: in Soviet prisons, 200; *see also*political/penal
Cronjé, Suzanne, 183–4, 185
cruelty/torture: and apartheid, 63, 65–7, 68–9, 70, 81–2; to chattel slaves, 15, 20–1, 23, 29–30; to children, 81–2, 91, 92, 95–6, 97; and debt bondage, 135, 136, 137; as fundamental human urge 234; to migrant/forced labour, 172, 180, 182–3, 188–9; in Nazi Germany, 36, 39, 42–3; of political/penal slaves, 198–9, 202, 208–9, 211–14; to tribal minorities, 147, 158, 162, 164; to women, 106–14, 116; *see also* accidents; disease; murder; starvation
Cubans, 75, 185
Cuellar, Perez de, 231
Cuenca, Rodolfo, 162
Czechoslovakia, 79
Daddah, Mokhtar, Ould, 17–18
Dahane Ould Ahmed, Mahmoud, 21
dam construction and tribal minorities persecution, 155–6, 161
Darwinism, 32
David, Kati, 109
Davies, Peter, 16
Davydov, Georgii, 204
death, *see* murder/execution
debt bondage and serfdom, 5, 7, 122–43, 233, 242–4; defined, 9, 122; in India, 124–30, 132–5, 141; in Peru, 135–40; *see also* Dominican Republic
decentralized industry, child exploitation in, 87
definitions and origins of slavery, 1–11, 237–8
Demba, Ahmed Salem, Ould, 23
deportation, *see* migration, compulsory
detention incommunicado without trial (South Africa), 67–8, 69, 70
diet, *see* starvation
Diogenes, 2
disease: of children, exploited, 84–5, 87–90, 92, 95, 97; and debt bondage, 133; and industry, 84–5, 87–90, 95; of migrant-forced labour, 172, 180; in Nazi concentration camps, 42–3; of women, exploited, 106; of political/penal slaves, 201, 203; of tribal minorities, 146, 148; *see also* cruelty
Disini, Herminio, 162
disposable asset, slave as, 8, 32–52, 237–8; *see also* children
dissidents in Soviet Union, wives of, 112–13, 114; *see also* Soviet Union,political/penal
divorce, male rights under Islam, 117
dolls, Russian, manufactured by prisoners, 202–3
domestic service: children exploited

in, 91–2, 93–4; debt bondage and, 138
Dominican Republic, migrant and forced labour in, 169–79, 190, 227
Doucara, Batou, 110
drugs used on prisoners, 194, 208–9, 213
Dutch, *see* Netherlands
Duvalier family, 170, 175, 183

Eastern Europe, 79, 228; forced labour from, 36, 38, 39
Ecuador, debt bondage in, 139–40
education: child exploitation and, 78–80, 82, 84–6, 90–1, 93, 96, 99; re-education centres, 192–3; in South Africa, 61, 73
Egypt, 115, 223
El Hor (emancipation movement in Mauritania), 19–20, 22–4, 26
electronics industry, political/penal slaves in, 201–2
Elizalde, Manuel, 160
emancipation: into debt bondage, 124; land reform and, 131–2; legislation, 7, 127; movements, 19–20, 22–4, 26, 132–4, 157; rejected, 141; women's, need for, 120–1
embroidery industry, children exploited in, 94–5
emigrants, *see* migrant; migration
Engen, Hans, 221
engineering industry, political/penal slaves in, 204
Epictetus, 2
Equatorial Guinea, migrant and forced labour in, 169, 179–86, 190, 227
Ethiopia, 188–9, 220
Europe: chattel slavery in, 27–8; children exploited in, 27–8, 79, 85–90, 188; colonialism, 4, 5–6, 8, 135, 140 (*see also under* Africa; Britain, Great); debt bondage in, 142; migrant and forced labour in, 187–8 (*see also* disposable asset); women exploited in, 102–3, 106–7, 110; *see also* Britain, Great *and individual countries*
European Economic Community, 46–7; migrant/forced labour in, 142, 187–8, 190; *see also individual countries*
excision, female, *see* genital mutilation
execution, *see* murder/execution
export of slaves, *see* trade
extermination, *see* murder/execution

Fang people of Equatorial Guinea, 179, 181
farms, *see* agriculture
Fascist governments, 46; *see also* disposable asset; totalitarianism
Feisal, Prince of Saudi Arabia, 13
Fernand-Laurent, Jean, 92–3, 101, 104
Fernando Po, 179–86
'Final Solution', *see* Jews
firms, *see* industry
forced labour in Nazi Germany, 34, 36–44; *see also* migrant workers; political/penal
foreign investment, *see* aid
forests, *see* timber
France: children exploited in, 188; colonialism, 17–19, 55, 179, 185; forced labour from, 36, 39; Jews in, 33; migrant labour in, 188; women exploited in, 110
Francesca (child slave), 88
freedom, *see* emancipation
Freiwillige ('volunteer workers' in Nazi Germany), 39
French Gabon, 179, 180–1
Frenkel, Naftaly Aronovich, 195, 196–8, 202
fruit growing and tribal minorities persecution, 160
FUNAI (Fundacao Nacional do Indio – Brazil), 147–53, 159

Gabon, French, 179, 180–1

Gandhi Peace Foundation, 126, 128, 131, 132, 134
General Act of Conference of Berlin (1885), 217
genital mutilation of women, 107–12, 241–2
genocide attempts, *see* disposable asset; tribal minorities
German South-West Africa (later Namibia), 57, 58, 75
Germany: chattel slavery, in 27–8; children exploited in, 27–8, 86–90, 188; colonialism, 55, 58; migrant labour in, 188; women exploited in, 102–3, 106–7; *see also* disposable asset; National Socialists
girls, exploited, 91–2; *see also* children; women
glass industry, political/penal slaves in 203, 207
glues, toxic, effect on children, 87–9
Goebbels, Joseph, 35, 45, 50
Goering, Hermann, 45
Greece, ancient, 1–2, 124
greed, 37, 86, 101–2
Gregory of Nyssa, St, 4
Guajá tribe in Brazil, 153
Guinea, 109
Gulag Archipelago, 48–9, 193–211 *passim*

Haiti, migrant and forced labour from, 170–9, 180, 183, 190
Hanbury-Tenison, Robin, 146
haratin (freed Mauritanian slaves), 19, 20, 23, 24, 27
Helfgott, Ben, 239
Helsinki agreement on human rights, 166
Himmler, Heinrich, 36, 41, 45
Hinduism, 154; child exploitation and, 94–5; debt bondage and, 7, 124, 127–9
Hispaniola, *see* Dominican Republic; Haiti
Hitler, Adolf, 32–5, 37, 43–8, 50–2, 58, 190
Hong Kong, 105, 192
Hoss, Franz, 41
Hottentots (Khoikhoim) of South Africa, 54–5
Huitoto people of Amazon basin, 136, 137
human rights: Helsinki agreement on, 166; Universal Declaration of, 166, 167, 191, 209, 225; *see also under* United Nations
hydro-electric: projects and tribal minorities persecution, 155–6, 161; components, political/penal slaves manufacture, 193

ideological justification for Russian prisons, 197–8
illiteracy of migrant/forced labourers, 172, 175
ILO, *see* International Labour Organization
immigrants to Great Britain, 27 *see also* migrant; migration; import of slaves, *see* trade
India: children exploited in, 94–8, 99; debt bondage/serfdom in, 5, 7, 123–34, 140, 141, 143; legislation, 124–5, 127, 129–30, 134; United Nations and, 223; women exploited in, 120
Indians, North American, 4, 187
Indians, South American, *see* Amerindians *and also under* Latin America
industry: child exploitation in, 82–3, 87–9, 91, 94–5, 97; debt bondage and, 132–40, in Nazi Germany, forced labour in, 36–44; political/penal slaves in, 193, 195–7, 202–7; and tribal minorities persecution, 159, 160, 162
Infanzón, Colonel, 29
inferiority of women, 100
Internal Security Acts (South Africa – 1976, 1982, 1984) 68, 70, 74
International Criminal Police

Organization (INTERPOL), 230, 232
International Labour Organization, 10; and apartheid, 62; and children, exploitation of, 77–9, 80, 99; and migrant/forced labour, 168, 171, 173–8, 187; procedures, 226–9, 233; and tribal minorities, 144; and women, exploitation of, 103, 107, 109
International Red Cross, 69, 146, 215
international trade, *see* trade
International Working Group on Women and Family, 119–20
interrogation, *see* cruelty/torture
investment, foreign, *see* aid
Iran, 120, 217, 223, 231
Iraq, 115, 231
irrigation, *see* dams
Islam, 7; and chattel slavery, 12, 14; and child exploitation, 94–5; and Chittagong Hill tribes, 154–5; and Crimean Tartars, 163–4; and debt bondage, 128; and genital mutilation, 109; laws, 15, 26, 200; in Philippines, 161; Shari'a, *see* laws *above*; women under, 109, 114–21; *see also* Bangladesh; Mauritania; Middle East; Pakistan
Israel, 72, 200, 228; *see also* Jews
Italy, 39, 98
ius gentium, 3
ius naturale, 3
Ivory Coast, 109, 115

Jaeger, Wilhelm, 39
Japan, 160, 227
Jews, 167: Nazi persecution of, 32–9, 44–5, 52, 145, 190; as Israelite slaves, 2–3, 124, 235–6
Jingbo, Huang, 193

Kaptai dam (Bangladesh), 155–6, 161
Karajá tribe in Brazil, 147
Keate, Governor, 72
Kennet, Lord, 111
Kenya, 112
Khailo, Vladimir, 208–9
Khan, Ayub, 155
Khruschev, Nikita, 200
Koran, *see* Islam
'Krumen' (labourers), 180–1
Krupp, Alfried, 37–46 *passim*
Krupp, Gustav, 42
kulaks, liquidation of, 196
Kuwait, 14
Kvartchevsky, Lev, 205
Kwazulu, 71

laboratory experiments in Nazi Germany, 36; *see also* cruelty
Lada cars, 205–6
land: enclosed by colonialists, 55; rights of tribal minorities, 151–2, 155–6; serfs tied to, 5, 123 (*see also* serfdom); tenure, reform, 131, 139–40, 188
Landaburo, Jean, 138
Latin America: chattel slavery, 28–31, 49; children exploited in, 79, 90–4; colonialism in, 4, 8, 135, 140; debt bondage/serfdom, 5, 123, 124, 135–9, 140; Indians, 4–5, 28–31, 49, 94, 137, 145–54; legislation, 90, 140; United Nations and, 227–8, 231; *see also individual countries*
laws, *see* legislation
Le Grange, Louis, 68
League of Nations, 218–20, 231
Lebanon, 103
Lederman, Joseph, 202
legislation/laws, 143, 217; Great Britain, 7, 111–12, 217; India, 124–5, 127, 129–30, 134; ineffective, 90, 96–8; Islamic, 15, 26, 109, 115–20, 200; Italy, 98; Latin America, 90, 140; Nazi Germany, 34; South Africa, 57, 59, 60, 68, 70, 72, 74, 80; Soviet Union, 112; Spain, 85, 89; Sweden, 110; *see also under* Islam
Lek (prostitute), 105

Lenin, Vladimir, 163, 166, 189, 196
Leopold II, King of Belgium, 8, 217
Lesotho, 60, 227
Letizia (child slave), 87
Liberia: migrant labour from, 180–1, 190, 220; women exploited in, 109
Linnander, Margareta, 109
logging, *see* timber
Lubarsky, Cronid, 201–2, 204, 206
Lugard, Sir Frederick (later First Baron), 219, 220

maalema (maîtresse), 83–4
Machel, Samora (President of Mozambique), 192
Macias Nguema (President of Equatorial Guinea), 179, 181, 182–4, 185–6
Macias Nguema (island), *see* Fernando Po
Mafia, 86–7, 142
Malan, D. F., 53, 59
Mali 109–10
Manobo people in Philippines, 160, 161–2
Mao Tse Tung, 193
Marcos, Imelda, 162
Marcos, President of Philippines, 159–60, 162–3
Marcus Aurelius, 2
Maria (child slave), 87–8
Marla, Sarma, 131
marriage: false, for prostitution, 102; miscegenation, 33, 59; servile forms of, 9–10 , 100, 116–21; *see also* women
Marx, Karl, and Marxism, 33, 47, 115, 196
massacres, *see* murder/execution
masseuses in Bangkok, 103–5; *see also* prostitution
master race concept, 32–3, 34–5; *see also Volk*
master-slave relationship, affectionate, 8, 12, 128
Matabele people of South Africa, 56
match industry, child exploitation in, 97
Mauritania, chattel slavery in, 14–27, 31, 37, 131, 232
media: advertisements for prostitutes, 102–3; in India, 134; on Islamic punishments, 15; in Nazi Germany, 50; in South Africa, 50, 54
Mein Kampf, 33–4, 45
Mercer, John, 15–16, 20, 23
Messaoud, Boubacar, 22–3
Middle East: chattel slavery in, 12–14, 218; children exploited in, 7, 10, 231; debt bondage in, 142; foreign aid from, 72; United Nations and, 217, 223, 228, 231; women exploited in, 103, 105, 115–20, 231; *see also individual countries*
middlemen/women: and child exploitation, 83–4; and debt bondage, 132–3; and prostitution, 102–6
migrant workers/forced labour, 168–90, 247–8; in Amazon basin, 136; children of, 79, 90; defined, 168; in Dominican Republic, 169–79; in Equatorial Guinea, 179–86; in Ethiopia, 188–9; in North America and Europe, 186–8; prostitutes, 102–4; *see also* migration
migration: and child exploitation, 80; compulsory, 61–2, 156, 161, 164–5; *see also* migrant; nomadic
Mikhalenko, V., 193
military *coups*, 19, 21, 23, 49, 70, 157, 182
minimum age for child labour, 78–9, 80, 81, 84
mining: political/penal slaves in, 195, 204, 207; and tribal minorities persecution, 160
miscegenation, attitudes to: by Hitler, 33; by South Africa, 59
Mokgoetse, Moyhkoane, 72

money: to abolish slavery, 14, 31; power and, 12, 31, 37
moneylenders, 5; *see also* debt bondage
Montesquieu, 6
Montgomery, Colonel, 27
Montsioa, Chief, 71
Moors (people of Mauritania), 17, 18, 19
Morocco, 19; children exploited in, 82–5; women exploited in, 120
Moses, 2; *see also* Jews
Moslems, *see* Islam
motor vehicle industry, political/penal slaves in, 203, 205–6
Mozambique, 192, 227
Multinational Development (South Africa), 59, 62, 65, 75
multinationals: child exploitation in, 82–3, 84; role in persecution of tribal minorities, 146, 159, 161–2
Münzel, Mark, 29–30
murder/execution: and apartheid, 82; of chattel slaves, 15, 20–1, 29, 30; of children, 81, 82, 92; of migrant/forced labour, 170, 182, 189; in Nazi Germany, 35, 38, 42–3, 44–5; of political/penal slaves, 197, 211; of tribal minorities, 146, 147, 152, 153, 157–8, 162, 164; of women, 116, 118, 120
Murton, Tom, 211
Muscat, 13
Mussolini, Benito, 46
mutilation, *see* cruelty; genital mutilation

nakedness, unnatural interest in, 149–50
Namibia (earlier German South-West Africa), 55, 75–6, 82
National Foundation of the Indian, *see* FUNAI
National Socialists (Germany), 8, 29, 47, 98, 135, 145; *see also* disposable asset
Native Areas Act (South Africa – 1945), 59, 60
Native Land Act (South Africa – 1913), 57, 60
Nazis, *see* National Socialists
neo-colonialism (Mauritania), 19, 21
Nepal, 140, 141
Nepotism, 162
Netherlands: children exploited in, 188; colonialism, 55, 56, 58; forced labour from, 36, 39; migrant labour in, 188
Nicaragua, 27
Niger, 109
Nigeria, 179; migrant and forced labour from, 181, 182–3, 190; women exploited in, 103
nomadic people, 14, 16–17, 55–6
Non-Governmental Organizations (NGOs), 230–1
North America (mainly USA): children exploited in, 79, 90; colonialism in, 4; Equatorial Guinea and, 185; independence, 6–7; Indians in, 4, 187; migrant labour in, 186–7, 190; penal slavery in, 211–15; and tribal minorities persecution, 160, 162; United Nations and, 223
Numeiry, President of the Sudan, 120
Nuremberg Trials, 36, 42
Nyerere, President of Tanzania, 98

Ocaina people of Amazon basin, 136
Oman, 13
Organization of African Unity, 184

Pakistan: Chittagong Hill tribes and 154–5; debt bondage in, 140–1; women exploited in, 116, 120
PANAMIN (tribal protection society in Philippines), 159–63
Paraguay, chattel slavery in, 28–31, 49
part slave status in Mauritania, 19
parties, *see* political parties
Paul, St, 3–4

PEN: Writers in Prison, 194
penal slavery, *see* political/penal slavery
peonage, 5, 124, 139–40; *see also* debt bondage
Pereira, Jesus de, 29–30
persecution, *see* cruelty; murder; tribal minorities
Peru, debt bondage/serfdom in, 5, 135–9, 140
Philippines, 230; tribal minorities persecuted in, 144, 146, 158–63
pimps, *see* procurement
Piro people of Peru, 138
Plant, Roger, 171
plantations, *see* agriculture
Poland, 36, 38, 228
police: corruption, 96; international, 230, 232; in Philippines, 160; prostitution and, 107; in South Africa, 68; totalitarianism and, 175, 176, 182
political parties: in South Africa, 67, 68, 74; *see also* National Socialists
political/penal slavery, 8, 11, 23, 169, 191–216, 233–4, 249–51; in China, 192–3; defined, 191; in South Africa, 62–70, 73; in Soviet Union, 112–14, 193–211; in United States, 210, 211–15
polygamy, 115, 116, 119
pornography, child, 10, 78, 90; *see also* prostitution
Portugal: colonialism, 4, 135, 140, 192, 227
poverty, 37, 86, 143, 145
power, lust for, 8
Primitive People's Fund, 146
prisons, *see* political/penal slavery
procurement of women for prostitution, 102–6
Promotion of Black Self-Government Act (South Africa – 1959), 60, 72
property, women as, 116
prostitution, 101–7; child, 78, 86, 90, 93–7, 188; need to curtail, 106–7
Protestants, *see* Christianity
psychiatric hospitals, political/penal slaves in, 194, 208–9, 212
Puerto Rico, 227
punishment: for recruiting bonded labour, 125–6; *see also* cruelty
purdah, 118–19
Putumayo rubber gatherers (Peru), 135–8, 147

Qatar, 115
quarrying industry, debt bondage in, 132–4

racism, 124; *see also* apartheid; disposable asset; tribal persecution
Rank Xerox, 206
Ravensbrück concentration camp, 44
Reagan, Ronald, Governor of California (later President of USA), 213
Red Cross, International, 69, 146, 215
reform, penal, need for, 214–16
rehabilitation and re-education centres, 192–3; *see also* political/penal
religion: imprisonment for practising, 194, 200, 204, 208; women persecuted by, *see under* Islam; women persecuted for, 112–14; *see also* Buddhism; Christianity; Hinduism; Islam
Rhodesia, 56, 57
rights: equal, demanded by El Hor, 24–5; of Israelite slaves, 3; of women, ignored, 108; *see also* human rights; women, exploitation; *and under* land
Rio Muni, 179–86
road construction: and political/penal slaves, 195; and tribal minorities, persecution of, 147, 150, 152, 153–4, 156, 161
Roman Catholics, *see* Christianity
Roman empire, 3

Rosenberg, Alfred, 35
Rousseau, J.-J., 6
rubber gatherers and debt bondage, 135–8, 147

sadism, *see* cruelty/torture
Sahel, 14; *see also* Mauritania
Saint-Germain-en-Laye Convention (1919), 218
Sakharov, Andrei, 165, 194
sale of slaves: chattel, 18–19, 23; children, 19, 20, 23, 27–8, 92, 98; *see also* trade
Sanderson, Lilian Passmore, 111
Sarakolé (people of Mauritania), 17
Sauckel, Fritz, 40, 45
Saudi Arabia, 13
scavengers, children as, 85, 92
Schindler, Oskar, 37
Schopenhauer, Arthur, 44
Searight, Susan, 86
Sebe, Charles and Lennox, 70
self-employed children, 85, 92, 97
Senegal, 19–20, 22
serfdom, 90, 122–3, 124, 141, 142–3; compared to imprisonment in USSR, 198–9; in India, 129–32; in Peru (peonage), 5, 135–9, 140; in Mauritania, 19; *see also* debt bondage
sex tourism, 96–7, 101; *see also* prostitution
Shaftesbury, Seventh Earl, 91
Shahila (Sri Lankan woman), 116
Shanti Bahini (Bangladesh Peace Force), 157
share-cropping, 142; -cum-bondage, 129
Shari'a, *see under* Islam
shifting cultivation in Bangladesh, 155, 156
shoemaking industry, children exploited in, 87–9
Siberia, *see* Gulag Archipelago
Siberian gas pipeline, 204
Sicily, 142
Sierra Leone, 109
Sin, Abraham, 203
slave-master relationship, affectionate, 8, 12, 128
slavery, *see* Anti-Slavery Society; apartheid; chattel; children; debt bondage; definitions and origins; disposable asset; International Labour Organization; migrant workers/forced labour; political/penal; tribal minorities; United Nations; women
Solzhenitsyn, Alexander, 186, 194, 198, 216
Somoza, President of Nicaragua, 27
South Africa, 239; children exploited in, 80–2; legislation, 57, 59, 60, 68, 70, 72, 74, 80; media and, 50, 54; political/penal slavery in, 192; *see also* apartheid
South America, *see* Latin America
South West African People's Organization (SWAPO), 75
Soviet Union: children, lack of data on, 79; disposable assets, slaves as, 47, 48–9; and Equatorial Guinea, 185; forced labour from, 36, 38, 39, 40; Jews in, 33; political/penal slavery in, 193–211; tribal minorities persecuted in, 39, 48–9, 163–7; United Nations and, 223, 224; women exploited in, 112–14
Spain: children exploited in, 85–6, 89; colonialism, 4, 15, 19, 22, 135, 140, 179, 181, 184–5; labour in, 228; legislation, 85, 89
Spanish Sahara, 15, 19, 22
Speer, Albert, 36, 45, 47
Stalin, Joseph, 47–9, 66, 164, 194–6, 199–200, 204
starvation, 42–3; inadequate prison diet, 202, 203, 204; of migrant/forced labourers, 172; *see also* cruelty
status symbol, slaves as, 12, 92–4
Stauffenberg, Count Klaus von, 50
Stolz, Jack, 30
Stowe, Harriet Beecher, 2

Streicher, Julius, 35
Sudan, the, 108, 120, 189
sugar growing: migrant/forced labour in, 170–9; and tribal minorities persecution, 160
Survival International, 138
Swaziland, 57, 60
sweatshops, 97; *see also* industry
Sweden, 110, 185, 223
Switzerland, 185
Syria, 10

Taew (prostitute), 104–5
Taiwan, 72
Tanzania, 98, 223
Tartars, persecution of, 49, 163–7
Technical and Optical Equipment Company, 202, 205
territorial bondage, *see* serfdom
Tevoedjre, Isabelle, 109
Thailand: children exploited in, 94, 95–8; women exploited in, 101–7
Third Reich, *see* disposable asset
Third World, *see individual countries and continents*
timber industry: debt bondage and, 138; political/penal slaves in, 203–4, 206; tribal minorities persecuted, 159, 160, 162
tool making industry, political/penal slaves in, 204
Tordesillas, Treaty of, 140
torture, *see* cruelty/torture
totalitarianism, 46–50; migrant/forced labour and, 169; police and, 175, 176, 182; *see also* disposable asset military *coups*; Soviet Union
tourism: sex, 96–7, 101; tribal minorities and, 148, 149–50
trade in slaves, 13, 18, 56; prostitutes, 105; suppressed, 217–18; *see also* sale
trade unions, prevented, 171, 172, 176
Transkei, 70, 74
transport, air, of slaves, 13; *see also* trade
Traoure, Bobo, 110
trial, detention incommunicado without (South Africa), 67–8, 69, 70
tribal minorities, persecution of, 10, 144–67, 244–7; in Bangladesh, 145, 154–8; in Brazil, 145–54; debt bondage and, 130–1; defined, 144; in Philippines, 145, 158–63; in Soviet Union, 49, 163–7, 196
tribal warfare in South Africa, 56
Trujillo, ruler of Dominican Republic, 170
Turkey: migrant labour from, 187–8; women in, 117
Txukahamaye tribe in Brazil, 153
tyranny, *see* totalitarianism

unemployment, 64, 98, 171
unions, *see* trade unions
United Nations, 12, 14–16, 251–2; and apartheid, 53, 62, 75, 231; and chattel slavery, 23–7, 29, 232; and child exploitation, 77–9, 97, 232; Conventions on Slavery, 24, 140, 218–21; and debt bondage/serfdom, 122, 123, 131–2, 134, 140, 143, 233; definitions, 9–11, 12, 53, 77, 100, 122, 191; Development Programme, 184, 186, 230; Economic and Social Council, 221–4, 226; and forced labour, 25–6, 62, 131–2 (*see also* migrant *below*); and human rights, 23, 29, 166, 167, 193, 209, 223–6 (*see also* Universal Declaration); and migrant/forced labour, 169–71, 173, 176–7, 184–8, 190, 233 (*see also* forced labour *above*); and political/penal slaves, 191, 194, 200, 209, 215–16; role of, 217–34; and totalitarianism, 50; and tribal minorities, 155, 166, 229, 231; and women, 100, 101, 107, 109, 186, 232–3; Working Group of Experts on Slavery,

180, 11, 14, 53, 79, 97, 134, 170–1, 177, 187–8, 224–34
United States, *see* North America
Universal Declaration of Human Rights, 166, 167, 191, 209, 225
Upper Volta (now Burkina Faso), 109
urbanization, 10
USSR, *see* Soviet Union

Vais, Michael, 203
Valcarenghi, Marina, 86–7
Valdez, Simeon, 162
Vega products from USSR, 201, 202
Venda, 70, 74
Verwoerd, H. F., 53, 82
Vicini family, 172
Villas Boas brothers, 150
Vins, Georgi, 205
Volga Tartars, persecuted, 164
Volk: in Nazi Germany, 45, 46; in South Africa, 58; *see also* master race

war captives, 8, 124; *see also* disposable asset; serfdom
War, First World, 58, 217
War, Second World: and Crimean Tartars, 164; and Gulag Archipelago, 198; and Nazi Germany, *see* disposable asset; and South Africa, 57–8; and UN, 219
Weltanschauung, 45–6
West Indies, *see* Central America
Wickham, Henry, 137
widow bondage, 129
Wilberforce, Lord, 77
Wilberforce, William, 7, 8, 194, 234
wives of dissidents in Soviet Union, 112–13, 114
women, exploitation of, 4, 10, 19, 100–21, 232–3, 241–2; chattel slaves, 14; debt bondage, 129, 134; definition, 9, 100; genital mutilation, 107–12, 241–2; in marriage, 9–10, 100, 102, 116–21; as political/penal slaves, 206–7; and religion, 112–21; sold, 23; in South Africa, 69–70; *see also* prostitution
wood, *see* timber
wooden products produced by political/penal slaves, 193, 202–3, 204, 206
Work, Birhane Ras, 109
World Bank, role in persecution of tribal minorities, 153–4, 156, 159, 161
World Health Organization, 110
Writers in Prison (PEN), 194

Xavante tribe in Brazil, 153
Xingu National Park (Brazil), 150–1

Yagua Indians of Peru, 138
Yanomami tribe in Brazil, 150–2, 153
Yemen, 115–16

Zanzibar, 217
zari embroidery industry, children exploited in, 94–5
Zia, General (of Bangladesh), 157
Zulus of South Africa, 56